Rex Hunt's
Fishing Australia

Rex Hunt's Fishing Australia

Rex Hunt

Pan Macmillan Australia

First published 2004 in Macmillan by Pan Macmillan Australia Pty Limited
St Martins Tower, 31 Market Street, Sydney

Copyright © Rex Hunt 2004

All rights reserved. No part of this book may be reproduced or transmitted in any form or by any means, electronic or mechanical, including photocopying, recording or by any information storage and retrieval system,
without prior permission in writing from the publisher.

National Library of Australia
cataloguing-in-publication data:

Hunt, Rex.
Rex Hunt's fishing Australia.

ISBN 1 4050 3619 2 (hbk.)
ISBN 1 4050 3640 0 (pbk.)

1. Fishing – Australia – Guidebooks. 2. Fishes – Australia. I. Reid, Darren. II. Title.

799.10994

Project manager: Darren Reid
Designed and typeset by Seymour Designs and Robyn Latimer
Cover design by Robyn Latimer
Cartographic art by Laurie Whiddon, Map Illustrations
Printed in Singapore by Imago Productions (F.E.) Pte. Ltd.

I dedicate this book to the future of fishing.

I have enjoyed this marvellous pastime since I was seven years old, and along the way I have fished in some of the world's most beautiful waterways.

I am very keen to see fishing prosper and grow. Despite moves from certain areas to restrict and in some cases to outlaw fishing, and recognising the unbelievable pressure that our modern world places on our waterways, I sincerely believe that fishing will play a big part in our lives for ever more.

Fishing will continue to hold an important role in kids' development by teaching them how to use and respect our delicate environment and its resources.

Finally, it is not the amount of fish that I see as the problem: it is looking after the environment in which they live.

I hope in some small way that I have made a contribution to the future of fishing.

Rex Hunt

Contents

Author's Note	ix
Port Phillip Bay	1
Western Port	21
Port Albert	29
Flinders Island	37
St Helens	43
Central Highlands	51
Lake Burbury	57
Strahan	63
Apollo Bay	69
Lakes Purrumbete and Bullen Merri	79
Warrnambool	87
Portland	97
Kangaroo Island	105
Adelaide	111
Marion Bay	117
Whyalla	123
Tumby Bay	129
Port Lincoln to Ceduna	135

Esperance	*143*
Dirk Hartog Island	*149*
Kimberley	*157*
Tiwi Islands	*165*
Cape Don	*175*
Mary River	*181*
South Alligator River	*189*
Liverpool River	*195*
Cape York	*201*
Lake Tinaroo	*209*
Noosa	*215*
Gold Coast	*223*
South West Rocks	*231*
Lord Howe Island	*237*
Hawkesbury River	*243*
Sydney	*249*
Snowy Mountains	*257*
Narooma	*265*
Mallacoota	*273*
Bemm River	*281*
Gippsland Lakes and Rivers	*289*
Eildon and Goulburn River	*303*
Photograph Sources	*313*
Index	*315*

Author's Note

Over the past 35 years I have written many books. Apart from my autobiography, *Rex: My Life*, they have all been on the subject of fishing, and in fact, *Rex* has its fair share of fishing, too! It is accurate to say that fishing is my life. I was once quoted as saying that I rarely think of fishing less than 16 hours a day. Now that I think about it, that is not too far off the mark. Fishing is my passion, my energy; it is the air I breathe.

Fishing is one of the few pastimes in life that can be enjoyed from the cradle to the grave. It can involve families, groups and individuals. The bottom line is that most people enjoy the relaxing free time that fishing brings, and even a bite on the end of the line is a bonus to some. Of course you can go right down to the other end of the spectrum and jump in boots and all, like me!

Whatever fishing is to you and however often you go, whether it is regularly as a fanatic or once in a lifetime as an enthusiastic dangler, the fact is that fishing gives a lot of happiness to a lot of people.

This book was spawned from my autobiography. I received requests for more fishing stories and information on great fishing spots. In my quiet times (yes, you guessed it, while fishing), I thought that I would like to write one last book that will be seen as my legacy to fishing, something that can be handed down through time and compared with the fishing in generations to come.

This book is about the places that I have visited, the people I've met along the way, the scenery, the environment and of course, the fish. These places are my favourite fishing spots. I have left some fantastic places out – I simply could not fit every location in the book. However, let me say this right here and now, I am and have always been conscious of my great satisfaction in assisting people to catch a fish in a nice place. I have without fear or favour unashamedly listed the places where I have, and would gladly, pay my way to go fishing.

There are of course places that will be out of reach to some, simply because of the cost involved and the difficulty getting there. Other places are more readily accessible and remain in my heart as special fishing places.

My journey in fishing throughout my life so far has been so good. I have been able to fish all of these places and get paid to do it! When you do for a living what you do on your day off – that is when you know life is really good.

I have for years now hoped to inspire kids to choose their journey and follow their heart and their passion. We must never forget that all great things in life have to start somewhere. That somewhere for me was a dream on the end of a pier on the shores of Port Phillip Bay in Melbourne. This is where this book begins, before travelling on a piscatorial journey right around Australia. I have had the time of my life fishing. I hope you too can enjoy my experiences fishing the greatest country in the world.

Thank you very much and good fishing.

Rex J. Hunt
Melbourne
Australia

Port Phillip Bay

This is my home water, where it all started for me back in the 1950s. I caught my first garfish off the Mentone Pier in the summer of 1956, the year of the Melbourne Olympics. At that stage, seven years old, I had only the original bent pin and string. My captures prior to that consisted of some modest-sized crabs caught on string baited with meat amongst the rocks opposite the Parkdale Yacht Club. I was always hanging around the beach, drooling over the small wooden boats that used to launch off the beach near the yacht club. Sniffing around their catches, I'd pick up any information I could. I did not have any introduction to fishing from my family – even now at family reunions people are amazed at my profile in fishing.

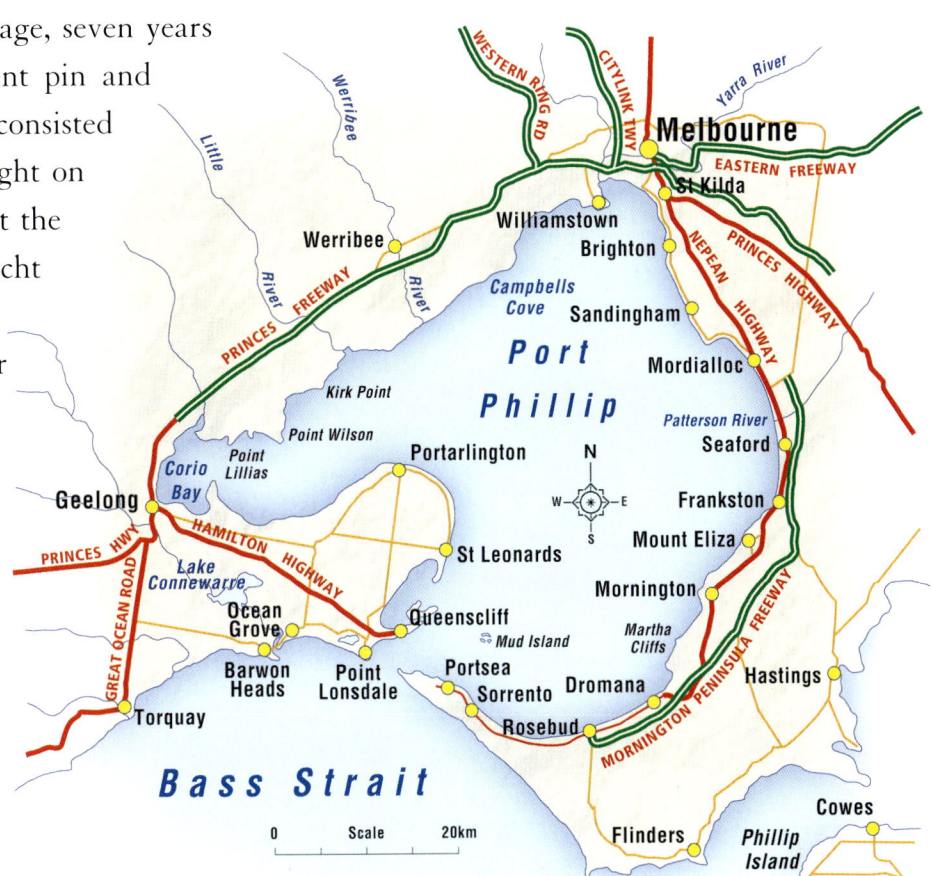

OPPOSITE: *One of my favourite combinations: an early morning off Carrum on Port Phillip Bay and snapper.*

TOP: *Dusk is a great time to get out on Port Phillip Bay and try your luck for big red. Fresh bait that you catch yourself is the go.*

ABOVE: *My son Matthew with a solid snapper. Note the Melbourne skyline in the distance.*

Port Phillip Bay is huge, covering 1950 square kilometres. It is an incredible 35 times larger than Sydney Harbour and has a coastline of some 260 kilometres. For a body of water this massive it is amazingly shallow, with an average depth of just 13 metres, and at its deepest point, not more than 26 metres. The bay's sheer size, unapparent from its small entrance, known as 'the Rip', would surely have amazed its European discoverer, John Murray, aboard the sailing ship *Lady Nelson* way back on 5 January 1802.

The 'bay' is in fact a giant estuarine lagoon, home to a wide variety of southern saltwater species from the mighty snapper that migrate into it each year, to the resident flathead and the 'ol' Chinese fish', the Whi-Ting! However, the bay has many secrets, and over the years I've been blown away at the sheer number of species (at last count 300!) to be found in its lime-green waters.

One thing that many people do not understand is the make-up of the bay. Being nearly fully enclosed and circular, it is fishable in any weather conditions, and it is these conditions that have formed the unique characteristics of this water over thousands of years. For instance, unlike in summer, when the winds can change direction by 180 degrees, the prevailing winds in the winter months come from the west and north. This means that for six months of the year, on the western side of the bay, the winds are primarily offshore. The lack of wave action that results from this allows the silt from streams like the Werribee, Yarra and Maribyrnong rivers to settle quickly on the sea floor. It is in this environment that the weed, which is so important to King George whiting, grows prolifically. These weed and sand patches form the very lifeblood of what the western side of the bay is all about. The polychaete worms thrive in these areas and are a terrific supply of food for the fish.

The eastern side of the bay also gets a fair thumping during the winter from these prevailing winds. Because of this there is more reef and rock than weed or sand patches. These reef areas offer excellent cover and food for the snapper that come into the bay each year.

While on the subject of fish coming into the bay, I would like to assure those folk who feel that 'the bay is being fished out', that this

ABOVE: *Broken ground off Sorrento in southern Port Phillip Bay. This is a prime place to hunt for King George whiting.*

cannot happen. We have a lovely seasonal run of fish each year, which replenishes fish stocks after each season. Of course there are also fish that are resident in the bay. That is, they are born in the bay and they live their entire lives in these waters. These fish include flathead (mainly sand and long-nosed, commonly called 'yanks'), flounder, stingrays, leatherjacket and rock cod. The seasonal fish include snapper, King George whiting, garfish and silver trevally, and Australian salmon can be caught throughout the year. The latter fish enter the bay from Bass Strait following schools of bait fish.

Water temperature plays an important part of the fishing in Port Phillip Bay. The ideal water temperature for snapper and whiting is 18 degrees Celsius and above. Sure, you can catch them when the water is colder, but for the main bites a higher temperature is ideal.

Contrary to popular belief, the water temperature does not rise with the outside temperature. The water warms when the ocean currents start to flow down the eastern seaboard of Australia, sending a huge warm current down south.

Snapper are by far the most sought-after fish in the bay. Apart from the annual influx of seasonal fish, there is a very healthy population of small to medium-sized fish commonly called 'pinkies', which inhabit the inner onshore reefs in areas like Beaumaris, Black Rock, Williamstown and Corio Bay. St Leonards always has a very good winter run of whiting (by run, I mean fish that do not leave the bay with the major schools).

The make-up and various fishing conditions of the bay can be divided into three categories: the sand and weed areas of the western seaboard between Williamstown and Corio Bay, the fast-flowing

BELOW: *View of Melbourne from the Docklands. In recent years there has been an explosion of sport-fishing activity from anglers keen to chase the bay's abundant population of bream.*

tidal waters of the lower bay south between a line drawn between Dromana and Portarlington, and the popular eastern seaboard between Mount Martha and Port Melbourne.

Deep Mornington through to Carrum

This area of the eastern seaboard is very popular. It is easily reached by launching at the Patterson River boat ramps or from Frankston or Mornington. Prior to the abolition of the scallop dredging boats in the mid 1990s, this area was a very well-worn path for the majority of the scallop fleet. The snapper fishing, even in the dredge days, was sometimes phenomenal. The problem was that the food was snapped up in a few hours of dredging and the schools of big fish moved on. The main areas seem to be from 14 metres' depth down to 18 metres.

ABOVE: *An aerial view of the Patterson River at Carrum.*

Selecting a place to try for snapper is a bit of a lottery. With the advent of the modern-day depth sounders, the job is a lot easier. Even more practical are the groups of boats that call each other into the 'hot spots'. My mentor Neil Thompson has had some ripper sessions in this area. Thommo's deep Seaford mark is located by looking straight down the Seaford Pier and at right angles to the Peninsula Centre at Frankston. X never marks the spot, but it is a great place to start. Well-known marks like Ansett's and the Gutway also are very productive at certain times.

The close-in areas between the mouth of the Patterson River and almost to the Frankston Pier are enormous areas for big fish after a strong and heavy south-westerly blow. This blow is onshore, and the reef and mussel beds here get a real stir-up. Immediately the winds start to abate, no matter what time of day, anglers move straight in to this magical area. Prior to bag limits there were cricket-score catches taken in this area. A well-known hot bite in the 1990s, named the 'Cup Day massacre', had a big bearing on the bag limits in place today. Some anglers just don't know when they have caught enough fish.

My advice for anglers fishing this area is to start in close at first light and then move out. If it is glassy calm, head straight for the 14–18 metre line. If the snapper are in the area you should be able to attract them to your boat. I am a great believer that fish are attracted to activity. Keep busy. Catch garfish and use them for bait, and catch flathead on the spot by using the latest soft plastic jig-type lures. Keep a constant berley over the side of the boat. Although whiting areas are scarce from Carrum to Frankston, there are several good 'patches' to be fished between Olivers Hill and Schnapper Point at Mornington.

For the best land-based fishing, try the banks of the Patterson River for bream and mullet. The best baits are sandworms, which can be gathered with a bait pump locally, and peeled prawns and pipis. You can fish for garfish off the Seaford Pier in the summer months. On some heavy onshore westerly blows the odd big snapper is caught here in October and November.

The Frankston Pier is also a very popular jetty for garfish. Best conditions are when a cross wind is blowing (north or south). Good catches of large salmon can be taken when the wind is in the west. From the end there are good catches of flathead and a few pinky snapper in the summer. I have also caught some nice six-spine leatherjacket here alongside the pylons.

The most popular and productive pier on the bay is at

LEFT: *The beautiful skyline of Melbourne from Port Phillip Bay, a view only anglers and yachties see.*

OPPOSITE: *An early photo of yours truly with some fine snapper taken off Black Rock.*

Mornington. The best asset is its close proximity to the deep water. When conditions are right, this allows large snapper to be taken right off the end of the breakwater section. Legend has it that the best conditions are when the waves are breaking over the top. Good solid catches of flathead and barracouta are also taken here, along with some huge garfish runs. At times King George whiting are caught inside the harbour.

Carrum to Ricketts Point

A prodigious area for snapper production, the region from Carrum to Ricketts Point is very popular with commercial long-liners early in the season (October to December). Deep marks are very productive on the change of tide. In close, there are many areas that contain what I call 'good snapper ground'. A mixture of mussels and weed along with some heavy reef make for an ideal snapper environment. The best times to fish there are just after the south-westerlies abate and the barometer starts to rise. There is some very good ground about two kilometres south-east of Mordialloc Pier. It has reef and weed patches that carry good populations of whiting and snapper, and in some good years the blue-spotted, or long-nosed, flathead are prolific here too. The area starts about 400 metres off the shore and runs out about a kilometre.

North of Mordialloc Pier is the start of a reef and weed area that extends right through to Ricketts Point. The area is known as Beaumaris Bay. Locals from the Mordialloc and Beaumaris Motor Yacht squadrons fish this area regularly. Famous marks like 'the Horsepaddock', 'Jack Shaws', 'the Mackerel', 'Brickies' and 'the Church' are readily recognisable as fine producers of whiting and small snapper. Large schools of garfish are prolific throughout Beaumaris Bay. In the winter, big Australian salmon chop up the bait schools that take refuge in the area during heavy northerly winds.

The Mordialloc and Beaumaris piers are probably the best spots for land-based fishing in this area. Mordialloc Pier is a very productive jetty and popular with a range of anglers. I first fished here in the late 1950s. Huge schools of garfish roam the surrounding areas, and serious garfish anglers entice them to the fishing area with liberal use of berley. The best method is an onion bag and bran, and tuna oil or bread. Allow a fine trail of feed to attract the fish. Small pinky snapper are also prolific, but watch the size limit of 27 centimetres. Flathead, snook, the odd catch of whiting, salmon and rock cod can all be taken here at times. Bream and mullet make up the bulk of the catches at the mouth of the creek and also up to the road bridge.

The Beaumaris pier is adjacent to the Beaumaris Motor Yacht Squadron, but it is a public jetty. There is some good fishing at times for southern calamari, garfish and small pinky snapper, and when they are prolific in the bay, there are good whiting to be caught, too. The best baits to try are fresh mussels and pipis. Many youngsters from the local area frequent this jetty. It is worth a go.

Ricketts Point to Yarra River

In 2002, a marine sanctuary was declared around Ricketts Point, however this stretch of the bay still has some great areas in close to shore and from the shore itself, outside the boundaries of the protected zone. The areas out wide in the deeper water carry the same conditions as all deep marks in the bay. Whiting and garfish are two very popular species targeted along these inner onshore reefs. The most sought-after fish are the pinky snapper, which range in size from 27 centimetres through to two kilograms. Most nights you will see clumps of small craft anchored over the reefs trying to catch these fish. The best time is immediately after an onshore wind has created big waves because these, in turn, create plenty of food for the fish. Whiting and garfish prefer settled conditions when the reef and sand patches are easily seen.

The area between Ricketts Point and the Sandringham breakwall is renowned as a late autumn and winter fishery. It is one of the best in Port Phillip Bay. Better areas for me have been the Clocktower reef out from Black Rock, Red Bluff reef close to shore

LEFT: *There is often excellent fishing for whiting and small snapper off the Brighton boat sheds.*

OPPOSITE: *My daughter Rachel with a huge snapper she caught in Port Phillip Bay.*

below the bluff, Yorkies reef out from Abbott Street, Sandringham, and Anonyma Shoal reef out from Yorkies.

Past the Sandringham breakwater there is the gully in close at New Street, where there are two groynes built to stop the shift of the sand covering the reefs. Try here for garfish, mullet, whiting and small snapper.

Past South Road and heading towards Brighton there is a great area of 'broken' ground: small areas of reef, weed and shell patches. This is a great environment for small pinkies and whiting. The Dendy Street reef is also a beauty, and inside Bonnet Rock at Brighton there are some nice sand holes that carry big whiting at times. I have caught dusky morwong here (also known as butterfish) and large schools of garfish inhabit the area, too.

Between the Brighton breakwater and the Yarra River mouth is a similar make-up of weed, reef, shell and sand. Many good catches of pinkies and whiting are taken along this stretch by members of the Elwood and Albert Park Anglers Clubs as well as keen public anglers. Early in the snapper season watch for boats fishing very close to shore at Brighton, St Kilda and off Pickle Street, Port Melbourne, to find out where the fish are biting.

The best land-based spots between Ricketts Point and the Yarra River mouth include Half Moon Bay Pier, which is a good area for

garfish. You might find a few leatherjacket around the pylons and some large flathead off the end in the summer. The rocks towards the Clocktower also produce small catches of pinky snapper in the summer. The best conditions are with southerly to easterly winds.

The Sandringham breakwater produces large snapper from the end on heavy onshore seas and flathead in the calm waters inside the harbour. Bream and mullet are regular catches from the small pier adjacent to the kiosk.

The New Street groynes are a recent addition and are proving to be very good land-based fishing platforms. Snapper, pinkies, whiting and flathead are the main catches. At times large garfish are taken and yellow-eye mullet are prolific in winter. The New Street reef itself offers some very good fishing in the summer. Wade up to your knees and fish from the rock ledges into the deeper (1.5 metre) water. Garfish, whiting and some very big 'yank' flathead are taken here. The soft plastic lures are very good fish-takers here. The best bait for the garfish is peeled prawn, yabby tail and maggots, or the inside of a freshly baked loaf of bread. Knead the inside into a dough and use small pieces.

The Brighton and St Kilda piers and breakwaters offer very

ABOVE: *Southern calamari squid caught off Sandringham. They are welcome as bait, but perhaps even more so as tucker.*

LEFT: *A mixed bag of whiting and leatherjacket, typical of the types of species you will encounter in the fast tidal water regions of southern Port Phillip Bay.*

OPPOSITE: *On location on the Werribee River, about to head out for some whiting action.*

good land-based fishing for garfish. Snapper are taken from the Brighton breakwater at times, and at St Kilda you may catch flathead, small salmon, mullet, and of course, toadies. When rough, you might get the odd snapper.

Adjacent to the Albert Park Angling Club is the highly productive Kerford Road pier. Garfish, whiting, mullet, warehou (also known as slimy, or snotty-nose, trevally) and flathead make up the bulk of catches here. The occasional big snapper is taken at night, with smaller pinkies after Christmas. Sometimes during winter large schools of salmon and trevally frequent the area.

There are also very good catches to be taken from Lagoon Pier. It is genuinely one of the best near-city jetties in the bay. Pinkies, flathead, trevally and salmon form the bulk of the fish caught. When the water is clear, garfish swarm in this area, and mulloway are sometimes caught on the full moon.

Nearby, the once very popular Station Pier is now closed to public vehicle access. Pedestrian access is allowed except when a cruise ship is in port, but it's a long walk with fishing gear. Pinky snapper, flathead, mulloway, bream, mullet, trevally and garfish are all taken off this pier. The waters around Station Pier are deep so as to allow ships to berth, therefore anything is possible.

Yarra River to Werribee River

This stretch is not as heavily fished as some others in Port Phillip. This is mainly due to the difficulty of travelling long distances from the available boat ramps. With the recent introduction of boat driver's licences in Victoria, it is hoped that there will be a big increase in the construction of boat-launching facilities, not only along this stretch but over the whole of Victoria in general.

Apart from the very good shore-based options around

RIGHT: *My long-time fishing mentor and friend Neil 'Thommo' Thompson with a pair of 'schoolie' size King George whiting caught off Kirk Point.*

OPPOSITE: *The first charter boat of Rex Hunt Fishing Charters, seen here at Beaumaris.*

Williamstown, the inner reef areas between Point Gellibrand and Point Cook offer some remarkable fishing, especially in the warmer months. King George whiting, snapper (pinkies), snook, garfish and sometimes large flathead are all taken. During the winter months small to medium-sized calamari squid swarm in these areas and are regularly caught by anglers drifting over the 'broken ground'. Very good catches of large snapper are taken offshore from this area. Well-known areas for big snapper are P2 and 3 buoys, the Spoil Ground mark and along the shipping channel. I have had very good captures late in the season (April) about four nautical miles due east of the plantation at Point Cook. Since the cessation of scallop dredging in the bay the growth has come back and the fish seem to stay in the area longer.

The stretch between the edge of the Point Cook marine park (introduced in 2001) to the mouth of the Werribee River brings back great memories for me. I first fished the area in 1967 with Geoff Fink. He had a shack at Campbell's Cove and we used to fish from a Carvel displacement hull in the local waters. I was involved in catching huge numbers of whiting here in the late 60s and 70s (though I must stress that we rarely saw many boats on the water in those days). The whiting grounds here are prolific. Anywhere from six to eight metres of depth will see patches of weed and sand, which are home to the millions of whiting that swarm in these areas. As I write I have found some new ground in this area that we never thought would hold whiting. It just goes to show that fish are where you find them.

At times in midsummer and late autumn, garfish swarm here literally in their millions. 'Gars' are a terrific table fish and so easy and such good fun to catch that all the family can have some action. This north-western part of the bay also has many species of flathead, but not the dusky variety, which is available in estuaries further north on the coast. In the shallows from, say, one to three metres, you'll encounter the long-nosed flathead, which takes both bait and lures readily. It stands out because its firm body is highlighted by brilliant blue spots. Many anglers frequent this area, often fishing together for safety and companionship. If you see a group of boats, they are probably on some fish action. Approach with care and respect and you will be welcome to join the party!

Because of the difficulty in reaching this part of the coast, except by boat, there are limited shore-based fishing opportunities. However, there are some spots that are recognised as proven producers of good fishing at times.

The lower Yarra and river mouth, for example, teem with fish, and the rock walls below Westgate Bridge are very popular with anglers. The outflow channel of the Newport Power Station is known locally as 'the Warmies' or from across the river 'the Hotties'. It is a sensational shore-based area where hundreds of anglers cash in on the good runs of bream, mullet, trevally and the winter run of tailor. There is no doubt that this area also produces some serious Mulloway on occasion. A live mullet, dead strip bait or large minnow-style lure is always worth a try.

The piers at Williamstown and Altona offer some good land-based opportunities, too. Check them for access: those that are open are well worth a look. Mussels grow along all the pylons and structures for the Williamstown piers. This attracts micro food offerings and, in turn, fish. Bream, trevally and mullet abound here.

BELOW: *Matthew Hunt with a solid elephant fish caught off Seaford. These fish are more regular visitors to Western Port, but still come in reasonable numbers to Port Phillip Bay.*

OPPOSITE: *Keen angler and Rex Hunt TV show presenter Lee Rayner with a monster snapper he caught on Port Phillip Bay.*

On the sea floor a flathead bait will always be taken. Several times a year the long rod brigade gather here to take advantage of a run of fish like mullet or garfish. It is worth watching.

Altona Pier is very popular for garfish, as well as leatherjacket and the occasional whiting. On rough days snapper can be caught from the end of the pier, and large flathead also frequent the area around the pier. Just after an onshore blow, when the barometer is rising, is the best time to have a go.

The area from Duncan's Road to the Werribee River mouth is also very productive for shore-based fishing. Long rods are needed to cast well into the water. Large flathead, some whiting and stingrays give good sport to novice and seasoned anglers alike. Towards the river mouth bream are taken regularly at night.

LEFT: *Many anglers today don't hesitate to put a big snapper back in the water. It's the way of the future.*

Werribee River to Bellarine Peninsula

This area, which includes Corio Bay, is very popular and easily accessible. Apart from the Werribee River ramps there are adequate ramps at Kirk Point and Avalon, and several other very good ramps in Corio Bay itself. Since my good friend Geoff Fink moved from his shack at Campbell's Cove over 20 years ago, I have spent countless hours in the stretch between the mouth of Werribee River and Avalon. I have found this area to be one of the most prolific in Victoria for whiting and small snapper, though X does not mark the spot, and the whiting have been anywhere of late. I have caught fish in seven metres of water seven kilometres from shore and in water about a metre in depth 100 metres from shore.

I fished in this area recently and was amazed at the number and large size of the swarming schools of garfish that I found in this stretch. Of concern for me as a flathead lover, catcher and eater, is the scarcity of 'yank' flathead over the past few seasons. I am hopeful it is only a cyclic phenomenon and that the good run of these fish will return.

There are a few safety measures that you should consider if

boating in this area. The extended mud and sand area known as 'Wedge Spit' can be hazardous. It pays to keep well out from the point. Be aware too that there are weed and sand patch areas right along this stretch.

Another potentially dangerous area is Long Reef. This reef extends out from the shore north of Kirk Point to a point where the cardinal mark is. It is a very heavy reef but well worth a look. I try to anchor close to the run-up to the reef and throw into the sand patches for whiting and leatherjacket. Outside the reef is an excellent area for pinky snapper. There are several experienced anglers who launch their boats from the shelly shore west of Kirk Point. While they have struggled over the past few seasons, they have years of experience. You will see their boats fishing these areas – give them plenty of room and courtesy and you are welcome to fish near them.

Arthur the Great is a long spit from the shore to a point nearly in line with Explosives Pier at Point Wilson. It is a prolific ground for whiting and snapper (both large and small). If you have a depth sounder you should use it so that you anchor just on top of the spit and throw into the deeper water (five to six metres) off the edge.

West of Explosives Pier is the commencement of Corio Bay with the outer harbour and Corio Bay proper. There are good whiting patches along the edge of the channel that runs into Corio Bay, and there are plenty of deep areas for anglers to catch the large snapper run that occurs here every year. Corio Bay has a genuine winter run of snapper, which is complemented by the annual run of snapper each spring into Port Phillip Bay. A legendary spot to catch them is Geelong Grammar School Lagoon. Fishing writer Geoff Wilson pioneered the big snapper fishing here. There are several anglers who specialise in this shallow-water, dark-of-the-night style. Corio Bay proper, right in Geelong, is a very good area to fish. Anglers should have a good knowledge of boating and port rules as there is a lot of shipping movement here every day.

There are plenty of bream and mullet to be caught from the jetties at Geelong. Between Bird Rock on the northern shore and

LEFT: *A fine bream caught on a lure in the Yarra River in the Docklands precinct.*

Point Henry in the south are some terrific broken ground and scattered reef areas. Whiting, snapper, large flathead, squid and the annual run of warehou (slimy trevally), are caught here. In the winter months large snapper are regularly caught in the deeper channels. Geoff Wilson believes that the snapper are trying to leave the bay, but take the wrong turn and end up giving us a terrific winter snapper fishery. Sounds good to me, Geoffrey!

The area between Point Henry and Portarlington is of shallow to medium depth, with the main shipping channel further out. There are a number of areas where 'spoil' from dredging is deposited.

Shortly after this there is always good fishing around these areas, because the spoil acts as a ground-bait type berley. Around the five-metre mark along this stretch there are prolific areas of weed and patches of sand. King George whiting, pinky snapper, leatherjacket, flathead and garfish are taken here in bag limit numbers. The area is also a very good place for snook (commonly called pike). I have caught these fish by slowly trolling a deep-diving lure like a CD 11 Rapala in the fluorescent pattern in these areas. I have found that anywhere there are squid, there will be snook, a great fighting fish and very good to eat.

Further south is the area stretching from the Prince George bank to Queenscliff. This is a beaut area. Averaging three to five metres deep, it has many qualities that make it a great spot to fish. Broken ground, reefs and mussel farms all add to the area's fish-attracting ability. I am keen on this area both at the start of the season (spring) and the end (autumn). The flow of water enables me to get a good 'set' on my mark. If I use a bridle-type anchor, I can sit in the one spot throughout the tide and with the aid of berley can have a very good session on whiting, garfish, flathead and squid. It's sometimes a lottery, though. Try a few areas and as soon as you get a sight, berley up and fish hard. If you see a boat or boats catching fish, it's best to move well away and set up your own area, I've found. I have rarely seen fish leave an area and go to another feeding spot, especially when they are biting.

Conclusion

Well there you are folks, my home patch, the magnificent Port Phillip Bay. 'The Bay' may not be the greatest big-fish producer on the planet, however it rarely fails to produce fish of some sort and all this whilst being surrounded by three million people in a temperate climate.

Piscatorial Compass

Port Phillip Bay, Victoria

How to get there: The metropolitan area of Melbourne and the regional city of Geelong surround Port Phillip Bay.

Where to stay: There is a huge range of accommodation available in greater Melbourne, from hotels to caravan parks and everything else in between.

What to catch: Snapper, King George whiting, flathead, garfish, Australian salmon, leatherjacket, rock cod, silver trevally, gummy shark, calamari squid, bream, barracouta, tailor, stingrays and yellow-eye mullet. Yellowtail kingfish and mulloway are occasional captures.

Gear to take: Use light and medium rod and reel outfits with mainly threadline reels. A variety of tackle is required to adequately cover all the main species in the bay.

When to go: October to May, and for snapper, October to December.

Guides and charters: A number of charter boats operate around the bay from St Kilda in the north to Queenscliff in the south.

Rex reckons: Concentrate on one species of fish at a time. Have one properly balanced outfit suitable for that species, have the freshest and best possible bait, find the fish and hopefully the fish will do the rest.

Western Port

Western Port is Melbourne's second biggest saltwater fishing playground after Port Phillip Bay. It is, in fact, east of Port Phillip Bay, and was so named by George Bass around 1798 as it was the western-most known port at the time along Australia's east coast. Many people rate the Western Port fishing as being better than Port Phillip Bay; in any case it is certainly one of my favourite waters.

Every part of this waterway tells a different story. It has a bad reputation of burning anglers because of the strong tidal flow and the myriad banks and channels. Every year anglers' boats are stranded on sandbanks as they take short cuts, thinking that safe navigable water is ahead. In fact, Western Port has an area of 680 square kilometres,

OPPOSITE: *In the 1980s I conducted beach-fishing schools right along the coast from Kilcunda to Venus Bay.*

but over 270 square kilometres are mud banks at low tide.

To view Western Port properly I believe it is essential to fish through the low tide. As such, the bible for fishing this water is the tide guide. I plan my trips to commence halfway down the ebbing tide and to finish halfway up the flood, which gives me a very good chance of catching a feed. There is less water over the banks at low tide; in fact, many of the banks that are covered at half tide come out at low tide. A good example is the large sand area known as the middle spit. To assist you to plan your trip to this water, I suggest you view or purchase chart number Aus 150. It shows the many channels and banks of Western Port, and can come in very handy.

Species

The most sought-after species in Western Port is the King George whiting, sometimes refered to here as 'channel' whiting. Most areas in this water carry this popular species. The whiting feed on polychaete worms, so where there is sand and a mixture of reef and weed, there will be whiting. At times a lot of sinker weight is needed to reach the bottom, but I prefer to allow a lot of line out

LEFT: *An early shot of the Hastings boat ramp and view to the channel. It was busy 20 years ago and even more so today.*

OPPOSITE TOP: *This bridge connects Phillip Island to the mainland in the south of Western Port. There is good fishing to be had in these highly tidal waters.*

OPPOSITE BELOW: *A sunrise and a set reel on Western Port.*

and have a direct feel on the rig rather than dropping a huge sinker straight down. Unfortunately the force in the tidal flow will cause a bow in the line and therefore it is difficult to feel the bites. Bigger fish can be caught in the deeper channels, and the best times to fish these deeper waters are an hour either side of the change of tide.

Snapper are also a serious consideration in this water. The main schools enter Western Port in early spring and leave at the start of winter. Whilst the change of temperature on the land has little to do with the fish biting, the water temperature does. There seems to be a trigger that sets the fish feeding in Western Port. My ideal water temperature is around the 16.5 degrees mark, but some of the best fishing occurs in the height of summer when the water can be 20 degrees plus.

Snapper are a deep-water proposition. Snapper love reefs, so it is wise to learn where the good ground is. There are plenty of areas in this water that hold good snapper for the entire season, such as Elizabeth Island at Corinella, offshore from Cowes, deep at Hastings and also around the edges of Crawfish and Eagle Rocks and Joe's Island.

Though whiting and snapper are the most common, other

BELOW: *Matthew Hunt with a huge gummy shark he caught in Western Port.*

BOTTOM: *Christi Worsteling with a fine snapper caught in Western Port.*

popular species include gummy shark, elephant fish (bag limit of three), snook (sometimes called pike), garfish, salmon and flathead. You might also catch the odd trevally, warehou and school shark.

In Western Port in particular, it is important to know how to work with the tide. When I was fishing hard as a competitor in the AAA, I always did very well on this water. I studied the tides and knew exactly where to go and fish at different stages of the tide. Tide is the operative word here; I have fished very few places in Victoria that are so affected by the stage of the tidal flow. I had marks for the complete cycle, but then, I was taught by two men who knew a lot about this water. Bill Copeland and Jack Wells were absolute champions in whiting fishing in these waters and I was fortunate in my early years to be able to go fishing with them and learn some of their trade.

When chasing whiting I would commence fishing halfway down the ebb from the flood. I would fish in areas that have seen about three metres of water at full tide, and I'd cast well away from the boat and use as light a sinker as possible. My leader would be quite long, about 75 centimetres, and I would use either fresh mussels, pipis or bass yabbies (also known as pink nippers), which can be pumped on the sandbank. If I was losing baits to toadies I knew I was in the wrong place or the fish were not there.

A short move of a few metres can sometimes put you onto the fish. If I encountered a good bite, I'd keep them busy with the liberal use of berley, which can be anything from pellets soaked in tuna oil, shell grit and mussel shells or sometimes just a handful of pellets.

As the tide reached its ebb I would move into the deeper channels and fish until the change of tide. I would then work my way along the edges of the channel near the exposed banks until I located the fish.

Flinders

Flinders is a ripper land-based location for youngsters to get out onto the pier and catch anything from big squid to snook, whiting and leatherjacket. For boaties, the deep channels offer some of the best fishing in Western Port with some seriously big King George whiting, snapper, gummy shark and yellowtail kingfish at times.

Sandy Point

At the start of the North Arm is a prime area for King George whiting between October and April. Fish the ebb tide in around three to four metres of water for best results with mussels, pipis or bass yabbies.

Bouchier and Boulton Channels

I have had some marvellous fishing at the intersection of the Bouchier and Boulton channels for small pinky snapper and some quite large King George whiting. It is also a good place to catch large leatherjacket on the low tide. I have caught some rippers here at times on pipis with long shank hooks. The biggest leatherjacket have been the six-spined and horseshoe varieties.

Stony Point

Some of my best days on Western Port have been within swimming distance of the Stony Point ramp. Many of us anglers tend to seek greener pastures and must travel over some great fishing spots in the process. Stony Point used to harbour a large fleet of boats that were only displacement hulls and therefore only capable of a few knots per hour in speed. In my early days on the water I fished really close to the ramp at Stony. The message here is, don't disregard any place that may hold a fish. It only takes a few minutes and an anchor drop to find out if the fish are in residence.

Kilcunda

I caught my first fish on Cemetery Beach at Kilcunda in 1967. I had just obtained my driver's licence and I can recall heading down the

BELOW: *Tackle shop owner and Rex Hunt TV presenter Paul Worsteling loves Western Port for obvious reasons.*

BOTTOM: *A nice pair of King George whiting taken off Flinders.*

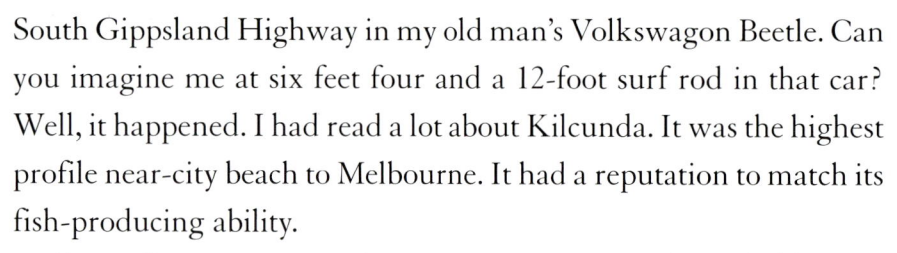

South Gippsland Highway in my old man's Volkswagon Beetle. Can you imagine me at six feet four and a 12-foot surf rod in that car? Well, it happened. I had read a lot about Kilcunda. It was the highest profile near-city beach to Melbourne. It had a reputation to match its fish-producing ability.

Later Gunnamatta on the Mornington Peninsula probably took over as a more popular beach, but in those days Kilcunda was 'the' place.

Ninety Mile Beach, between Woodside and Marlo was a hot spot as well, but it involved an overnight trip. Kilcunda was popular with day-trippers and many angling clubs used anything from buses to furniture vans to take them to this beach. The main fishing area was Cemetery Beach. You would park in the area and walk past the cemetery, over the train line and then onto the beach. Not much has changed today! Fish three hours leading up to the high tide. Take the tide from Port Phillip Heads, use a paternoster rig with pipis on the top and half a pilchard, whitebait or surf popper on the bottom, and you are in business.

I found that there are no half measures at Kilcunda. I fished the beach well past the mouth of the Powlett River. I found good fishing

ABOVE: *A fine catch of Western Port 'fast water' King George whiting.*

LEFT: *One of Hastings Marina's many charter boats prepares to leave for a day's fishing.*

OPPOSITE: *The unusual-looking elephant fish are a consistent visitor to Western Port in March and April.*

all along as long as there were gutters and holes. Weed can be a problem after a big onshore swell, which can dislodge huge clumps of kelp that float onto the beach. Salmon are the main target here, with yellow-eye mullet and silver trevally also being caught. In the summer months there are large flathead and small pinky snapper to be taken as well.

There were regular reports on my radio show in Melbourne from this area. Colin Gilmartin owns the local caravan park and used to relay reports to Paul Worsteling. Kilcunda is still a very good surf-fishing beach area within easy drive of Melbourne.

Conclusion

I've taken the TV cameras to Western Port many times, mostly in pursuit of King George whiting and in more recent times the elephant fish, which has become a unique fishery each March to April for Melbourne anglers. There is plenty of good information available on fishing Western Port, including a very detailed book by Paul Worsteling. Get to the know the tides and the channel areas, and you won't be disappointed.

Piscatorial Compass

Western Port, Victoria

How to get there: Western Port is approximately 60 kilometres south-east of Melbourne via the South Gippsland Highway. Hastings is one of the major launching points.

Where to stay: Anglers can base themselves in Melbourne or stay locally. Phillip Island has a very wide array of accommodation available.

What to catch: Snapper, elephant fish, King George whiting, gummy shark, Australian salmon, calamari squid, flathead, garfish and silver trevally. There are also several shark species that inhabit Western Port.

Gear to take: Use light to medium rods to cater for the variety of species.

When to go: Like Port Phillip Bay, you catch fish year round in Western Port, but the best times are between October and May. March and April is the prime time for elephant fish.

Guides and charters: Western Port is well served by a large number of charter boat operators.

Rex reckons: The fast tides of Western Port can be a navigational challenge, so it is best to learn about the tides and obtain a quality map or chart.

28 REX HUNT'S FISHING AUSTRALIA

Port Albert

Port Albert is an historical town in South Gippsland about 250 kilometres south-east of Melbourne. It was once a thriving port in the gold rush days of the 1850s and 1860s when gold was discovered at Walhalla and Omeo. Today its industries comprise a modest commercial fishing fleet and an emerging tourist trade, which anglers contribute to in ever-increasing numbers.

OPPOSITE: *The boat ramp at Port Albert provides good access to inshore and offshore fishing.*

TOP: *Dolphins are frequent visitors to the waters off the South Gippsland coast.*

ABOVE: *The western shoreline of Wilsons Promontory offers great fishing in a spectacular environment.*

I've taken the TV film crew here a few times to fish offshore for snapper aboard Sharon E Charters with charter boat skipper Mark Radon. We've enjoyed some good success on the snapper when the wind permits, but this is southern Australia, folks, and the wind is king. Luckily you can always fish inside the islands that offer Port Albert some protection. The main ones include Sunday, Dog and Clonmell Island, the latter named after a steamer that was shipwrecked there in 1841.

Based in Port Albert you can fish the entire coastline in relative protection, from McLoughlins Beach in the east through to Port Welshpool in the west. The area is made up of small islands, channels and sand flats. Species found throughout here include big flathead, King George whiting, 'pinky' snapper, trevally, garfish, juvenile salmon and tailor, flounder and many others. The flounder love bass yabbies (as do most species), which can be pumped from the banks that are exposed at low tide. These are some of the best yabby banks I have seen anywhere.

There are several entrances to Bass Strait: at McLoughlins Beach, Manns Beach, Kate Kearney, Port Albert and Singapore Deep (Port Welshpool). All except the entrance from Port Welshpool through Singapore Deep are often treacherous and should only be crossed by experienced boaters who have local knowledge. You can still get yourself into trouble in Singapore Deep, although there is at least a main channel to follow, which is reasonable in fair to good weather conditions.

McLoughlins Beach

McLoughlins is situated inside the estuary and there is, in fact, no actual beach there – the area consists mostly of shallow marshes and weed beds. There is a very good boat ramp, but the best boat-launching conditions are limited to about three hours up the flood tide then two hours after the change. Fishing inside the estuary offers whiting, flathead, flounder and silver trevally. For best results, use fresh bait in low-light conditions.

ABOVE: *The jetties in Port Albert house the local commercial fishing fleet and provide great opportunities for land-based anglers.*

The channel is marked all the way to the entrance, but again, the bar is dangerous and whilst it is the shortest to get through, it can be very difficult to get through, particularly when afternoon sea breezes pick up.

Offshore at 14–18 metres depth is good for snapper up to nine kilograms, plus gummy shark, school shark, flathead, silver trevally and in some places King George whiting up to one kilogram, which will take whole pilchards. Look for reef areas on the depth sounder. If you encounter gurnard and barracouta, it is usually best to move on unless you are confident the snapper are there.

Surf fishing can be very good across from the footbridge near the McLoughlins Beach boat ramp. This footbridge gives access to the famous Ninety Mile Beach, one of the longest continuous beaches in Australia. (McLoughlins is in fact its starting point.) Australian salmon, flathead and gummy shark (at night) are the main targets. In late spring there is a real chance for big snapper as they move into spawn, and smaller snapper, which also make for good fishing and eating, tend to stick around for a while after Christmas.

ABOVE: *Blue-throated wrasse are an unusual addition to the South Gippsland angler's bag.*

LEFT: *Double-header of flathead and snapper caught offshore from McLoughlins.*

OPPOSITE: *Yours truly and Paul Worsteling with two fine snapper caught offshore from Port Albert.*

Manns Beach

Manns Beach is accessed via the road from Tarraville. There is a fairly poor boat ramp available, however I would not advise using the entrance to the ocean from here in any case — it's just too dangerous in my opinion.

On the 'inside' around Farmers Channel, whiting, garfish, flathead and trevally are on offer. The deeper sections of the channel sometimes produce big snapper, gummy shark and large stingrays. Small pinky snapper turn up after Christmas. Another good location is around St Margaret Island, where all of the major estuarine species can be caught, including estuary perch.

Robertsons Beach

Further west of Manns Beach is Robertsons Beach, also accessible from Tarraville. Robertsons does not have a reasonable boat ramp and is usually fished by anglers who have launched elsewhere, or who fish from the beach. The big channel that runs past Robertsons carries good fish. I once caught the biggest garfish I have ever seen from the shore here whilst filming for the TV show: it was a double-header that weighed 600 grams between the two of them.

The entrance to Bass Strait past Dog Island is known as Kate Kearney, and as far as I'm concerned it falls into the same category as Manns Beach – too dangerous.

Port Albert Channel

Port Albert Channel offers some very good fishing. I've filmed here both inside the estuary and offshore, and usually managed to produce some good TV. Port Albert has a good two-lane concrete boat ramp and several jetties to fish from. The entrance to Bass Strait via the marked Port Albert channel has a very long and sometimes dangerous bar. If you are new to the area, using a charter boat is a very good way to learn the ropes of crossing the bar at Port Albert.

There are good runs of whiting between October and April in the estuary. Fish the edges and the drop-offs where gutters enter the channels. The best times to try are halfway down the ebb and halfway up the flood tide. Keep an eye out for the number three channel marker known as the Basket Beacon, which is famous for its early-season run of big snapper, usually in November. Gummy shark and some big flathead are caught throughout the system, with Snake Channel and Sunday Island Channel both very good spots to try. On a high flood tide you can navigate your way through to Port Welshpool.

The approach to the offshore scene is similar to that at McLoughlins. Most anglers fishing offshore from Port Albert will head east towards McLoughlins anyway, sometimes as far up as Seaspray, in search of the best reefs for snapper.

ABOVE: *Lee Rayner with a solid South Gippsland snapper.*

OPPOSITE: *Anglers fishing the famous Ninety Mile Beach.*

Port Welshpool

Port Welshpool is the other major town along the coast in this area. The facilities for anglers are excellent, with a very good boat ramp and a jetty that provides access to Corner Inlet, Singapore Deep and the waters and islands off Wilsons Promontory. The jetty fishes well for many species including flathead, silver trevally and whiting. There is good shore-based fishing all around Port Welshpool – you could even make a cast from the front bar of the pub. A note for boat fishers: some of Corner Inlet's mixture of channels and sand flats are now part of a marine park, but there is still a considerable area open to anglers, who fish mainly for whiting.

Singapore Deep, which runs past Snake Island, is the large channel that connects Port Welshpool and Corner Inlet with Bass Strait. In good conditions it is worth fishing for flathead, gummy shark, other sharks and large snapper. Heavy sinkers are the go in Singapore Deep as the tide can run very fast.

When fishing offshore along the western shoreline of Wilsons Promontory, one of the prime places to try is Rabbit Island. Apart from the usual species there are some huge King George whiting to rival even South Australian whiting, with at least one recorded capture of a two-kilogram specimen. Large flathead are also very good around Rabbit Island.

Many of the island groups that are found between the bottom of Wilsons Promontory and Tasmania's Flinders Island produce yellowtail kingfish in summer when water temperatures are at the highest. Other species to be caught around these islands include snook, blue-throated wrasse and very big squid.

Conclusion

Port Albert offers a great diversity of fishing within the confines of its uniquely protected estuarine system. It would take years to fully explore the islands and channels that make up this complex environment. The offshore snapper scene is one of the finest in Victoria, however it is not without its dangers as the weather can get very rough.

Piscatorial Compass

Port Albert, Victoria

How to get there: Port Albert is approximately 235 kilometres from Melbourne via the Princes Highway. Take a right turn at Traralgon onto the Hyland Highway and then follow the signs to Port Albert via the South Gippsland Highway and the Yarram–Port Albert Road.

Where to stay: A wide variety of accommodation is available, from caravan parks and units to holiday cabins and hotel/motel rooms.

What to catch: Snapper, King George whiting, gummy shark, flathead, flounder, garfish, silver trevally and Australian salmon.

Gear to take: Use light to medium rods and threadline reels.

When to go: September to May.

Guides and charters: Several charter boats operate out of Port Albert.

Rex reckons: If you're fishing inshore, take plenty of insect protection as the sandflies and mosquitoes in the mangroves are bigger than some countries' air forces.

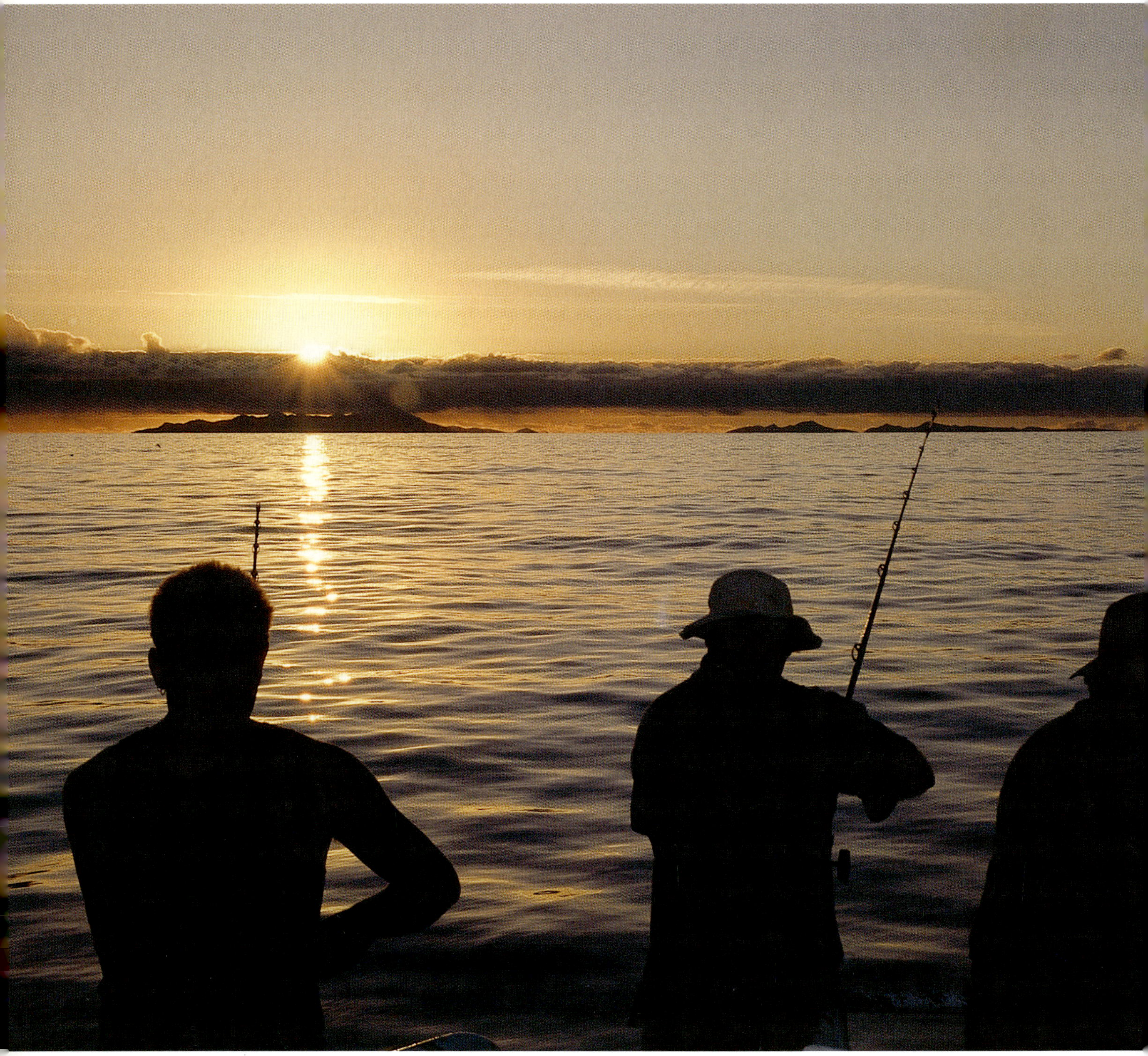

Flinders Island

Flinders Island is the largest of 52 islands that form the Furneaux Group off the north-east tip of Tasmania. The island was named by the ubiquitous Matthew Flinders who, along with George Bass, circumnavigated Tasmania to prove it was separated from the mainland by a large body of water, subsequently to be known as Bass Strait.

Flinders is 64 kilometres long and up to 29 kilometres wide, covering almost 1400 square kilometres. Its main industries are farming, commercial fishing and tourism. The tourism blurb boasts that the island has more sunny days than the Gold Coast, with a fairly temperate climate in winter.

The islands in the group offer some of the best-

OPPOSITE: *Bass Strait vista of Flinders Island.*

sheltered fishing in Bass Strait. The disappointment that the big schools of snapper and whiting seem to avoid this area is compensated for by the beauty of the rugged landscape and the wilderness environment that Flinders has to offer.

For the land-based angler, the waters around the island are home to some very good fighting species such as Australian salmon, silver trevally, gummy and school sharks, and large flathead (tiger and sand). On a lighter note, it is also the home – and perhaps the only home – of the red gurnard. They seem to be everywhere.

North East River

My favourite fishing spot on the island is at the entrance to North East River in the extreme north. I have had some of the best salmon fishing I have experienced here, and the time of year doesn't matter.

Fish to nearly four kilograms have been taken off Elephant Rock, which is a large platform facing the ocean. It is relatively safe, but – like all rock platforms – you should never fish alone and be always on the lookout for freak waves.

The best methods for catching the salmon are during a flood tide, preferably in the afternoon, using baits such as pilchards or whitebait fished on a paternoster rig, or by casting and retrieving silver metal lures. There are also very good-sized silver trevally and flathead in this area. Floundering is popular here at night using a spotlight and spear.

Pot Boil Point

An excellent land-based area is the 'Pot Boil', located on the southeast corner of Flinders Island and accessed via Pot Boil Road from Lady Barron. It can be reached by a two-wheel-drive vehicle; however, a 4WD is advisable. This is a very churned-up, rough sea area, as the name suggests. Big flathead are the go here, with gummy shark in the late afternoon to evening. Silver trevally, Australian salmon and mullet are also present and will take baits of fresh squid and pilchard.

Trousers Point

Trousers Point is a rock platform at the foot of the Strzelecki Peaks in the south-west of the island. This is one of the most picturesque parts of Flinders, with high peaks surrounded by clear aqua-coloured waters. There is excellent fishing for salmon and large snook using lures on an incoming tide. Snook can also be caught on whole pilchards fished under a running bobby float.

Lady Barron

A very good land-based spot is the wharf located in the port town of Lady Barron. There is deep water near this jetty, as large vessels

ABOVE: *Big flathead are common right around Flinders Island.*

ABOVE OPPOSITE: *Beautiful Trousers Point and Strzelecki National Park, a top spot for a range of beach species.*

BELOW OPPOSITE: *A nice Australian salmon taken on a lure cast off Trousers Point.*

bringing supplies to the island berth here. My son Matthew and I filmed a segment for the TV show a few years ago where we took some lovely silver trevally using squid for bait. I have also taken good catches of salmon and calamari squid, particularly at dusk. Kingfish and gummy shark are also taken from the wharf by anglers who put in the time.

Offshore

The boat fishing is unlimited. I have always fished with Captain James Luddington aboard his boat *Strait Lady*. Jim has always put us on the best areas. Whether it is the large flathead drifting off the many islands, large gummy or school sharks in the deeper channels on the change of tide, or fishing for striped trumpeter on the Continental Shelf, we have always caught a feed.

Cape Barren Island, the second largest island in the Furneaux Group, lies directly south of Flinders and has a small settlement of people, but is otherwise uninhabited. Seven gill sharks haunt the passage between Cape Barren and Clarke Island. They can be berleyed at night when the tide will take the scent into a deep hole. When the action begins, it is battle stations all round.

The Continental Shelf also offers the opportunity to catch game

LEFT: *Thumping Tasmanian or striped trumpeter caught in 200 metres of water off the eastern coast of Flinders Island.*

BELOW: *Seven gill sharks can be found in good numbers around Flinders, in particular between Cape Barren and Clarke Islands in the south.*

BOTTOM: *A couple of lady anglers with a salmon and a silver trevally they caught from Elephant Rock, North East River.*

OPPOSITE: *Lady Barron jetty and port.*

fish trolling skirted lures or live baits. Striped and blue marlin and yellowfin tuna are present from January to April when the warm currents flow down from the north. Albacore and striped tuna are quite reliable when the larger game fish aren't around and will also respond to trolled skirted lures.

The waters around the Continental Shelf also offer deep-sea fishing, with the emphasis on deep. Blue-eye trevalla, harpuka and other deep-sea monsters lurk at depths of over 300 metres in the canyons that dot the shelf. The further east you go, the deeper it gets and the longer the haul to retrieve lines. The potential is untapped but only when the weather is right, as you are in the middle of Bass Strait.

Conclusion

I think the magic of this island lies in the fact that it's not easy to get to. Not everyone enjoys travelling in light planes. Once on the island, it is fun driving to places such as Killiecrankie Bay, West End, Red Bluff and Cameron Inlet to explore the fishing opportunities.

Piscatorial Compass
Flinders Island, Tasmania

How to get there: Island Airlines and Dreamtime Flights operate a regular air service out of Melbourne. Flights also depart from Launceston.

Where to stay: There is a range of accommodation available on the island in the towns of Lady Barron and Whitemark, including a hotel, bed and breakfasts, cottages, holiday units and guest houses.

What to catch: Striped trumpeter, Australian salmon, gummy shark, sand and tiger flathead, barracouta, silver trevally, sweep, snook, various species of wrasse, garfish, calamari squid, striped and blue marlin, yellowfin and striped tuna, albacore, blue-eye trevalla and seven gill shark.

Gear to take: You'll need a light threadline rod and reel for jetties and estuaries, a ten-kilogram overhead rod and reel for deep-sea fishing, and surf-fishing gear for the beaches.

When to go: Year round. The best weather is from January to May.

Guides and charters: I would recommend Jim Luddington and his boat **Strait Lady**.

Rex reckons: You don't need a boat to get amongst the fish on Flinders Island, as there is a wealth of fantastic land-based fishing spots right around the island.

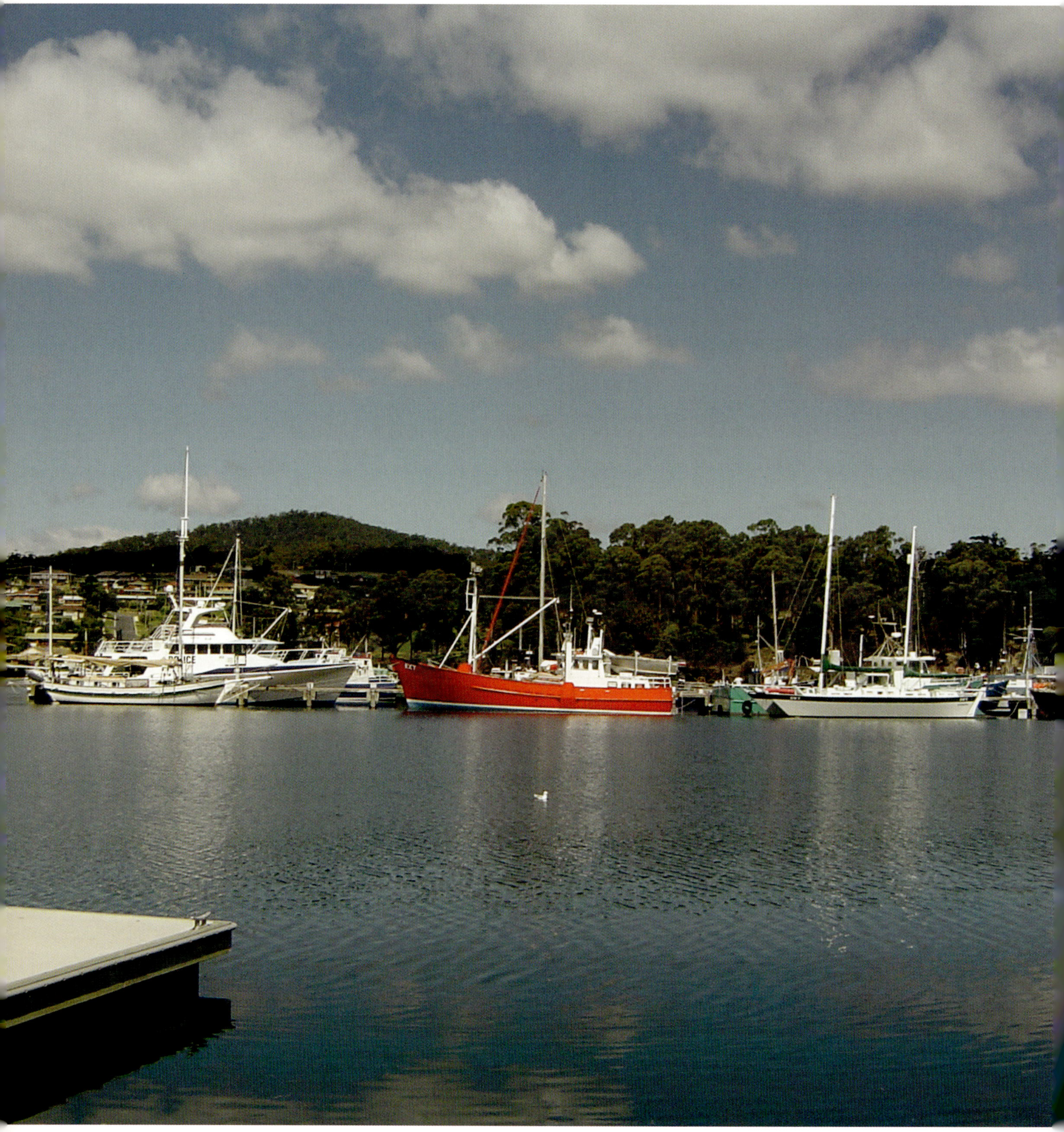

St Helens

St Helens is the largest town on the east coast of Tasmania, and has an interesting history. Tin mining and the exporting of the native timber from the hills behind the town ensured that plenty of traffic flowed through the port in the early days, and as the supply of tin tapered off in the 1940s, boat-building became a serious industry. Two large 100-foot-long trading boats were built from local Tasmanian oak on the foreshore of the harbour. After the Second World War, fishing boats boomed and there are still good commercial catches of deep-sea trevalla, scallops, abalone and orange roughy made today.

The fastest-growing industry for St Helens is tourism. With the warm, pleasant climate and sandy beaches, St Helens and other towns along the 'Sun Coast' are now attracting visitors. Tourists fish with the local charter boats, bushwalk, swim or just lounge around and take in the local scenery.

St Helens offers the whole gamut of fishing experiences, from shore-based fishing to deep-sea and game

OPPOSITE: *The beautiful port of St Helens on Tassie's east coast.*

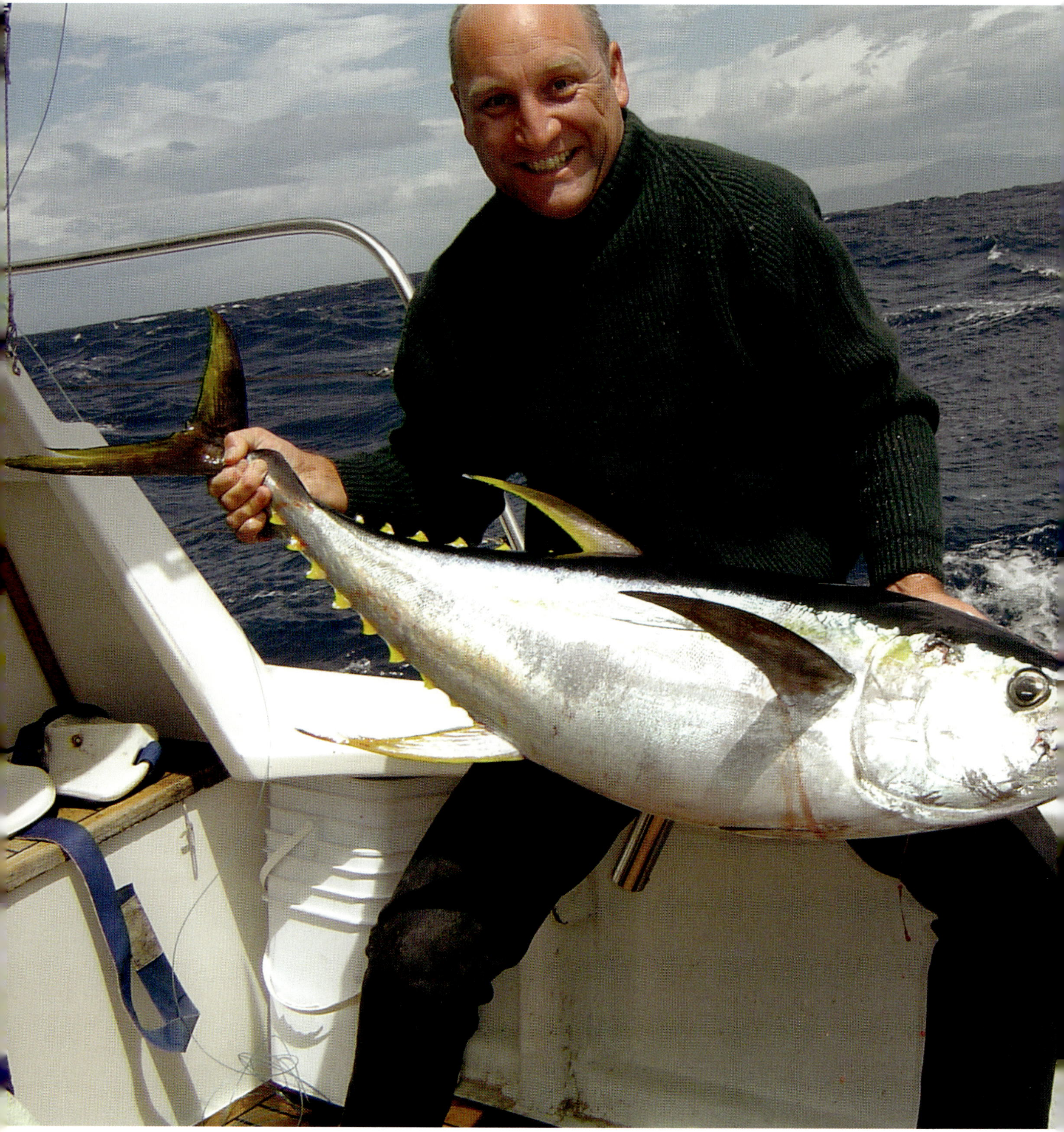

fishing, from just offshore out to the continental shelf some 30 kilometres away. There are some superb beaches, a magnificent estuary in Georges Bay and rock fishing along the coast.

Offshore

The TV crew and I fished offshore of St Helens with local charter skipper Rocky Carosi of Professional Charters. We headed out to the continental shelf, hoping to get amongst the striped trumpeter, a deep-sea reef fish common in the waters off Tasmania and occasionally encountered off the south coast of New South Wales.

We fished very deep at 200 metres with heavy gear comprising 70-kilogram Gelspun for the main line and 180-kilogram Jinkai for the trace. The trace has to be tough, as barracouta and other toothy critters create havoc at times. To get this whole rig to the bottom I usually anchor it with half a brick, or in this case, three large snapper leads.

As soon as my rig hit the bottom it was taken by something. The long haul of pump and wind began and folks, it really took the wind out of my sails to find a barracouta on the end of the line. That was it for the Bearded Burbler; 200 metres of winding is not my idea of fun! Rocky took over and soon showed the TV cameras and me the kind of quality fish that can be caught in the waters off St Helens. He hauled in a magnificent striped trumpeter of around eight kilograms – a beauty. These fish are great to eat and can grow up to 16 kilograms.

Then things got very interesting. The dorsal fin of a mako shark broke the surface just metres away from Rocky's boat. These streamlined sharks are very curious and it wasn't long before I rigged a strip of striped tuna, started a berley trail and cast the bait out into the trail with great expectation.

Bang! The mako took the bait, ran, and when I set the hook it leapt into the air like an acrobat. These sharks are classified as game fish for a good reason. They are tenacious, never giving up, and jump

OPPOSITE: *Yellowfin tuna turn up most years out on the continental shelf offshore from St Helens.*

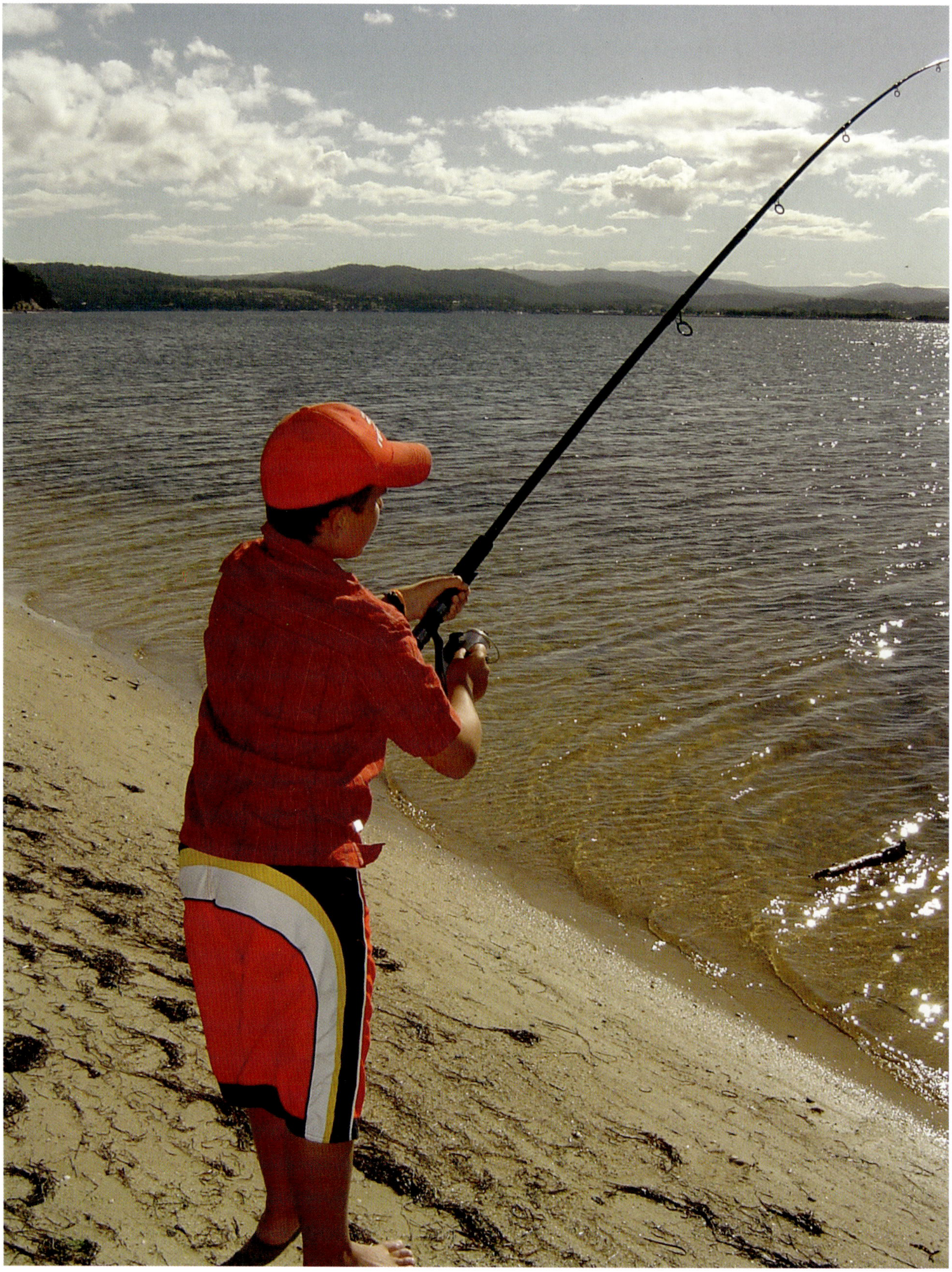

frequently into the air, occasionally even landing in the angler's boat. Just remember to duck! Makos have been known to completely destroy the inside of a boat. Our mako jumped and ran hard, but luckily decided to stick to the water. I soon brought the shark alongside, cut the wire trace and bid our finned friend farewell.

There are a number of varieties of game fish to be caught in the waters off St Helens. Striped marlin come here late in the autumn when the warm ocean current reaches these waters. Yellowfin tuna and albacore are reliable visitors and these fall to both live baits and trolled skirted lures.

Georges Bay

On another trip to St Helens with the TV crew we fished Georges Bay aboard Rocky's charter boat. Georges Bay is a tremendous body of water that provides protection to the port of St Helens, and is an excellent choice when the weather offshore is too rough. Featuring deep channels, sea grass beds and sand flats, it provides anglers with the opportunity to catch a variety of species including Australian salmon, tailor, flathead, silver trevally and garfish.

Lee Rayner and Paul Worsteling joined Rocky and myself for an entertaining session chasing salmon and tailor on lures around Georges Bay. Schools of these fish were so thick that we had multiple hook-ups of all four anglers at one time. It made for good television and was a great dancing lesson, as we had to duck and weave around each other to land the salmon, which averaged three kilograms, and the tailor, which weighed in around the 1.5-kilogram mark. It is a bit unusual to catch big tailor in waters this far south, as they mostly prefer the warmer waters of New South Wales and Queensland and of course, Western Australia.

The salmon and tailor took any lure, from a bibbed minnow to pieces of plastic tube on a bare hook. This was a terrific session that highlighted the healthy state of the inshore fishery in Tasmania, which, unlike on the Australian mainland, faces only limited commercial pressure.

TOP: *Rocky Carosi with a superb albacore caught off St Helens.*

MIDDLE: *Striped trumpeter are a prized table fish in Tasmanian waters.*

ABOVE: *A ripper salmon caught in Georges Bay.*

OPPOSITE: *Fishing the magnificent Georges Bay.*

Ansons Bay

Located approximately 40 kilometres north of St Helens is Ansons Bay. This unique estuary is in pristine condition; I can honestly say that I have never fished for bream in a better environment, and have never caught fish of such quality anywhere in Australia. This estuarine lake has clean water covering vast patches of weed beds.

I fished here with Michael 'Comet' Haley of Gone Fishing charters. Comet is a top bloke who knows his bream fishing, and boy, has he got a great office. This was serious bream fishing, folks, where a one-kilogram fish was almost a 'throwback' and those of two kilograms or more were 'good' fish. We fished various spots around Ansons Bay using bass yabbies or nippers for bait, and Comet wasn't afraid to move if the action was slow or when we encountered small fish.

ABOVE: *Charter and other moored boats at St Helens.*

I cut my teeth on bream fishing on the Patterson River in Melbourne and then on the Gippsland Lakes. We used long rods with light tips. These rods act like shock absorbers and with a finely tuned drag you should never a lose a good bream. The session on Ansons Bay proved once again just how effective long rods can be.

Conclusion

St Helens has a lot to offer, from game and deep-sea fishing offshore to light estuary, rock, beach and jetty fishing. The weather is fairly mild compared to other parts of Tasmania and the east coast is protected from prevailing south-westerlies, so you can usually find somewhere to fish.

Piscatorial Compass

St Helens, Tasmania

HOW TO GET THERE: Situated on the east coast of Tasmania, St Helens is approximately 250 kilometres north of Hobart along the Tasman Highway.

WHERE TO STAY: There is ample accommodation all around St Helens. The TV crew and I stayed at the Bayside Inn on our visits.

WHAT TO CATCH: Yellowfin tuna, albacore, striped marlin, mako shark, striped trumpeter, Australian salmon, tailor, black bream, garfish, barracouta and flathead.

GEAR TO TAKE: Use light threadline gear for estuary, rock and inner offshore fishing, and medium overhead gear for reef work. Take game gear up to 80 kilograms for marlin and yellowfin tuna.

WHEN TO GO: October to May.

GUIDES AND CHARTERS: I've fished with Rocky Carosi of Professional Charters on several occasions, and recommend him highly as a reliable charter boat skipper. Nothing is too much trouble for Rocky and his lovely wife Angela. Fishing guide Michael Haley of Gone Fishing also knows his stuff.

REX RECKONS: This is a top spot with a good variety of fishing environments and plenty of options if the weather offshore shuts you down. One of Australia's secret fishing jewels.

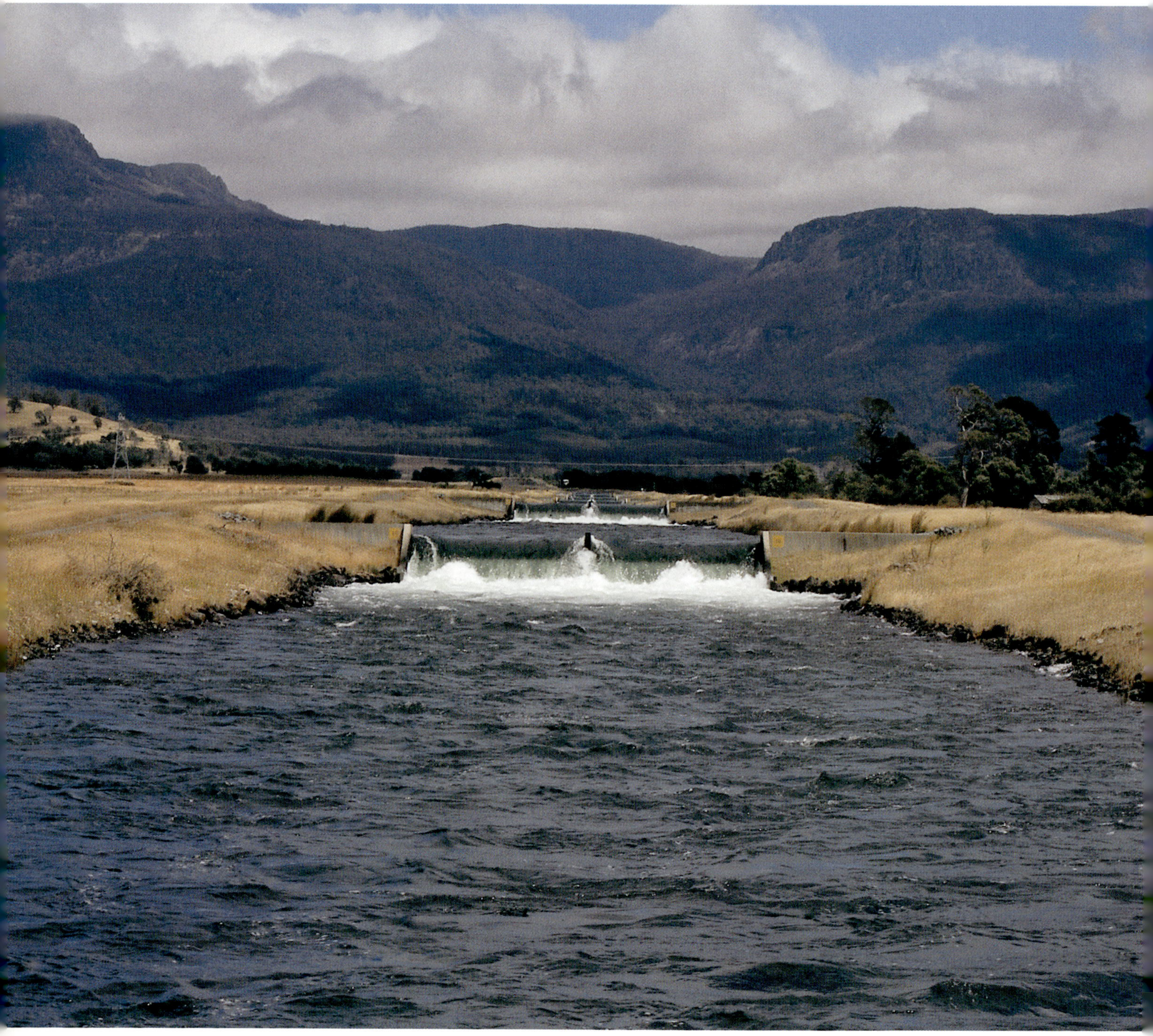

Central Highlands

The Central Highlands region of Tasmania is the most famous brown trout region in Australia. It is also a major hydro-electric power generation area much like the Snowy Mountains in southern New South Wales.

The region has been popular with anglers chasing trout for well over a century, although in the early days, road access was often difficult in this remote part of Tasmania. While there are literally hundreds of lakes, the best known and probably most productive are a couple of my favourites: Arthurs Lake and Great Lake.

OPPOSITE: *Highlands vista!*

Arthurs Lake

Arthurs Lake was formed when two natural lakes (Sand and Blue), along with the Morass Marsh, were flooded. Brazendale, Neil and Hawk islands are all that remains of the land that originally separated these two natural lakes. The lake is about 12 kilometres long from north to south and up to nine kilometres wide. It is around 950 metres above sea level when full.

There are many treed areas as well as open stretches which provide a perfect trout environment. The original lake area was stocked with trout as early as the 1870s, although it didn't receive serious liberations until the mid-1940s. Today, it is a fully self-supporting wild brown trout fishery.

I first fished this area in 1992 and found Arthurs to be full of small to medium-sized brown trout that took trolled lures very well. Arthurs is Tassie's most popular lake. There is an amazing population of trout in its waters. (Top trout guide Peter Hayes described the browns here as underwater rabbits.) Each year I visit Arthurs just to catch these beautiful brown trout.

There is a closed season from early May to late July or early August each year to allow the fish to spawn. There are three or four

ABOVE: *You can teach an old dog a new trick, as this nice brown taken on a soft plastic lure in Great Lake proves.*

LEFT: *Stripping fly line for a wily Arthurs brown trout.*

major spawning streams that replenish the stocks very well indeed. The lake is open to all methods of fishing. One popular method is trolling slowly in the main lake areas, with the favourite lure being the old-faithful Tasmanian Devil.

Another popular method is fly-fishing. Cow Paddock Bay, in the far north of the lake, is famous for its mayfly hatches between November and February and is known for its tailing trout. Of course, in any lake you have to find the fish and one sure-fire way is to drift-fish a wind lane. The froth of the water gathers beetles, midges and the like, and you will always find a feeding trout there.

Unfortunately, Arthur's isn't a good shore-based spot; however, those that do fish with worms take big trout every year around the launching ramps at Pump House Bay, in the south-east of Arthurs, and at Jonah Bay, about halfway up on the western side of the lake.

Some of my best days have been polaroiding the shallow waters along Brazendale Island. The most productive days are with a cloudless blue sky with the sun behind you. The best fly for me has always been the Red Tag. I have caught trout on the Red Tag all over the world. Has there been a more successful universally used dry fly than the Red Tag?

ABOVE: *Devoted saltwater angler and good friend Neil Thompson with his first Tassie brown trout.*

BELOW: *A lovely Central Highlands brown.*

BELOW LEFT: *Lynne Hunt and John Fox with a monster brown trout caught in Arthurs Lake whilst drift-spinning with lures.*

Of late the use of mudeyes (dragonfly larvae) in the lake has become more popular. These are suspended under a float and fished amongst the timber near the weed beds. When I go to Arthurs, now twice a year, I fish all three methods and usually end up with a fine lot of fillets to bring home. The brown trout of the Tasmanian Highlands are the best trout I have eaten. Together with King George whiting they are my two favourite fish to eat.

Over the last ten years the brown trout of Arthurs seem to have grown in size, from an average of 750 grams to well over a kilogram. This puts this lake right up there as a consistent quality fish producer. While I have heard of and seen the odd monster up to five kilograms, the biggest fish I have taken in over 30 trips was just under three kilograms.

Great Lake

At approximately 23 kilometres long from north to south and up to 13 kilometres at its widest point but averaging seven kilometres, the Great Lake is truly one of the marvellous big waters around. The lake is vast and exposed to inclement weather, being some 1020 metres above sea level.

The quality of the fish is great, with a good supply of both brown and rainbow trout. I have done well fishing large bushy flies at dusk in wind lanes, as well as right out in the middle of the lake fishing for cruising trout in the waves. This lake is open all year round to fishing with the exception of Canal Bay (near where the Liawenee Canal enters the lake), which has a closed season from late March to late October.

There are countless bank-fishing opportunities for anglers. I have done particularly well floating mudeyes under a bubble float off the shore. With the wind behind, it offers peaceful and at times frantic fishing. Casting wobblers and spinning blade-type lures from the shore is also very productive, with the best colours in my opinion being silver and gold.

TOP: *A brace of fine Central Highlands' brown trout.*

ABOVE: *Lynne and our dog Mister with a lovely brown from Arthurs.*

Other lakes

I have also had magical fishing in Lake Sorell, but that lake has suffered some problems with water quality and the infestation of European carp so it may be some time before it can return to its former glory. However, it was once the Mecca of brown trout fishing in Tasmania. An 'artificial lure only' water, it produced the best-looking and conditioned brown trout I have caught anywhere in the world. The best method for me was to wade the shallow stone areas and cast and retrieve a wet fly, either a green Matuka, Yellow Peril or a Tom Jones fly.

I have also fished Penstock Lagoon, a small lake several kilometres south of Great Lake, and Little Pine Lagoon, again a small water to the south-west of Great Lake. They are both 'fly only' waters and the fish can be extremely difficult to catch. However, as with all trout fishing, a careful approach, sighting the fish and a good presentation usually results in a trout.

Conclusion

The Highlands of Tasmania remain one of my favourite all-time fishing destinations. It can be cold, with the weather downright hostile at times, but this creates a tremendous contrast to my other favourite fishing holiday locales, which are predominantly in the tropical Top End.

Piscatorial Compass
Central Highlands, Tasmania

How to get there: From Hobart to Miena is around 130 kilometres via the Brooker, Midland and Lake highways. From Launceston it is 115 kilometres on the Midland, Meander Valley and Lake highways.

Where to stay: There are several fly-fishing lodges scattered throughout the Central Highlands which are run by local fishing guides. Anglers can also base themselves at Launceston which has ample accommodation.

What to catch: Brown trout and rainbow trout, some brook trout and chinook salmon.

Gear to take: Use four to seven weight fly-fishing tackle, and a baitcaster rod and reel combo for casting or trolling lures.

When to go: November to April. The main Tasmanian closed season for trout runs from May to late July. Check with Tasmania's Inland Fisheries Service for relevant regulations for particular waters.

Guides and charters: John Fox, Peter Hayes and Ken Orr are all quality fishing guides who operate in this area.

Rex reckons: Arthurs Lake is one of the most angler-friendly impoundments for trout in Australia. It is a very good location for the novice angler to try to catch a trout when visiting Tasmania.

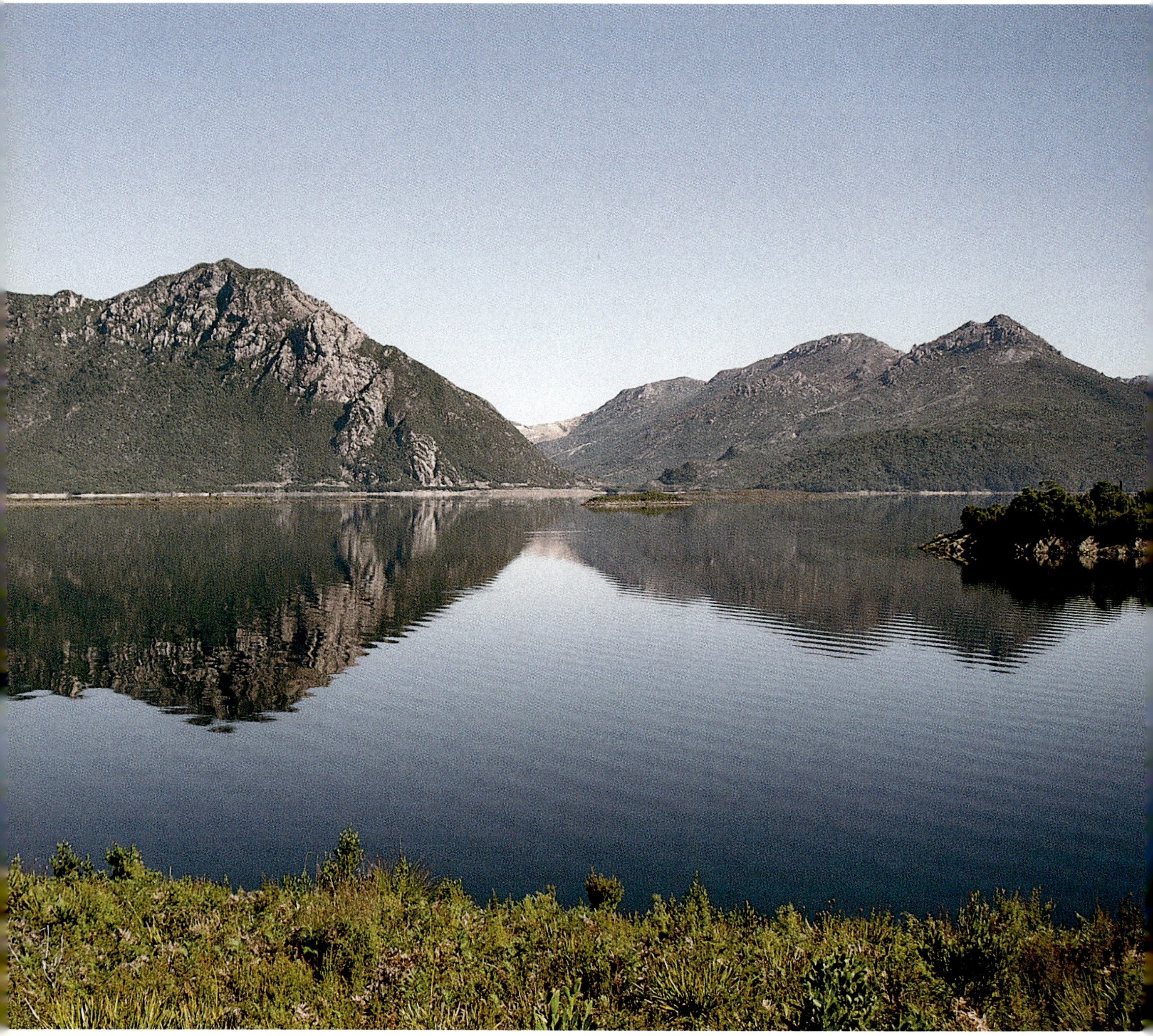

Lake Burbury

Lake Burbury is a man-made impoundment, formed when the King River was dammed near Queenstown, a copper-mining township on the west coast of Tasmania. It is fairly new, opening up for 'business' in the early 1990s. After the construction of Crotty Dam and the subsequent filling of the lake to its total capacity, the lake is 235 metres above sea level with a total surface area of around 50 square kilometres.

Burbury was stocked with massive amounts of brown and rainbow trout fry in 1992 and 1993 by the Inland Fisheries Department of Tasmania, because the general feeling was that there were insufficient self-sustaining stocks in the river to service the lake. Additionally, the King River stocks were mostly polluted by copper tailings, so Fisheries stocked the lake.

These days the lake has a self-sustaining population of trout. When I fished here with my wife Lynne and Tassie guide John Fox in the late 1990s and early

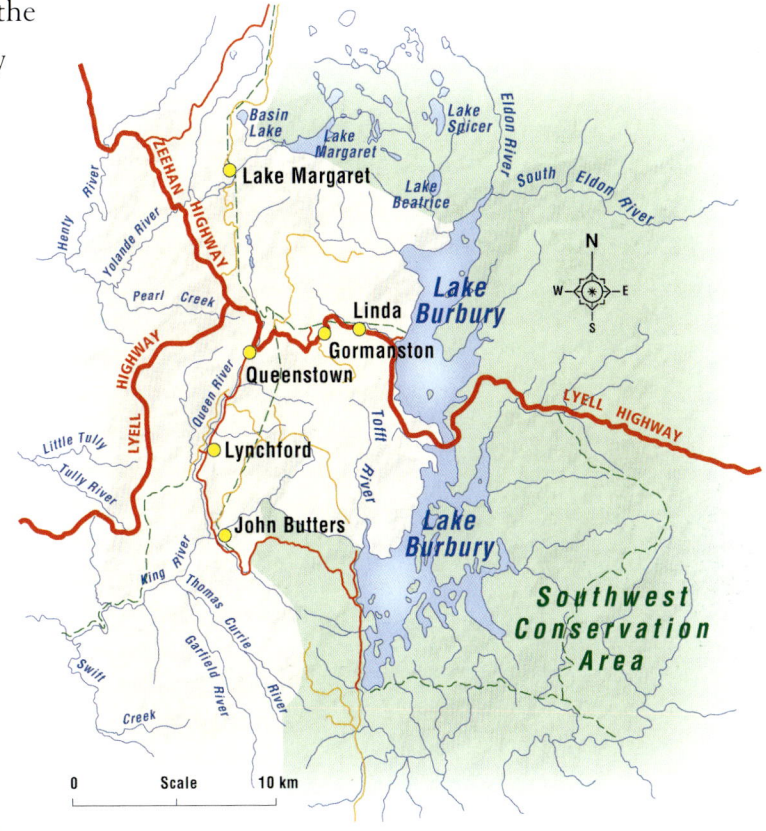

OPPOSITE: *Lake Burbury on a picture-perfect day.*

LEFT: *A lovely brown trout taken by yours truly whilst trolling on Burbury.*

OPPOSITE: *Lake Burbury offers only limited bank access for bait-fishing or spinning lures.*

2000s we had some extraordinary fishing using mudeyes under floats. Every backwater, and there are hundreds of miles of shoreline here, contained fish. We also had some very good days driftspinning, fly-fishing 'wind-lane' style and slow-trolling in the upper regions of the lake where the Eldon and South Eldon Rivers run in.

There are several boat ramps that service many parts of the lake, but note that the water is tannin-coloured (the colour drains from the button grass plains in the area during rain and flood) and the depth can be quite deceiving. Exercise caution at all times and be prepared for any weather conditions: the wild nature of the west coast can see the lake change from a millpond to a raging surf.

Land-based Opportunities

Much of the coastline of Burbury is rugged and inaccessible as it is surrounded by mountains, but there are some nice banks to fish from near road access points that are quite clear of vegetation. The western shoreline offers some of the best land-based opportunities, especially around Bradshaws Bridge.

A good bait-fishing strategy is to rig your bait with the use of a float, even when using grubs or worms, as it is ideal to allow the bait to get off the bottom, which for the most part is strewn with twigs and small bushes. Bubble floats that can be part-filled with water are best, as the trout can move away with the bait with only minimal resistance.

Live mudeyes are by far the best bait, and these can be collected at the lake. A mudeye is the larval stage of a dragonfly and trout can't resist them, no matter where you are fishing. Again, rigging them under a float using a small hook, say a number 12, will give you every chance of success.

Trolling Lures

One of my favourite forms of trout fishing is trolling, as you can cover so much ground and it is a relaxing way to fish. My good friend John Fox is an expert troller, and we never seem to fail to get some action. I've always had success trolling spinners with a

LEFT: *The lake has superb boat-launching and picnic facilities.*

OPPOSITE: *The mining township of Queenstown and the Queen River, which flows into the King River and eventually Burbury.*

revolving blade, or small bibbed minnow lures with a tight body action that replicates the movements of a bait fish. Tassie Devil or Cobra-style lures are also highly effective on Tasmanian trout in trolling situations. The best areas of Burbury to troll are around the edges, following the contours of the shoreline and around submerged trees and their branches.

Other productive lure-fishing methods include drift-spinning from a boat. Foxy and I have practised this method on many occasions. As with trolling, you can cover plenty of ground, but perhaps be more precise with the lures when drift-spinning, as the lure can be twitched or worked around likely trout holding areas such as snags.

Fly-fishing

As bank access is mostly restricted, the best way to practise fly-fishing at Lake Burbury is from a boat. This is where wind-lane fishing comes into its own. On clear days with light wind, wind lanes form when winds come from slightly different directions, creating gaps in the wind or 'lanes' of calm glassy water. They can also be created when a current of water is going one way and the wind is going the other. Beetles, midges, spent mayfly hatches, leaves and other insects and debris are blown into these wind lanes.

As a natural slick of food for trout, the fly-fisher can drift in a boat and cast into these wind lanes with an above average chance of success. One of the best flies in these circumstances is the Royal Wulff. Summer and early autumn are the prime months for wind-lane fishing at Lake Burbury, with early morning the best time to try.

Conclusion

I must say that the drive from Hobart or the Highland Lakes area across Derwent Bridge to Lake Burbury is the most beautiful I have experienced anywhere in the world. Tasmania is a compact state with some wonderful natural attractions; Lake Burbury is well worth a visit for the travelling angler.

Piscatorial Compass

Lake Burbury, Tasmania

How to get there: Lake Burbury is approximately 240 kilometres west of Hobart via the Lyell Highway.

Where to stay: There are only basic camping facilities around the lake. The nearest town with accommodation is Queenstown, some ten kilometres west on the Lyell Highway.

What to catch: Rainbow trout and brown trout.

Gear to take: Use light threadline rods and reels for bait-fishing, spinning and trolling lures. Fly-fishing gear ranging from four to seven weight is best.

When to go: October to May.

Guides and charters: Fishing guides will travel to Burbury from locations all over Tasmania to fish here.

Rex reckons: Take plenty of warm clothing and a good expectation of catching some nice trout, especially when trolling, drift-spinning or bait-fishing with mudeyes.

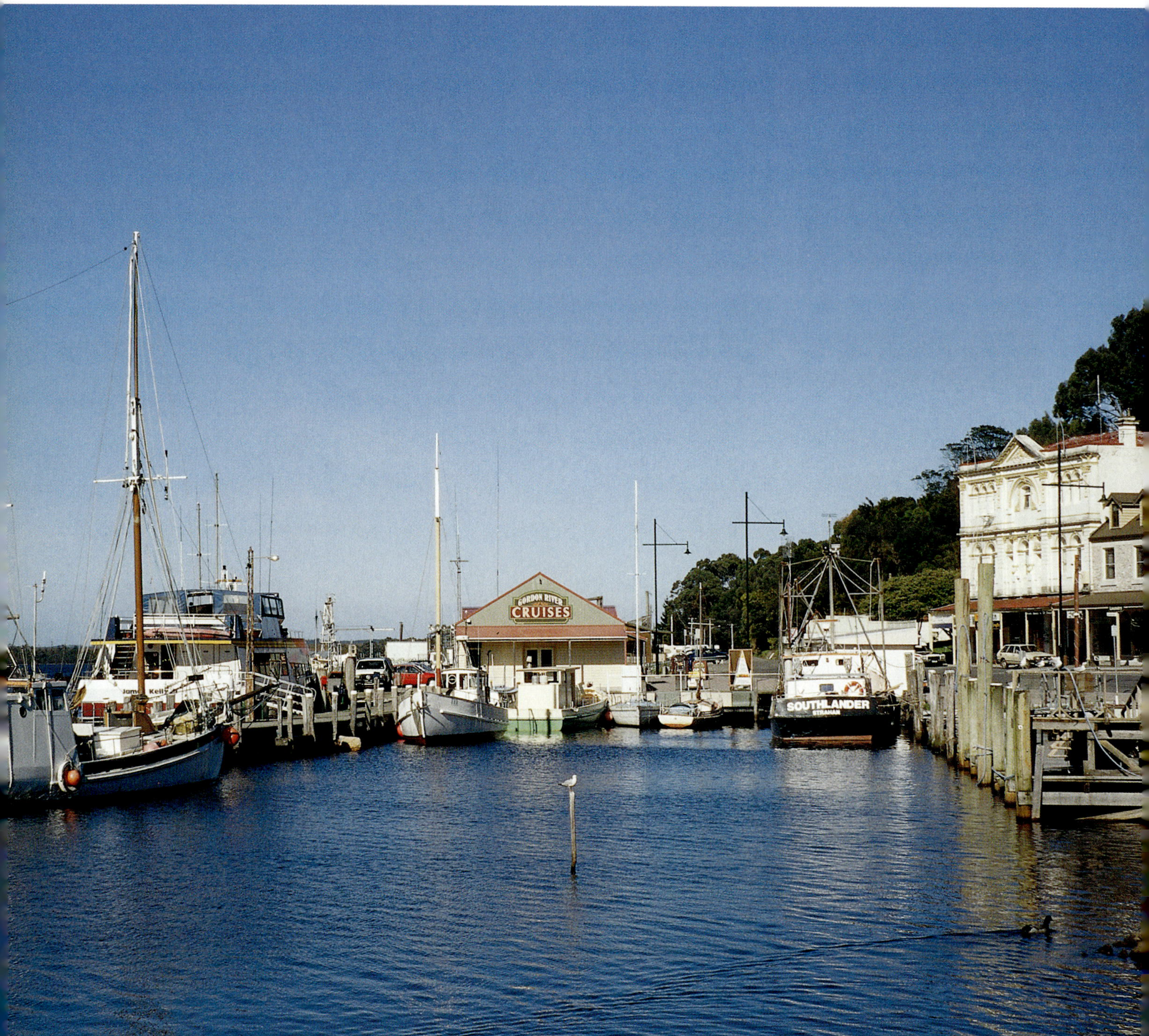
GORDON RIVER
CRUISES
SOUTHLANDER

Strahan

A visit to the west coast of Tasmania and the historic township of Strahan on the banks of Macquarie Harbour is a step back in time. Macquarie Harbour was first discovered by Europeans in 1815. They were immediately impressed by the amount of timber around the harbour, in particular the magnificent huon pine, as it was an excellent source of wood for ship-building.

However, Macquarie Harbour's big claim to fame in the early days was its convict settlement on Sarah Island in the 1820s. The poor souls housed there were worked to death in this cold and barren place, a climate that gets only 30 fine days a year. Sarah Island was largely acknowledged as one of the cruellest places on earth.

Into the 20th century Strahan's various industries continued to develop and the town served as an important port for timber and mining. In 1983 it was the staging platform for one of Australia's most famous environmental protest rallies when the Tasmanian Government proposed to dam

OPPOSITE: *The main dock at Strahan.*

the Gordon River. Fortunately, the 'greenies' won the fight on this occasion and the pristine Gordon River has been preserved for future generations, including us anglers.

The fishing environments on offer whilst based at Strahan include Macquarie Harbour itself, the Gordon River, which flows into Macquarie Harbour from Tasmania's beautiful World Heritage Area, the Henty River just north of Strahan, where sea-run trout make an annual run, and the beaches along the coast.

ABOVE: *An angler displays some brown trout he caught in the Gordon River.*

LEFT: *The fish pens of Macquarie Harbour.*

Macquarie Harbour

In the late 1990s I took the TV crew down to Strahan to meet local fishing guide Ken Orr. Ken had arranged for us to fish the tannin-coloured waters of Macquarie Harbour for rainbow trout. Macquarie Harbour is a huge body of water, two and a half times bigger than Sydney Harbour. Rainbow trout are naturally not native to Macquarie Harbour nor Tasmania – these fish were 'escapees' from the fish farms located in protected bays on the north-western coast of the harbour.

We fished outside the rainbow trout pens and caught rainbows to 12 pound in the old scale (5.5 kilograms), using tiny hooks with small fish pellets for bait. This was a good lesson in fish behaviour. These trout were territorial inside the net with the constant flow of feed. Once outside the net they were happy to hang around the same area and eat the feed that fell through the net. As caged fish they could not look after themselves when they were set free in the wild.

When feeding began the trout inside the net would get excited and even jump free of the one-metre-high fence around the pens, but most of the fish escaped due to damage from storms or from seals tearing gaping holes in the nets to get at the fish. Our target was the escapee trout underneath the nets, which were attracted by the berley and constant flow of pellets.

This was an unusual fishery and it made for fantastic TV. A 5.5-kilogram rainbow is a monster in anyone's book, but Macquarie Harbour has produced trout to over eight kilograms, surely the biggest trout regularly caught anywhere in Australia.

Once we'd had our fun with the trout, our guide took us to 'Hells Gates', the entrance to Macquarie Harbour. We caught some parrotfish on lures here and tossed lures to Australian salmon. We caught some monsters at around three kilograms, and also caught luderick on pipis. The best time to get onto the salmon is on the

TOP: *Fly-fishing the Henty River for sea-run trout.*

ABOVE: *Ken Orr and yours truly with a couple of superb rainbow trout of around 12 pound in the old scale.*

LEFT: *'Hells Gates', the entrance to Macquarie Harbour.*

flood tide, when a wash of green water enters the harbour. The 'black backs', as they are known in Tassie, enter the harbour chasing schools of whitebait.

ABOVE: *Anglers troll along the majestic Gordon River.*

Gordon River

The Gordon River meanders through Tasmania's World Heritage Area and flows into Macquarie Harbour. As the mouth of the Gordon River is some 30 kilometres from Strahan across Macquarie Harbour, it is very remote. Many anglers stock large trailer boats with provisions and head up the river for several days each spring to troll for big trout, both rainbows and browns, as well as Atlantic salmon. Brown trout over nine kilograms have been caught from this river, but on average fish weigh in between two and four kilograms. These trout or salmonids are typical of their northern hemisphere cousins in that they spend up to ten months a year in the open ocean, only coming into estuarine waters each spring.

Henty River

North of Strahan along the Zeehan Highway is the Henty River. Anglers have two choices here; enter via 4WD and make your way across the sand dunes to fish the banks on foot, or launch a small tinnie at the highway bridge and motor up. The main attraction is the seasonal run of sea-run trout each October and November. These fish literally follow huge whitebait schools up the river from the ocean to raid their numbers.

For bait, lure or fly anglers this is paradise. The annual run is legendary in Tasmanian fishing and a good friend of mine, Bill Classon of *Freshwater Fishing* magazine, has caught fish up to eight kilograms in the Henty River. Bushy and I fished here with the TV cameras, and using both fly and lures we took some nice trout of around two kilograms.

Ocean Beach

Ocean Beach is a vast open beach approximately six kilometres west of Strahan. The beach is mostly white sand, hard and fairly flat, thus suitable for 4WD vehicles. The main piscatorial target is the black back Australian salmon, along with the odd shark and ray. As at Hells Gates, you generally need green water to be successful, so avoid the tannin-coloured waters from Macquarie Harbour that wash along Ocean Beach.

Conclusion

Strahan, Macquarie Harbour and the Franklin–Gordon Wild Rivers National Park offer some of the finest scenery I've seen in our magnificent country. It is a privilege to be to able to fish in these places.

Piscatorial Compass
Strahan, Tasmania

How to get there: Strahan is located on the west coast of Tasmania approximately 290 kilometres from Hobart via the Lyell Highway. Alternatively, if you are flying into Burnie/Wynyard, it is around 200 kilometres via the Murchison Highway and Henty Road.

Where to stay: As an international tourist destination, Strahan has a very wide range of accommodation from backpacker style to luxury apartments.

What to catch: Rainbow trout, brown trout, Atlantic salmon, Australian salmon, flounder, luderick and mullet.

Gear to take: Use light threadline rods and reels. The best fly-fishing gear is four to six weight.

When to go: October to March. Fish for sea-run trout from October to December in the Henty River.

Guides and charters: Several fly-fishing guides operate in the area.

Rex reckons: The wind blows hard in this part of the world; take adequate clothing and be prepared for any weather.

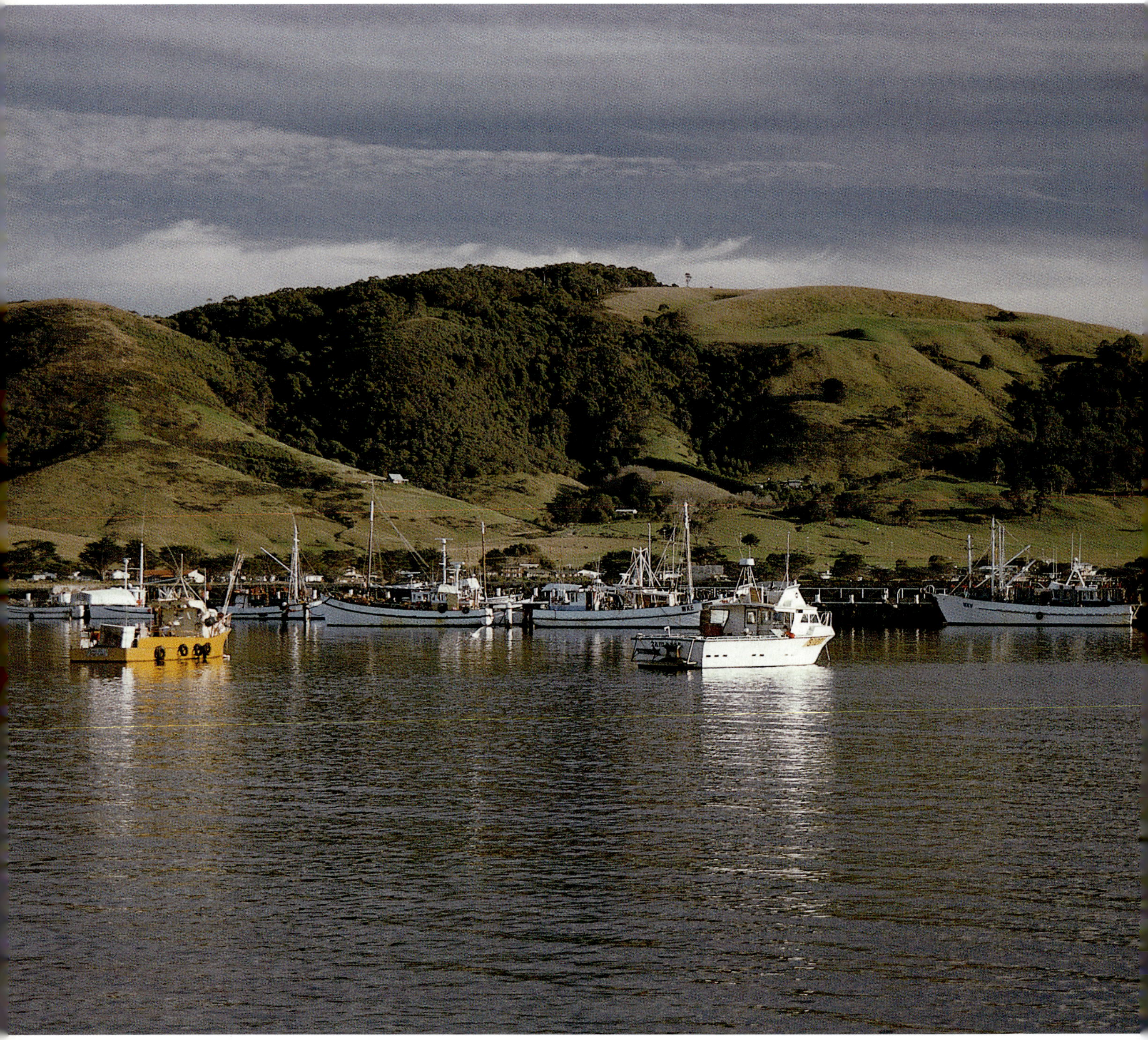

Apollo Bay

Nestled on the southern coast of Victoria, just east of the Otway Ranges and approximately halfway along the Great Ocean Road is the delightful seaside town of Apollo Bay. Now folks, I don't know if *Apollo 11* astronaut Neil Armstrong ever visited the place, but I can tell you the fish most certainly do!

Once known as 'Krambruk', an Aboriginal word meaning 'sandy place', Apollo Bay was settled in the mid-1800s by whalers and sealers, who declared the bay 'the finest harbour on the Otway Coast'. The eventual opening of the Great Ocean Road in the early 1930s saw the town prosper as viable transport links opened up with Melbourne for the bustling commercial fishing industry, mainly supplying crayfish.

I first visited Apollo Bay in

OPPOSITE: *The picturesque Apollo Bay Harbour.*

the late 1970s whilst fishing the AAA tournament circuit. I was immediately struck by the diversity of fishing options from the magnificent boat harbour to the spectacular coastline, which is dotted with many wide sweeping beaches and rock formations.

Both the land-based and boating angler are well catered for at Apollo Bay. Land-based options include the breakwalls of the harbour itself and the beaches, rock ledges, river banks and small estuaries. Trailer boats can launch within the protection of Apollo Bay Harbour and venture offshore in search of such piscatorial quarry as snapper, silver trevally, whiting, big flathead and sharks.

Based at Apollo Bay, the angler can comfortably day-fish from Cape Patton to the east, through to the Otway Ranges and Johanna surf beach in the west.

ABOVE: *Silver trevally are probably the most common species caught around Apollo Bay Harbour.*

OPPOSITE: *The harbour itself is worth a try, as many species venture in and out with the tides.*

Cape Patton

The ships *Mary Cummings* and *Speculant* came to grief in the vicinity of Cape Patton in 1872 and 1911 respectively, which gives you some idea of the ruggedness of the coast in these parts. From an angler's perspective though, this means a good fish-holding structure both from the shore and offshore.

The rock ledges around Cape Patton are renowned for good snapper and sweep, but these areas should only be fished in calm conditions, which are rare in the Southern Ocean. The best time is from February to May.

Fishing from a boat is a good option as you can drift bait along the bottom, particularly in depths of 30 metres, until you find fish. The snapper average from one to three kilograms, with the odd bigger fish up to six kilograms. The area off Whalebone Creek along the shallow reefs is also worth a look for snapper, but only in good weather. The run from the Apollo Bay boat harbour is approximately 30 minutes in reasonable conditions.

Skenes Creek

When taking the short cut to Apollo Bay from Melbourne via Birregurra and Forrest, you will intersect with the coast and the Great Ocean Road at Skenes Creek. There is good beach fishing at Skenes Creek for King George whiting, salmon, silver trevally and mullet, particularly at low tide. Access to the beach is via the car park near the bridge.

Wild Dog Creek

West of Skenes Creek along the Great Ocean Road is Wild Dog Creek, a popular small estuary and beach for anglers. Salmon and silver trevally are the main targets in the surf, although the salmon can be small at times. Anglers fishing at night will often encounter bigger fish, particularly trevally.

Upstream on Wild Dog Creek is a good population of small

brown trout, which will readily take a spinning lure or live baits fished on the drift. This is also a good water for fly-fishing with a coachman pattern.

Apollo Bay Harbour

Constructed in the 1950s, Apollo Bay Harbour is home to the town's commercial fishing fleet. Tucked inside the boat harbour in the south-west corner is a two-lane concrete boat ramp for trailer boats. As one of the few protected offshore fishing ramps in Victoria, this harbour is unique in Victorian fishing.

I first fished the Apollo Bay Harbour at Easter in 1979. The harbour itself is a fish-attracting structure, and a wide variety of species have been caught from the breakwalls and jetties that form it. The main species include King George whiting, small snapper, barracouta, mullet, silver trevally, leatherjacket, Australian salmon, wrasse and calamari squid. The outer breakwall fishes well year round, but as it is more exposed to the mighty swell of the Southern Ocean it can be difficult to fish and stay dry.

On heavy-weather days, boating anglers can fish inside the

harbour with a reasonable expectation of catching a feed from the salmon and whiting schools that move in and out. Resident species such as leatherjacket, barracouta, trevally, wrasse, mullet and sometimes squid can also be expected.

Offshore options are almost unlimited. The best strategy is to seek out the reefy ground with the aid of a depth sounder. The area known as 'the Waterfall', which is situated between Wild Dog and Skenes creeks, is a regular producer of good snapper and big trevally. Schools of Australian salmon can be encountered by trolling around Apollo Bay and Mounts Bay, between the harbour and Marengo. Some parts of the Henty or Marengo reefs are protected in a marine sanctuary, but anglers can still fish outside these areas with a reasonable expectation of catching a variety of species, including whiting and snapper.

Barham River

The picturesque Barham River winds its way down from the nearby Otway Ranges and provides the angler with a diverse range of species

OPPOSITE: *The outer breakwater of the harbour provides a sturdy platform to fish for salmon and other species.*

BELOW: *Magnificent Marengo Beach produces good salmon fishing and even better views.*

to target, with brown trout in the upper reaches, estuary perch and bream in the middle, and yellow-eye mullet and some bream in the lower reaches. Live bait presented under a float will take most estuarine species here. There is good access to the bank of the lower reaches at the Great Ocean Road bridge, with a car park located on the ocean side. When the entrance is open to the sea, sea-run trout sometimes enter the river, providing great sport on lure and fly.

Marengo

The beach at Marengo produces some excellent Australian salmon and at times King George whiting. There are many reefs just offshore, some coming right in close, particularly around Hayley Point, where the Hayley and Henty reefs extend into the Southern Ocean. Some of the reefs are part of a marine park, so check up-to-date regulations for where you can fish.

There are multiple rock ledges that run right around Hayley Point and Marengo, and these fish well for small snapper, whiting, trevally and salmon. The best time to try your luck is at the beginning of the run-out tide, and for the next two hours or so. Fresh squid and pipis are the prime baits.

Cape Otway

Cape Otway, with its famous lighthouse, built in 1848, is one of the most striking parts of the Australian coastline. A national park, Cape Otway is still as remote as when it was first discovered by Europeans two centuries ago, and that's good news for anglers. Blanket Bay is one of the areas you can access via the Cape Otway Road and it has a great picnic ground and camping facilities, though you'll need to check on the road status. The fishing off the rocks and beaches is often superb for a range of species from sweep and snapper to whiting, salmon, garfish and gummy shark.

ABOVE: *The Barham River provides a contrast to the nearby ocean, with bream and mullet the main targets.*

Aire River

The Aire River is something of a secret spot! The river descends from the Otway Ranges, widening to form Lake Craven before running to the coast as a small estuary. Road access is via Horden Vale off the Great Ocean Road. An old wooden bridge crosses the Aire at the camping ground and is a good land-based fishing spot for mullet and bream. Small tinnies can be launched either side of the bridge, allowing access both up- and downstream. The latter fishes well for most estuarine species, including juvenile Australian salmon and tommy ruff, plus the odd sea-run trout. There are estuary perch upstream and small populations of trout that will fall to small lures and flies.

OPPOSITE: *The Red and Blue Johanna beaches west of Apollo Bay have a deserved reputation for producing big salmon, mainly due to their unusually deep gutters.*

BELOW: *The rocks at Hayley Point near Marengo produce small snapper at times, but can be difficult to fish with the amount of kelp in the area.*

Johanna Beach

Further west along the Great Ocean Road is the turn-off to the Red and Blue Johanna beaches. Overshadowed by huge cliffs and rock formations, the deep gutters of Johanna Beach offer some of the best surf fishing along the entire Victorian coast. Big Australian salmon, snapper and gummy sharks (at night) dominate catches here, particularly on a rising tide.

Conclusion

Apollo Bay's bountiful angling opportunities are not the limit of its attractions. The nearby Otway Ranges have a number of pristine rainforests and waterfalls to visit and of course the sensational Twelve Apostles are only 90 minutes' drive away.

Piscatorial Compass
Apollo Bay, Victoria

How to get there: Located along the Great Ocean Road, Apollo Bay is just under 200 kilometres from Melbourne via Geelong on the Princes Highway and then through Forrest across the Otway Ranges.

Where to stay: There is ample accommodation at Apollo Bay with multiple motels, holiday units and caravan parks.

What to catch: Australian salmon, small snapper, silver trevally, barracouta, sand flathead, pike, shark species and King George whiting. Bream, mullet, estuary perch and brown trout can be found in the upper reaches of the rivers.

Gear to take: Use light to medium rods and threadline reels, and beach-fishing rod and reel.

When to go: Year round.

Guides and charters: There are several charter boats operating out of Apollo Bay.

Rex reckons: When the weather is crook, the harbour is a great option for boat- and land-based fishers.

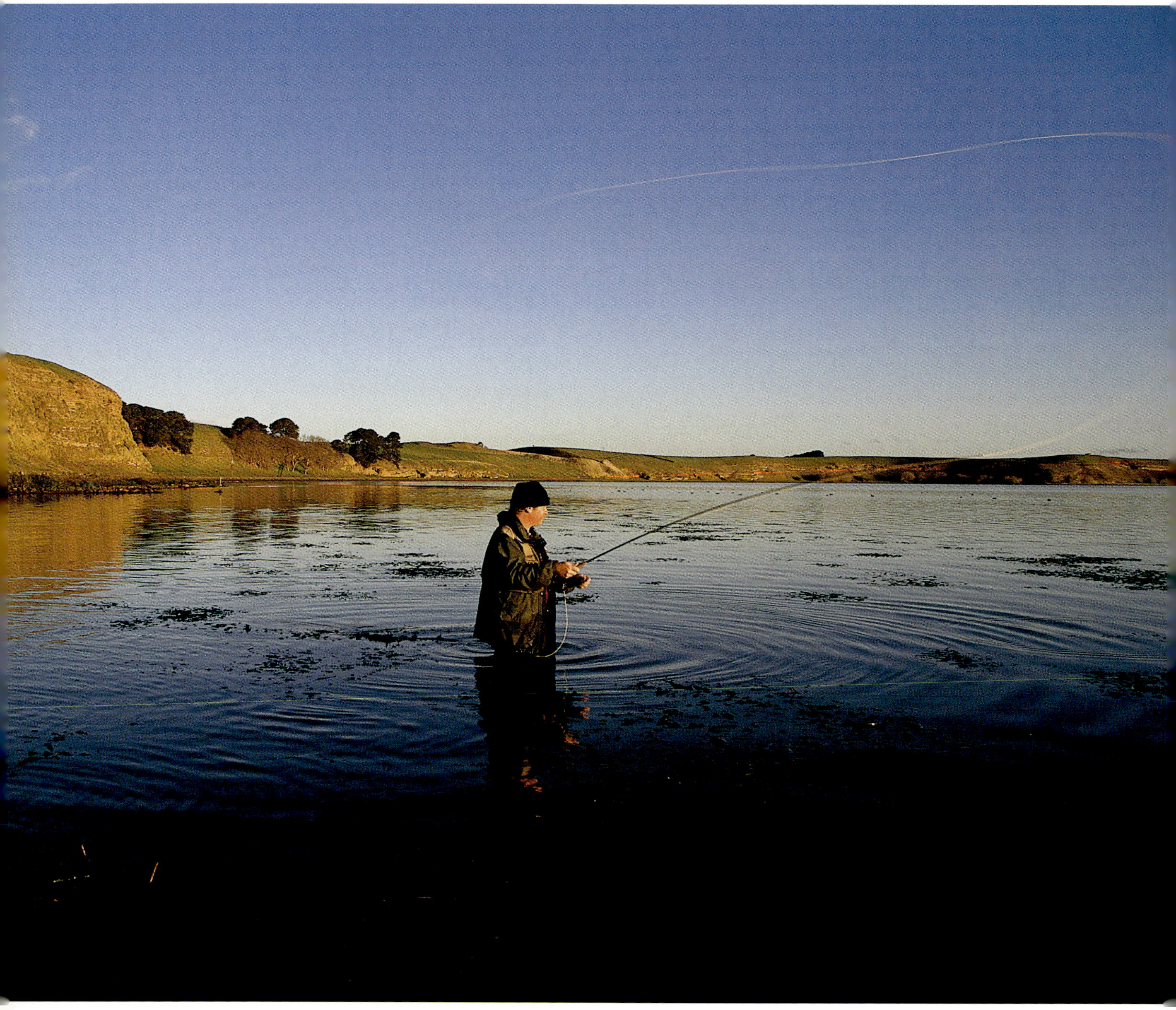

Lakes Purrumbete and Bullen Merri

Situated near the township of Camperdown in south-western Victoria, the 'twin' volcanic lakes Purrumbete and Bullen Merri have been popular for several decades, producing some massive trout and other salmonids (trout and salmon species).

Camperdown, with a population of around 3500 people, is the major town in the district and a centre for agriculture. It has many old buildings, including the famous Manifold Clock Tower, and is well kept with beautiful gardens and parks. Its main claim to fame, however, is its location at the centre of the volcanic lakes region, with Purrumbete,

OPPOSITE: *Fly-fishing the eastern shore of Purrumbete is very productive in winter.*

Bullen Merri and Lake Gnotuk the best known. The town offers all the necessary amenities for visiting anglers and their families.

There are some 30 crater lakes, or maars, in the region. These are formed by fragments of rock and ash that cool over time, forming a crater with steep sides. The lakes are natural, and are fed by underground water. Purrumbete and Bullen Merri are the star attractions and are the two main lakes where fishing occurs. Bullen Merri holds many records for fish growth of salmonids due to its prodigious stocks of bait fish, whilst Purrumbete has always produced some trophy-sized specimens. The trout cannot spawn in either lake, so a stocking program is maintained by Fisheries.

Lake Purrumbete

Each year Purrumbete receives liberations of brown trout, rainbow trout and chinook salmon. Because on occasion too many fish went into the lake, resulting in fewer food sources and consequently smaller fish, fisheries experimented with not supplying the lake with brown trout over a period of time. As a result, the fish have grown in average size, and there has been some magnificent fishing, with brown trout over five kilograms being taken.

The chinook salmon used to be called quinnat salmon in the early days, and are also known as king salmon in some parts of the world. They are a very good sporting fish that can be caught on a variety of methods. One of the most productive is to fish bait on the lake bed. This involves lowering the bait (live minnow, pilchard fillets or whole whitebait work well) down to the bottom. You then lift the rig (running sinker) up about two to three metres from the bottom. The best rod to use is a whiting-type rod with a slow, almost sloppy, action that will allow the fish to mouth the bait without feeling any resistance.

Many anglers actually berley on Lake Purrumbete when chasing the chinook salmon, using small pieces of whitebait, glassies or pilchards, in a scene more at home on Port Phillip Bay. As the berley has to sink down to depths in excess of 40 metres in some cases, a good technique is to crush the berley into a tight ball with the aid of tuna oil and breadcrumbs.

Mudeyes fished about one metre under a bubble also take many trout, particularly browns. This method is best employed near the margins of the lake, over weed beds and near drop-offs. Good spots

LEFT: *There are excellent boating facilities at Lake Bullen Merri.*

OPPOSITE: *Boats can be launched onto Purrumbete from the Lake Purrumbete Caravan Park.*

to try include Horans Point, which is on the right as you enter the main lake from the boat ramp; opposite the trees at Rainbow Point and anywhere close in along Hoses Rocks through to Shags Rocks.

The rainbows tend to be caught in the main body of the lake. Trolling with flat lines in the cooler months and downriggers in summer always produces quality rainbow trout. Tassie Devil lures are popular at Purrumbete as they can be trolled on the surface or with a downrigger without any swimming problems.

I have found that deep-diving lures imitating small trout take quality fish, but sometimes you have to use a downrigger or a paravane to get down deeper. The operative word here is depth.

ABOVE: *A fine brown taken on fly from the margins of Lake Purrumbete.*

OPPOSITE: *Yours truly with a rainbow trout caught on a lure in Lake Bullen Merri, about 1980.*

Purrumbete is a very deep lake indeed, and the fish can be anywhere between the surface and 40 metres' depth.

Unlike the rainbow trout, the browns concentrate on the shallow margins where the weed is thick. Therefore sight-fishing with small flies is often very good. The eastern shoreline offers good fly-fishing amongst the weed beds, as the lake gently shelves away into deeper water, allowing you to cover some ground and cast your fly out beyond the thick weed beds where trout often cruise. Starting just below the quarry you can work your way north towards the cliffs and the old windmill. Winter is a prime time to fly-fish here.

Lake Bullen Merri, 'The Bull'

I first became aware of Lake Bullen Merri in the early 1960s. Lance Wedlick wrote in the *Melbourne Sporting Globe* about the phenomenal growth rate of the trout and salmon in this lake. In those days the trout were rainbow and the salmon were chinook.

Today the lake receives many fish as liberations continue. Apart from the lake's native minnows and gudgeon, there are brown and rainbow trout, chinook salmon, Atlantic salmon and Australian

LEFT: *Bruce Smith with a lovely brown trout caught in Lake Purrumbete.*

OPPOSITE: *The floating pontoon at Bullen Merri is a popular place for anglers collecting minnows with bait nets.*

bass. The latter are a more recent addition to fish stocks, and Victorian Fisheries surveys have now revealed that the bass are doing well, having reached the legal size limit of 25 centimetres and beyond. In years to come, these fish will give Victorians a taste of what anglers from the northern states have known for a while: Aussie bass are a top freshwater sports fish.

Lake Bullen Merri can be subject to intermittent fish kills where the fish apparently die suddenly. This is caused by a release of sulphur from deep in the old volcanic crust. The sulphur enters the water and removes the oxygen, thereby killing fish. I can remember total fish kills where all the fish died. In recent times it appears that only a small number of fish die before the lake rights itself again. One thing that I find amazing is that the food chain is never affected when the fish kills take place: the bait fish like minnows and gudgeon are never found dead. They survive, more fish are stocked, and away we go again.

Bullen Merri is even deeper than Purrumbete, with depths in excess of 60 metres. Unlike Purrumbete though, Bullen Merri is a little more 'bland' in its features or marks in which to find fish.

Many of the methods that work on Purrumbete work here as

well. Mudeyes, crickets or twin gudgeon rigged under a bubble float will often take quality trout. Trolling Tassie Devil style lures, deep-diving minnows on flat lines and trolling with the use of the downrigger and attractors is also successful. A depth sounder is a terrific aid.

The best trolling runs are around the margins of the lake. Some spots to try include around Wurrong Point, which is to the right of the main boat-launching ramp; off the black sand of East Beach at a depth of between ten and 15 metres; just off the rock wall at the 'Coral' and around Potters Point on the western side.

Conclusion

To be quite frank, these two waters have frustrated me immensely over the years. I can tell you that I spent many hours trying to master the art of angling here. The rewards are well worth the effort when they come, though, as a potential trophy trout awaits the patient angler.

Piscatorial Compass

Lakes Purrumbete and Bullen Merri, Victoria

How to get there: Camperdown is 190 kilometres from Melbourne via Princes Highway. Eight kilometres short of Camperdown is Lake Purrumbete. The turn-off is well signposted. Bullen Merri is three kilometres south of Camperdown on the road to Cobden.

Where to stay: There are excellent caravan and camping parks at both lakes, and accommodation at nearby Camperdown.

What to catch: Rainbow trout, brown trout, chinook salmon, redfin, Australian bass, Atlantic salmon and short-finned eel.

Gear to take: Try a light threadline rod and reel with two-kilogram monofilament line. Fly-fishing gear from five to seven weight is best.

When to go: Year round. Note that Lake Purrumbete is subject to a closed season for boat fishing for trout from midnight on the Monday of the Queen's Birthday weekend through to the first Saturday in September.

Guides and charters: Some fly-fishing guides take their clients to the lakes. Good local knowledge can be gleaned from the Lake Purrumbete Caravan Park.

Rex reckons: These lakes are very deep, so anglers need to concentrate on finding fish at various depths. A downrigger aided by a depth sounder is a great asset.

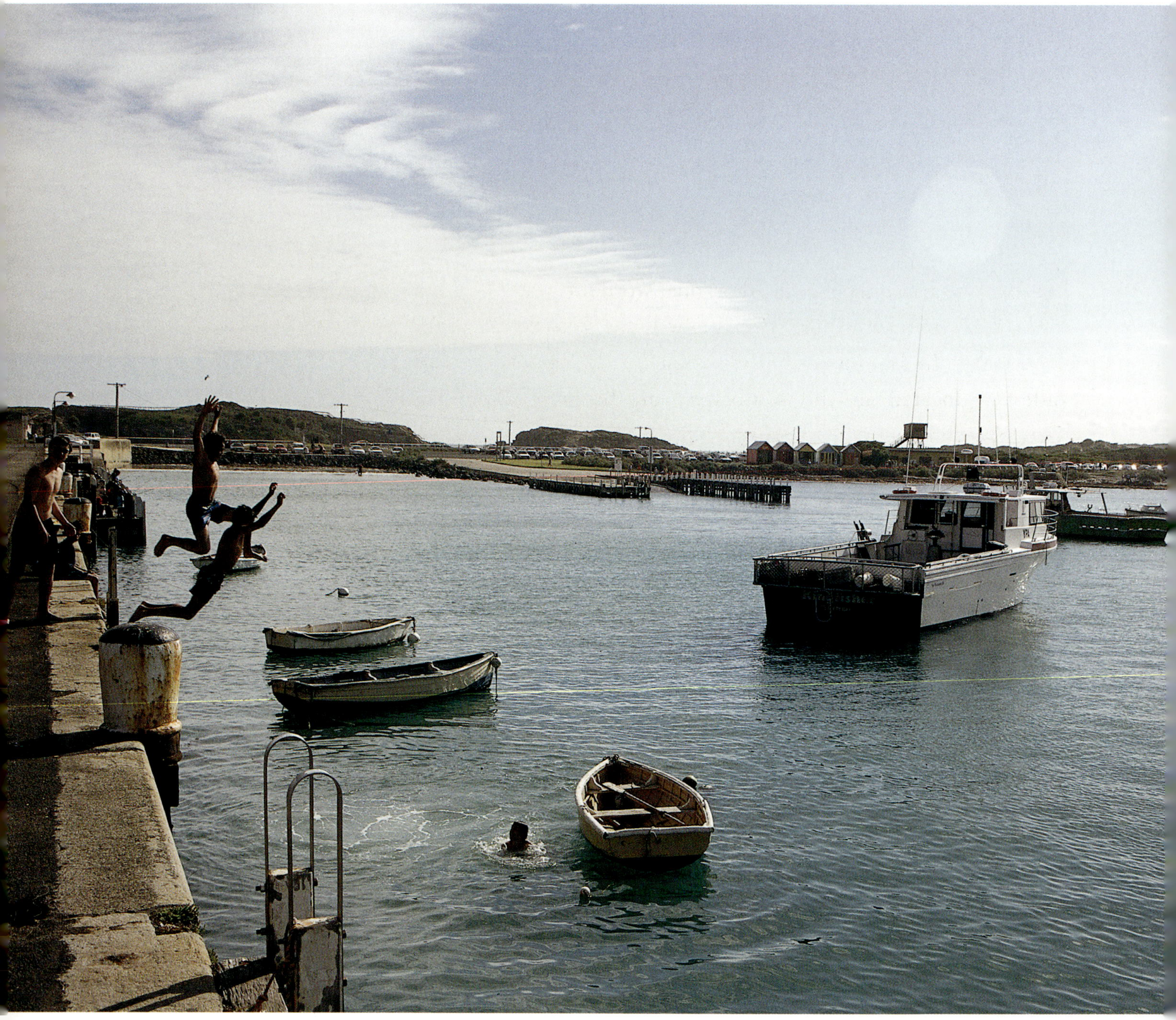

Warrnambool

Warrnambool is an Aboriginal word for 'water between two rivers', and that is exactly the scenario the angler finds on arrival at this coastal city – one of Victoria's oldest – located in the south-west of the state along the Great Ocean Road.

I fished extensively here way back in 1979, competing at the AAA National Titles, where my wife Lynne won the Australian Ladies Estuary Championship from a star-studded field. I was a member of the Australian champion estuary team. The Hopkins River fished very well that year and we showed the locals how good it was by 'importing' sandworms from Gippsland. There were a few coppers in the team and together with the paper trucks and the paddy wagons we managed to get a delivery of sandworms on each day of the competition! Lynne, the kids and I used to stay with Bernie and Fran Lourey of Noorat, near Terang. Fran is an auntie of Lynne's and Bernie is a keen angler

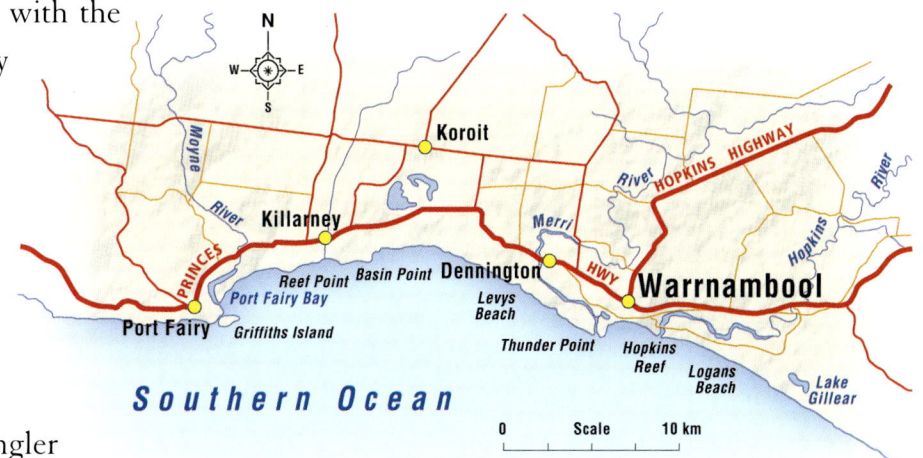

OPPOSITE: *The offshore boat ramp is tucked up inside the Warrnambool breakwall, but can still become exposed to ocean swell depending on prevailing sea conditions.*

LEFT: *The Hopkins River provides excellent casting opportunities for bream and estuary perch, especially with soft plastic lures, which can be worked into shallow weedy areas.*

ABOVE OPPOSITE: *The famous 'Kings Head' mark a few kilometres upstream from the mouth.*

BELOW OPPOSITE: *The breakwall at Warrnambool is a terrific place for kids to fish for silver trevally, leatherjacket, squid and salmon.*

and secretary of the Terang Angling Club. For many years Bernie gave reports on the district on my radio fishing show.

I have fished the Warrnambool area for some time, including a trip to do some filming for the TV show. The fishing environments at Warrnambool are varied and include the two major rivers, the Hopkins and Merri, as well as Lady Bay and several good surf beaches including Levys and Logans, with East Beach towards Port Fairy a hot spot for salmon.

Hopkins River

From the mouth to the upper reaches near a major rock formation called Tooram Stones, a distance of some nine kilometres, the Hopkins River offers some of the finest estuary fishing for bream and estuary perch available in Victoria. Trout are also to be found in the fresh water, which is plentiful as the entrance is closed more often than open.

The river has extensive beds of pod worms. These are soft sandworms that can be collected with a bait pump. There are also shrimp, grey-back gudgeon (like whitebait) and shell in the river.

The black bream is the most popular species sought by anglers on the Hopkins, and these will fall readily to bait, lures and flies like

Matukas and Woolly Buggers. Estuary perch are also encountered in large numbers, and these can be taken on fly, live shrimp, soft plastics, minnow lures and crickets. Sometimes when the river mouth is open to the sea, large schools of small to medium-sized mulloway come in and give great sport on light tackle. Ever present are the yellow-eye mullet. They can reach weights of nearly a kilogram when trapped in the river. They are also great sport and easy to catch, making them a very good beginners' target.

There is good access for shore-based anglers, with plenty of open

ABOVE: *The Hopkins bream love a well-presented soft plastic lure.*

LEFT: *Local fishing writer Marty Ellul with a nice bream he caught in the Hopkins.*

OPPOSITE: *Levys Beach is a consistent year-round producer of salmon and mullet.*

bank areas and small jetties dotted along the lower reaches in particular. Local knowledge can be obtained at tackle shops and bait shops that sell sandworms. Good marks along the river include Kings Head, Hen and Chickens, Selby's and Jubilee Park before Tooram Stones. When targeting bream or estuary perch, look for areas with weed beds and cast your bait or artificial lures into that area.

Merri River

The Merri River is predominantly a freshwater fishery, recognised for its major brown trout populations. It also receives regular liberations of brown trout. There is, however, a small population of estuarine species located in its lower reaches.

The Merri snakes its way inland from the mouth near the Warrnambool breakwall, running almost parallel to the coast, and it is in these reaches that some of best big brown trout in the whole state can be caught. All methods work, from live baits to lures and flies. When the entrance is open, some magnificent silver-coloured sea-run trout can be caught in the middle and lower reaches. Anglers should note that the mouth of the river is part of a marine park.

Upstream, past the Dennington area, the Merri has small trout in good numbers, along with some estuary perch and bream, although it does not fish as well as the Hopkins for estuarine species. Some good spots include Cassidy's Bridge and Hogies Hole.

BELOW: *In 1987 I took a busload of anglers down to Levys Beach for one of my fishing schools and they didn't come away disappointed.*

OPPOSITE: *Warrnambool's surf beaches are very productive and a great place to get away from it all.*

Lady Bay and Offshore

A large concrete breakwall offers considerable protection to an offshore boat ramp and Warrnambool's commercial fishing fleet. Whilst the boat harbour and launching facilities are not in the same league as those at Portland or Apollo Bay, the ramp does offer offshore access for trailer boats to snapper grounds when the weather conditions are reasonable to good.

The breakwall is a good land-based platform allowing you to fish Lady Bay on the northern side with light tackle and the Southern Ocean on the south side with heavier surf tackle. Species that inhabit the area include King George whiting, mullet, leatherjacket, garfish, Australian salmon, silver trevally, gummy shark and barracouta.

Fishing in a boat around Lady Bay is generally more productive than off the breakwall, however particularly for schooling fish like whiting, snapper, garfish and mullet. Look for patches of reef and sand whilst being prepared to move around to find the fish.

The offshore scene is very specialised and should only be undertaken with a solid knowledge of the weather and the conditions that are likely to be encountered in the Southern Ocean. Large trailer boats are definitely preferential and if your intention is to go a considerable distance offshore, it is best to fish in groups. Seek local advice from tackle shops and fishing clubs. Species to be found include snapper, whiting, sweep, shark, yellowtail kingfish and gummy shark. Depths in excess of 40 metres are reached from only a few kilometres out from the breakwall. Nannygai and blue morwong can be caught here, and bigger snapper are often taken at these depths compared to those caught inshore.

Surf Beaches

The surf beaches around Warrnambool are very good for Australian salmon. The beaches stretch for some distance, to Peterborough in the east and Port Fairy in the west. I conducted bus trips and fishing schools to this area for many years. Salmon, mullet, and sometimes silver trevally, gummy sharks and the odd small to medium-sized mulloway were our quarry.

Logans Beach

Logans is perhaps most famous for its whale watching, as visitors flock there from around May through to October to observe one of nature's giants – the southern right whale. Logans is just east of the mouth of the Hopkins River and usually has deep gutters. A reef offshore sometimes draws in snapper, mulloway and sharks, thus providing the angler with considerable variation. When the Hopkins River entrance is open, anglers in the know fish in this area as schools of mulloway, salmon, trevally and mullet move through the mouth. Fresh bait is the order of the day here.

Levys Beach

Levys Beach is a noted salmon fishery and consistent producer. Levys is west of the Warrnambool breakwall, about five to six minutes' drive from the city centre and a short walk through the sand dunes.

BELOW: *The Moyne River at Port Fairy produces its share of fish, from bream and mullet to trevally and salmon.*

The beach is quite long, offering plenty of room for everyone. When the fish are on, though, anglers congregated together tend to really get the salmon in the mood as more bait in the water will also attract more of these fish. Even when Levys is a bit quiet there is always some sort of action from juvenile salmon and mullet.

Port Fairy

Some 30 kilometres west of Warrnambool is the picturesque little town of Port Fairy on the Moyne River. The beaches around Port Fairy are some of the best in the state, most notably East Beach and Killarney Beach either side of the golf course.

Anglers can launch their trailer boats in the protection of the Moyne River and then head out offshore in search of snapper, salmon, flathead and sharks, using the protected breakwall sheltered by Griffith Island. There is excellent fishing at Lady Julia Percy Island and its surrounding reefs for snapper, sweep, sea bream (warehou), sharks and morwong. This island is a considerable run west of Port Fairy, though, and the trip should only be undertaken in excellent conditions.

Conclusion

So there you go. Warrnambool has much to offer the angler, with its variety of fishing environments and species. It is a sizeable town of some 25,000, meaning plenty of accommodation, restaurants, parks and other activities to keep the whole family entertained.

Piscatorial Compass
Warrnambool, Victoria

How to get there: Situated on the south-west coast of Victoria, the major coastal town of Warrnambool is approximately 270 kilometres from Melbourne via Geelong along the Princes Highway.

Where to stay: There is ample accommodation at Warrnambool, with multiple caravan and holiday parks, motels and units.

What to catch: Black bream, estuary perch, mullet, Australian salmon, gummy shark, snapper, King George whiting, yellowtail kingfish, silver trevally, a variety of sharks, snook, sweep and blue morwong.

Gear to take: Use light to medium threadline tackle for river and estuary fishing, and light to medium beach-fishing gear. Take ten-kilogram medium tackle for reef work.

When to go: Year round.

Guides and charters: There are several offshore boat charters.

Rex reckons: The Hopkins River offers some of the best sport fishing for bream and estuary perch in Victoria.

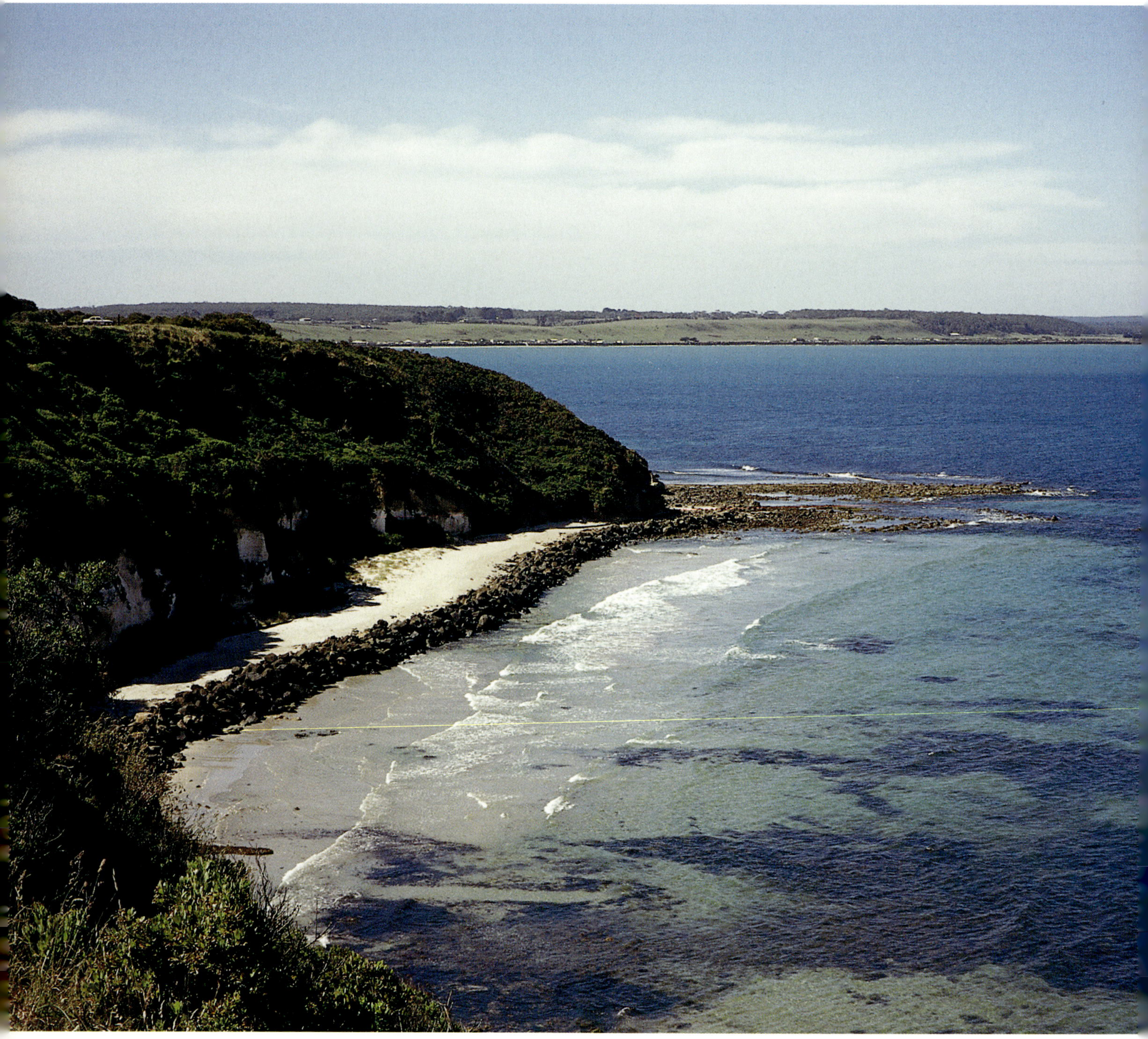

Portland

Portland is on the far west coast of Victoria and is a major commercial deep-sea port. Settled in 1834, Portland was named by the Royal Navy's Lieutenant James Grant after the Duke of Portland, and is widely acknowledged as Victoria's birthplace. It features many historical buildings and is the ideal base from which to explore this part of Victoria's coast.

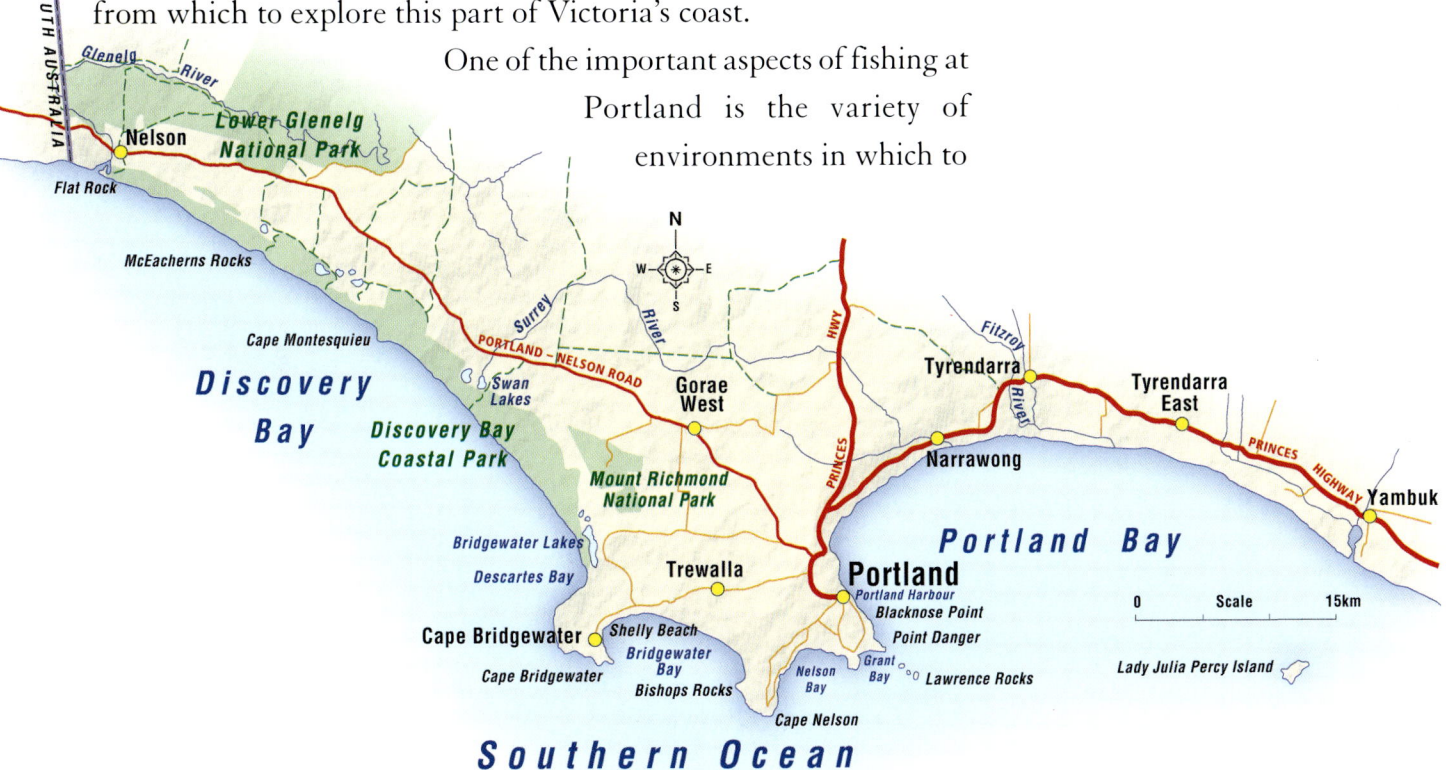

One of the important aspects of fishing at Portland is the variety of environments in which to

OPPOSITE: *The patches of sand and reef along the north shore at Portland provide excellent ground for snapper and whiting.*

catch fish, from remote white sand beaches to the protected Portland harbour, rivers and offshore.

The fishing kicks off from the Narrawong Beach area, a known snapper and gummy shark haunt, then heads west to the north shore in Portland Bay, the harbour and its tremendous land-based fishing opportunities, Bridgewater and Discovery Bay beaches, through to the mighty Glenelg River.

The range of species is likewise varied, with snapper, huge King George whiting, Australian salmon, gummy shark, mulloway, yellowtail kingfish, bream and plenty of big sharks to keep any angler happy.

Portland Harbour

Tucked up into the western corner of Portland Bay, the harbour is formed by two long man-made breakwaters known as the Lee and Main breakwaters. The Main breakwater is off limits to anglers, but the Lee breakwater can be fished right along its length. A small marina and an excellent two-lane boat ramp suitable for boats up to seven metres are found on the town side of the harbour. Anglers can

LEFT: *Anglers fishing from the Lee breakwall catch snapper, trevally, salmon and whiting.*

ABOVE OPPOSITE: *A pair of lovely King George whiting from Portland Bay.*

BELOW OPPOSITE: *Big calamari squid are common around Portland Bay and in the harbour itself.*

drive their cars onto the Lee breakwater and fish either side of it, that is, into Portland Bay or inside the harbour itself. On the harbour side of the breakwater, the Patterson tanker berth platform is worth a try for salmon and leatherjacket, but by far the best and most popular fishing is on the Portland Bay side.

The Lee breakwater has produced some remarkable catches over the years, with big snapper, King George whiting and yellowtail kingfish being caught by anglers fishing into water depths exceeding ten metres. Other species caught off the Lee breakwater include salmon, silver trevally and barracouta; it really depends on which school is about on the day. Fresh squid or pilchards snare the majority of the fish, although the humble fillet of chicken is an extremely popular bait with the locals.

If the weather is too rough to fish offshore or in Portland Bay, there are plenty of other opportunities. The harbour can really turn on the fishing, with resident pinky snapper, King George whiting or mobile schools of salmon on a year-round basis, and warehou, or snotty-nose trevally, which move into the harbour during winter. Mullet, silver trevally and a variety of estuarine and oceanic species congregate in Portland Harbour from time to time. Simply anchor up and start fishing in the harbour whilst being careful not to obstruct any shipping.

Portland Bay

Portland Bay is one of the few accessible offshore locations on the Victorian coast that is protected by prevailing south-westerlies, which dominate this part of Australia. The fishing can be superb, with good small to medium-sized snapper, thumping King George whiting, yellowtail kingfish and mulloway off the reefs that dot the area, some in only five to eight metres of water. The best spots are off Dutton way, along the north shore through to Narrawong Beach on the east side of the harbour, and Blacknose Point and Point Danger on the west side.

A depth sounder is an added advantage, especially when trying to find the reefs further out in Portland Bay, such as the mark known as 'the Cod Splatt', which is approximately 3.5 kilometres out from the harbour entrance. This spot is renowned for snapper and some quality kingfish, which can be taken on surface lures on calm days. Sharks are also common in many parts of the bay and will soon respond to berleying.

Lawrence Rocks is a rock formation some eight kilometres from Portland Harbour, past Danger Point. This is the dividing line for boating anglers from the relative protection of Portland Bay to the swells of the Southern Ocean. Bait fishing with squid and a pipi cocktail bait will produce big King George whiting. Pilchard baits will catch a variety of reef species and some monster arrow squid. From autumn to winter, warehou is the target species. Trolling around the rocks will produce salmon and the rare hit from a stray southern bluefin tuna!

Offshore

Blue, mako and thresher sharks are the main game quarry offshore from Portland. Wire traces and big baits suspended under a float

LEFT: *Silver trevally provide great sport and Portland Harbour is a great place to catch one.*

ABOVE: *Young Michelle Reid with an Australian salmon she caught using a paravane and lure in Portland Harbour.*

work best, in conjunction with a steady stream of berley or chum. The other game species are the mighty southern bluefin tuna, which turn up around late May and June each year to provide Victorian anglers with their only pelagic fishery of note.

Lady Julia Percy Island is a 35-kilometre boat trip south-east from Portland Harbour, or around 20 kilometres from Port Fairy. Well known as a feeding ground for the protected Great White shark, I fished here in the late '70s in the AAA championships held at Warrnambool. I saw one of the great displays of power fishing by Dave Bateman from Queensland and the Garven brothers, Ross and John, from New South Wales. They bailed a huge school of warehou. With the aid of berley and hand-line skills, they landed fish up to two kilograms in weight.

ABOVE: *A superb bream caught upstream on the Glenelg River using cut black crab – the secret to big bream fishing.*

RIGHT: *Beginning the day's filming on the mighty Glenelg River.*

Beaches

Starting from the east of Portland township, productive beaches stretch from Portland Harbour to the estuary mouth of the Fitzroy River. These beaches turn on big salmon, snapper, mulloway and gummy shark. The mouth of the Surrey River at Narrawong

Beach is probably the most productive, with some good holes and gutters to fish, especially at night. Pilchard, mullet and bluebait are the best baits.

Heading west around Cape Nelson there is Bridgewater Bay and Shelly Beach, only a short drive from Portland township. This beautiful bay regularly yields gummy shark, salmon and mulloway. I've been told that snapper have been seen on Shelly Beach feeding in the shallows at night.

Further west the vast Discovery Bay opens up along the coast and heads towards the mouth of the Glenelg River. The beaches are only accessible by 4WD, however no vehicles are allowed on the beach. The best access from Portland is via the Swan Lake camping area. Monster salmon hunt these beaches, along with excellent gummy shark. Mulloway are always a chance at night near the mouth of the Glenelg River if the entrance is open.

ABOVE: *Neil Shelton owns the local pub. He's a good bloke and loves his fishing, especially trolling lures or live baits for mulloway.*

Glenelg River

The best place to do some estuary fishing when based at Portland is the Glenelg River, 70 kilometres west of Portland along the Portland–Nelson Road. A marvellous waterway, the Glenelg stretches from its source in the Grampians to the mouth at the tiny township of Nelson. The river is navigable for some 70 kilometres in its lower reaches, but has an overall length of around 440 kilometres. There are some terrific fishing platforms in Nelson, and boat ramps are spread along the entire navigable section of the river.

The main attraction here is the mulloway. There is a very good population in the river all year round, but when the mouth has a deep enough channel from the ocean, the mulloway come in en masse and provide some sensational fishing. The best method is to slowly troll live mullet. Mulloway can also be caught on trolled deep-diving bibbed lures. At first and last light dead baits and strip baits such as mullet, fillets of salmon and pilchards are all good, successful baits. The best time to fish is around the new moon.

Bream are also found in large numbers in this system and can stretch right up to the freshwater section. Soft bait like sandworms can be very good, however they do attract the undersize bream and mullet. Bigger fish are taken by anglers who use local black crabs. Visiting anglers from Warrnambool and Portland also use bass yabbies (nippers). For the daytripper and tourist the humble peeled frozen prawn will always get a response.

The locals will gladly assist you. Good information can be gleaned from the boat hire place and the local pub, run by Neil Shelton.

Conclusion

So there you go, folks. Portland and the surrounding area is a great place to take the family and gee, the fishing can be superb. Best of all, you don't need a boat, with the Lee breakwater, beaches and Glenelg River to choose from. If you do have a boat, some of the best offshore fishing is available to you, and you can utilise the terrific boat-launching facilities within Portland Harbour.

Piscatorial Compass

Portland, Victoria

How to get there: Located on the far south-west coast of Victoria, historic Portland is approximately 365 kilometres from Melbourne via Geelong along the Princes Highway.

Where to stay: There's a full range of accommodation available, including numerous caravan parks and holiday units that accommodate trailer boats.

What to catch: Snapper, King George whiting, bluefin tuna, yellowtail kingfish, mulloway, gummy, thresher and other sharks, Australian salmon, flathead, leatherjacket, warehou, calamari and arrow squid, silver trevally, pike and barracouta.

Gear to take: Use light to medium tackle for boat- or land-based fishing. Game-fishing gear is best if you're targeting bluefin tuna in the winter months. Take medium to heavy gear for beach fishing.

When to go: Year round, but best from December to April.

Guides and charters: There are several boat charters operating out of Portland, some on a seasonal basis only.

Rex reckons: Fresh bait in the form of the southern calamari squid is the best if you want to get amongst the fish at Portland.

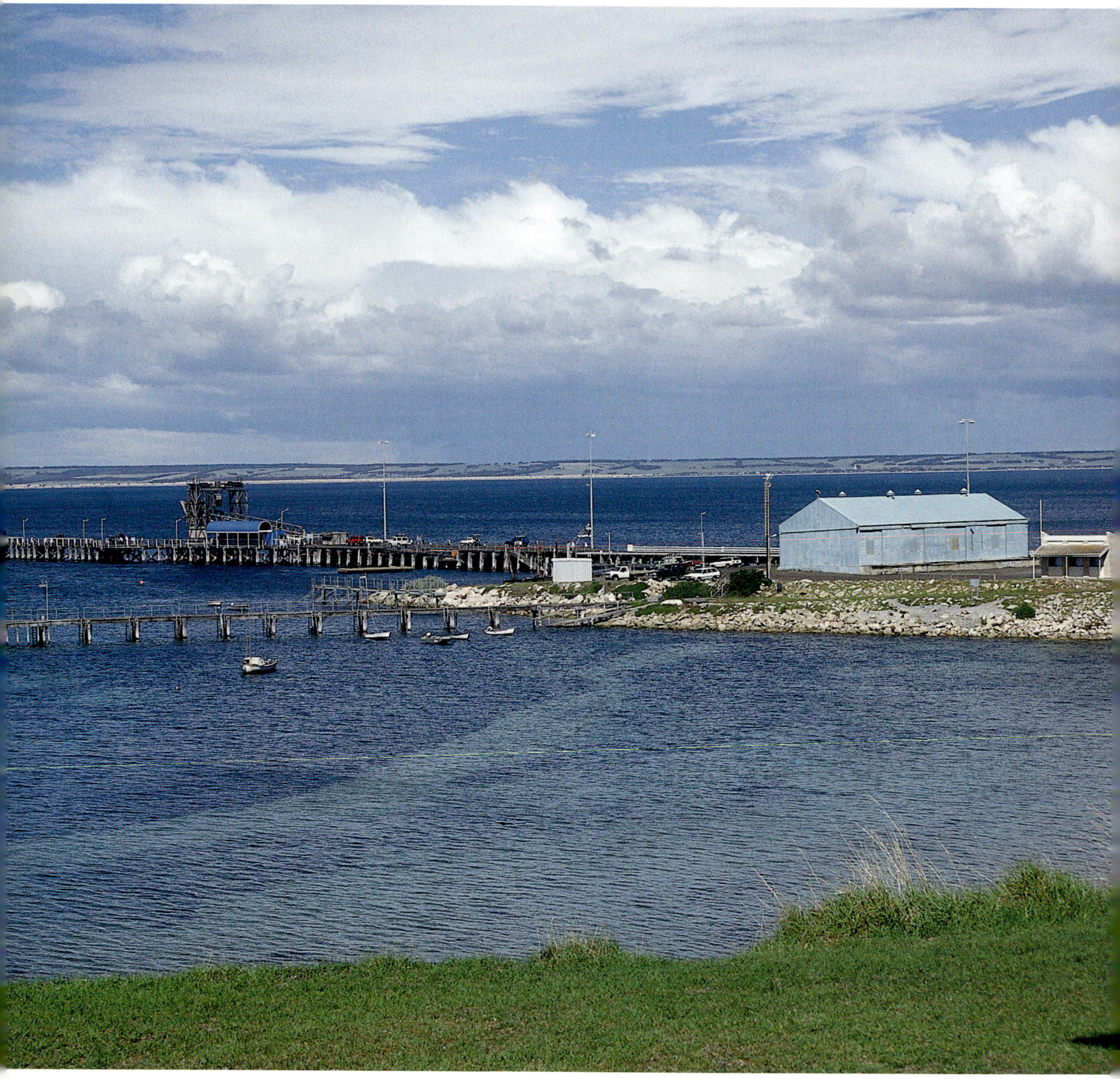

Kangaroo Island

Kangaroo Island is possibly South Australia's most famous tourist destination. It's a big island at 155 kilometres long and 55 kilometres wide. In fact, it is Australia's third largest island behind Tasmania and Melville Island north of Darwin in the Top End.

I reckon they should have named South Australia 'Matthew Flinders', as this bloke explored and named most of the South Australian coast during his circum-navigation of Australia in 1802. Early that year Flinders spotted the island

OPPOSITE: *Kangaroo Island's Kingscote jetty is one of South Australia's very best land-based locations. It consistently produces trevally, tommy ruff, King George whiting, snook and squid.*

LEFT: *Smooching up to a sweep caught off Cape Jervis, the gateway to Kangaroo Island from the Fleurieu Peninsula.*

ABOVE OPPOSITE: *Merrilyn Mensforth with a pair of giant whiting from Kangaroo Island's western end. Both fish are well over a kilogram.*

BELOW OPPOSITE: *Big silver trevally like this pair of ten-pounders are often caught off Kangaroo Island. These came from Western River Cove.*

and came ashore, naming it Kangaroo Island for obvious reasons – lots of kangaroos. He just beat a French explorer, Nicolas Baudin, to the island, and whilst technically the two countries were at war they agreed to share information. As a result, many of the place names around the island are French in origin.

Being relatively close to Adelaide, the island offers the visitor the full range of scenic vistas, outdoor activities and accommodation options, and the local wildlife is truly amazing. To protect the wildlife and natural beauty of Kangaroo Island there are some twenty national and conservation parks.

Fishing is at the forefront of the possible activities on Kangaroo Island, with the full gamut of environments to choose from: rivers, beaches, jetties, rocks and offshore.

Jetties

Kangaroo Island is blessed with some of the best jetties to fish from in the state, with jetties and wharves at Kingscote, Vivonne Bay, Penneshaw and American River all providing excellent fishing at times.

The pier at Kingscote, which juts out into Nepean Bay, is the pick with silver trevally, tommy ruff, garfish and squid all on the chew for most of the year. This is a great place to take kids, as you have a good to very good chance of catching a fish. Armed with fresh bait and fishing around high tide should see you amongst the action.

American River, named after American sealers that settled in the area, is located on the western shore of Eastern Cove. The wharf here is a good spot to dangle a line for most of the usual species, with the added bonus of some lovely King George whiting. This is a beautiful spot to take the family.

Beaches and Rocks

An extensive road network on the island means the angler has a multitude of choices when looking for a secluded beach on which to get back to nature. Australian salmon and mullet are commonly taken at Snelling Beach, Stokes Bay and Emu Bay on the north coast. D'Estrees Bay in the south-eastern corner of the island offers good flathead on either bait or rubber-tail jigs cast off the beach.

During winter big salmon hunt the beaches at Hanson Bay, located on the southern coast near the eastern tip of the island, with Pennington Bay and Mouth Flat beaches on the Dudley Peninsula popular with the locals.

The north coast of the island is generally better protected from the prevailing ocean swell, and consequently anglers can usually find a calm and safe place to fish off the rocks for sweep, salmon, leatherjacket, silver trevally and the usual pests like parrotfish and other species of wrasse.

The south coast has more rock platform options, but is naturally less protected and in some cases fairly inaccessible. A good spot to try is at Cape Du Couedic on the far south-western corner of the island, where trevally and sweep are the main targets along with some very big blue groper for the angler with gear heavy enough to land them.

ABOVE: *Blue morwong (also known as queen snapper) are common in South Australia's deeper areas. This beauty came from Investigator Strait near Kangaroo Island.*

LEFT: *Snug Cove, at the western end of Kangaroo Island's north coast, is a terrific anchorage in most weather.*

OPPOSITE: *Anglers cast bait for mullet from the beach at Western River, on Kangaroo Island's north coast.*

Offshore

There is some great deepwater snapper fishing to be found off the north coast of Kangaroo Island, with fish around nine to ten kilograms quite common. Charter boats are generally the go for visiting anglers, where you can tangle with the local snapper plus other monsters such as huge samson fish that pull like trains, and the delicious nannygai or red snapper. Other deep-sea species include yellowtail kingfish, blue groper, queen snapper and various species of cod.

The charter boats all have their GPS marks and these locate reefs or 'lumps' that rise off the bottom. Reef species usually hover around the top of these peaks. The best option is to drift over the top with the tide and use braided line to eliminate the belly in the line that is common when using monofilament. When fishing in deep water you need to feel the bites and the braid is just sensational.

The bays around Kangaroo Island also produce some terrific King George whiting fishing. The best spots include offshore from Middle River, Western River, Stokes Bay and Snug Cove. Investigator Strait is the prime producer of big whiting. It has a fast current and is deeper than usual whiting territory, so heavier terminal tackle is required. My good friend Shane Mensforth and I spent time trying to catch the one-kilogram variety on our last visit and we fell just short, but these fish are magnificent.

For anglers with their own boats, salmon, snook and the odd southern bluefin tuna are taken on trolled lures at various points around the island. Look for birds working the water or troll around rock bommies and, in good conditions, around rocky outcrops. Places to try include North Cape, Cape Cassini and Cape Dutton along the north coast.

Conclusion

Kangaroo Island has many surprises, including some excellent river systems that hold good populations of big bream to tempt the bait or lure angler. The variety to be found at K.I. is such that you would need a lifetime to sample all its piscatorial pleasures. As a bonus, it is also one of the most scenic places in the country.

Piscatorial Compass

Kangaroo Island, South Australia

HOW TO GET THERE: From Adelaide to Cape Jervis by road is via the Southern Expressway and Main South Road. From Cape Jervis, connect with the Kangaroo Island Sealink ferry for a trip across Backstairs Passage, arriving at Penneshaw on K.I. Several regional airlines also fly to Kangaroo Island from the mainland.

WHERE TO STAY: There's a huge range of accommodation to suit all budgets. Check out the Kangaroo Island tourist site at www.tourkangarooisland.com.au for details.

WHAT TO CATCH: Snapper, King George whiting, southern bluefin tuna, Australian salmon, mulloway, sweep, nannygai, queen snapper, yellowtail kingfish, shark, tommy ruff, trevally, flathead, garfish, bream, mullet, leatherjacket, blue groper, cod, squid and snook.

GEAR TO TAKE: Light estuary gear is best for the rivers and jetties. Use surf gear for beaches and a ten-kilogram rod and reel set-up for reef species.

WHEN TO GO: Year round.

GUIDES AND CHARTERS: Boat and game charters vary in size, however several operators are capable of full game fishing and deep-sea fishing expeditions.

REX RECKONS: One of the best spots to snare yourself a one-kilogram whiting!

YAMAHA
SaltwaterSeries II
MUSTANG
2000 TOURNAMENT
SIGNAGE BY
Regal Display
YAMAHA
LOWRANCE

Adelaide

Adelaide is a beautiful city situated on the Torrens River and the eastern shoreline of the magnificent Gulf of St Vincent. The Adelaide cricket test is always a highlight each year and for me the fishing around Adelaide is equally impressive. Even though the city has a population of over a million people, it is blessed with some of the best metropolitan fishing in Australia due to the vastness of the coastline and some sensible fisheries management.

Unlike in Victoria and other states, bag and size and boat limits have been set to allow popular species such as snapper and whiting to attain a reasonable size before they can be legally taken. In Victoria, an angler can keep a snapper over 27 centimetres (that's a tiddler). In South Australia a snapper has to be over 38 centimetres. This type of fisheries management has seen snapper thrive all along the coast and has become a major drawcard for the visiting angler.

South Australians have embraced artificial reefs with great enthusiasm, and many reefs have been created in the waters off metropolitan Adelaide.

OPPOSITE: *Myself and Shane Mensforth getting stuck into the whiting on the Grange tyre reef off metropolitan Adelaide.*

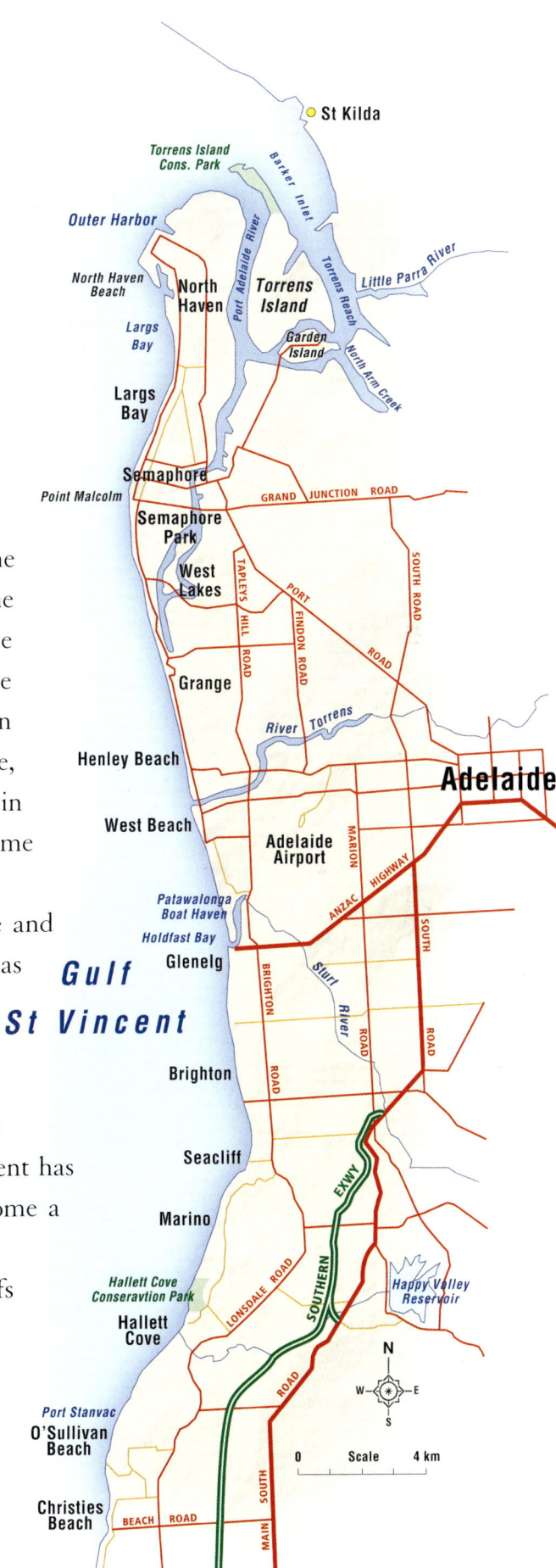

These reefs act as natural hideouts for bait fish, which in turn bring the predators and of course, big red.

Adelaide has also been blessed with some excellent boating facilities and launching ramps for offshore access, for example at North Haven and O'Sullivan Beach marinas. These facilities cater for big trailer boats with multiple-lane ramps and ample car parking.

OPPOSITE: *Brett Mensforth with two thumper King George whiting taken on a charter boat in lower Gulf of St Vincent.*

RIGHT: *Adelaide Crows star, Andrew McLeod, with a nice snapper from one of Adelaide's artificial reefs.*

Offshore

The Outer Harbour Channel and artificial reefs offer some of the best snapper fishing off Adelaide. Shane Mensforth and I have fished the Glenelg tyre reefs for snapper with great success. You have to be fishing right over the reef to get snapper, though. If you are off to the left or right you'll get the 'rubbish' fish like wrasse and gurnard. This is where a quality sounder and good anchoring technique are paramount to success.

It took me a while to get used to the way the snapper bite in South Australia. It is different from back in Port Phillip Bay: the bite is more of a rattle, and the next thing you know you are on! We let the fish run a bit in Port Phillip. I also discovered that winter is the best time to fish for reds off Adelaide.

I recall one time fishing with Shane. I'd been calling a footy match for the radio between AFL teams Essendon and Port Adelaide on the Saturday and was invited out the next morning to chase snapper. It was five degrees Celsius in the middle of winter and I thought, you've got to be kidding! But we caught our bag limit in no time. Again this was totally alien to my thinking back home.

The artificial reefs off Adelaide also produce some ripper King

ABOVE: *The Torrens Island power station just north-west of Adelaide is a great place to chase bream and mulloway.*

LEFT: *Kylie Peake displays a couple of lovely bream from North Haven Marina right in the middle of Adelaide.*

George whiting. The Grange tyre reef is a particularly good spot. A cockle (pipi), perhaps combined with some fresh squid, will often get hammered. The Grange reef is also very accessible, being only a short distance from the North Haven Marina launching facility.

Land-based Opportunities

The jetties around Adelaide are very good, and I have caught some fine garfish and tommy ruff from them. Berley is often the key ingredient. Some of the best jetties around Adelaide include those at Glenelg, Brighton, Grange, Largs Bay and Semaphore. These jetties poke out into the fishy waters of the Gulf of St Vincent and literally any type of fish could swim by. The most common species caught are garfish, tommy ruff, whiting, squid and blue swimmer crabs.

There is excellent whiting fishing along the many areas between the Port River mouth and south of Glenelg. Shore-based anglers can also have some great fun by 'berleying up' schools of mullet on the sandy beaches.

Port River

The Port River in northern Adelaide has some excellent bream fishing amongst the man-made structures in the river. Strictly speaking, the river is more a canal connecting the outer harbour, Port Adelaide and West Lakes. It is a big system that offers black bream and mulloway to the angler willing to put in the time with the right baits and techniques.

The best times to fish the river are around dawn and dusk, with times of low light absolute prime time. Don't cast out into the middle of the river; stick to the wharves and pylons, which is where the big fish lurk. I remember we used nine-kilogram monofilament line to prevent the bream from cutting us off on the barnacles around the pylons, as their first run is straight back into cover and that is usually right around the nearest pylon. The best baits to try are pipis, prawns and small crabs.

A boat is helpful but not a necessity on the river, as there are some very good spots for land-based fishers, particularly the wharf at Tragedy Dock and Snowdens Beach. Boat-based anglers have the luxury of mobility and can move to find feeding fish right along the Port River and outer harbour.

Conclusion

I've fished around Adelaide quite a few times for the TV show with the support of top local fishing expert and good friend Shane Mensforth. I've had some memorable moments fishing for snapper and whiting and have always enjoyed fishing with many of the Adelaide Crows footballers from time to time. Fishing and football South Australian style – what a great combination.

Piscatorial Compass

Adelaide, South Australia

How to get there: Adelaide, well known as the city of churches, is the capital of South Australia and is located on the east coast of the Gulf of St Vincent. There are regular flights from all major capital cities and major highway linkages from east and west.

Where to stay: As you can imagine, a city of a million people has no shortage of accommodation to suit all budgets.

What to catch: Snapper, King George whiting, tommy ruff, leatherjacket, Australian salmon, black bream, garfish, mullet, calamari squid, blue swimmer crabs and sharks.

Gear to take: Use a ten-kilogram medium overhead rod and reel for snapper, and light threadline combos for estuarine species.

When to go: Year round.

Guides and charters: There is a huge range of fishing charters eager to take customers out onto the Gulf of St Vincent in search of big red.

Rex reckons: There are many tyre reefs off metropolitan Adelaide that have 'manufactured' excellent areas for snapper, whiting and leatherjacket.

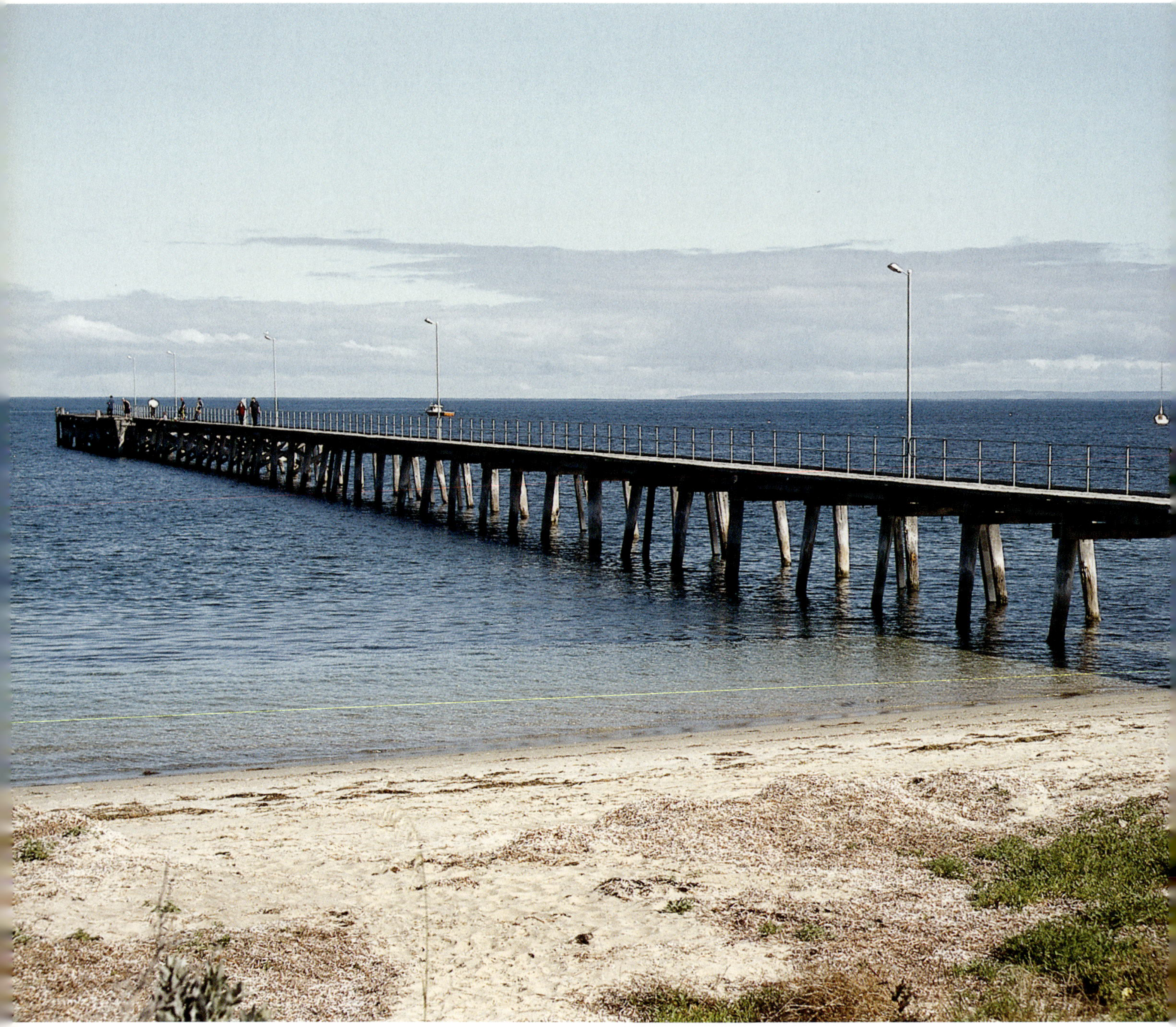

Marion Bay

Marion Bay is at the southern tip of the foot-shaped Yorke Peninsula, often referred to as South Australia's 'little Italy'. The Yorke Peninsula divides South Australia's two main gulfs, the Gulf of St Vincent with metropolitan Adelaide on its eastern coast, and Spencer Gulf, which runs from Port Augusta in the north to Port Lincoln in the south.

Originally inhabited by the Warri clan of Narranga Aborigines, Marion Bay was named after a ship that was wrecked on nearby Troubridge Shoal in 1851. The area was popular with sealers in those days, and with the discovery of copper, Marion Bay became an important sea port.

My first impressions of Marion Bay, aside from its natural beauty, were a bit grim. This is where my producer Bob Grieve nearly lost his life. We were filming in this area with Bill Kelly when we

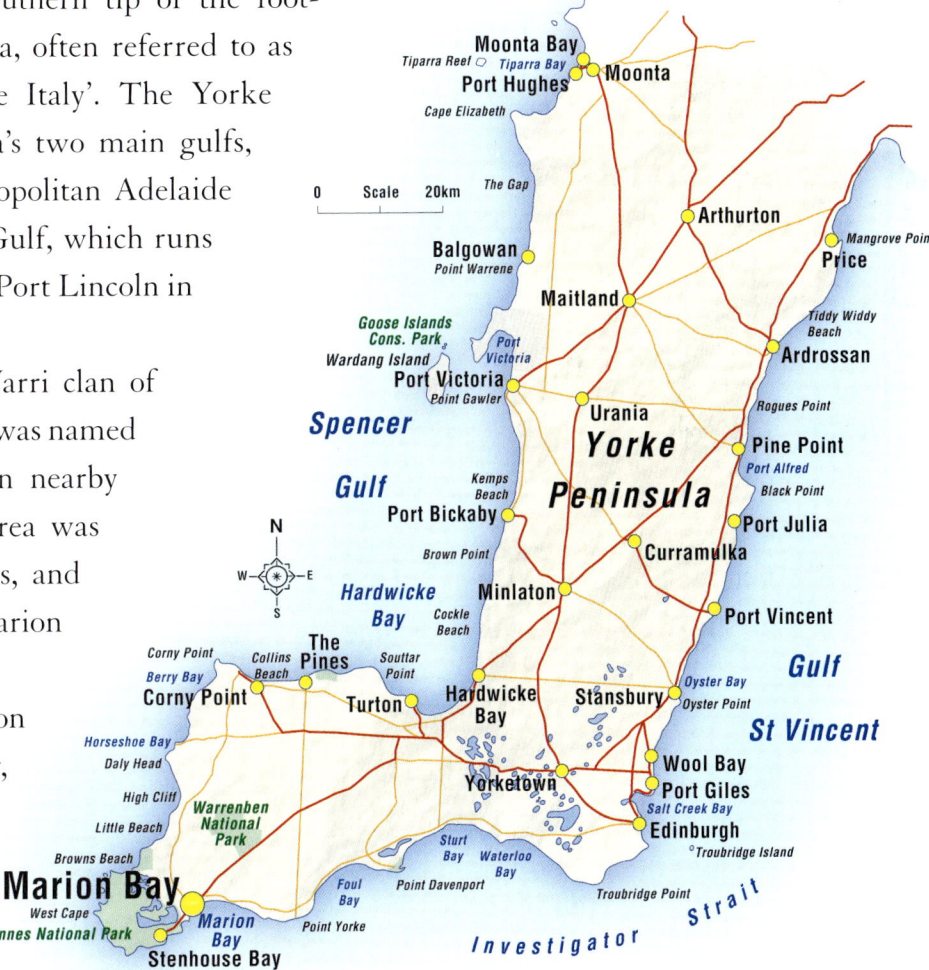

OPPOSITE: *The Marion Bay jetty, the step-off point for our piscatorial adventures. It also fishes well for garfish and squid.*

were hit by a huge wave that came from nowhere. Apart from a few bruises everybody was fine, except Bob. He was obviously very badly injured and as it turned out it was life threatening.

I sent out a mayday call via the seaphone to the South Australian Coastal Rescue Service, and within half an hour there were three helicopters hovering over our boat. Unfortunately none of them was the sea rescue team – they all happened to be from the commercial television networks!

Finally, the yellow sea rescue helicopter turned up with a paramedic and a doctor on board. The paramedic, Leonie, lowered

RIGHT: *Paul Worsteling with a huge Marion Bay King George whiting.*

OPPOSITE: *The nannygai, or red snapper, is one of the finest table fish to be caught from southern Australia waters.*

herself down the rope ladder and assessed that Bob was in big trouble with a collapsed lung. Bob was also going a deathly grey colour. Something needed to be done and quick.

Next down to the boat was Dr Bill Griggs, a trauma surgeon. He also quickly assessed Bob and immediately made an incision into Bob's chest. He placed a tube through it and then began to pump air into Bob's collapsed lung. Bob was then stabilised, lifted into the chopper and flown back to Adelaide.

The long story ended six months later when Bob, after lengthy and painstaking rehabilitation, returned to work.

Four years after that frightening experience we returned to Marion Bay with Bob as producer and my South Australian correspondent and good friend Shane Mensforth, who had also been with us on that fateful day. Our objective was to finish what we'd started four years before – a piscatorial adventure into the deep to chase a range of bottom-dwellers including nannygai, blue morwong, samson fish, snapper and possibly some big deepwater King George whiting, which are all commonly found in these waters.

ABOVE: *South Australian whiting – simply magnificent!*

Investigator Strait

Investigator Strait is the body of water between the Yorke Peninsula and the northern coast of Kangaroo Island. It contains some seriously deep water, which makes for great fishing.

On this particular trip, we boarded the charter boat off the Marion Bay jetty and steamed for more than an hour before reaching our mark in the middle of the strait. We were fishing at a depth of 65 metres, folks, and we knew that standard monofilament line would form a belly in the ocean current and any bites would simply go unnoticed unless an express train of a fish hit the bait. So, in the deep we used braided line that has little or no stretch. This line was spooled on ten-kilogram rods coupled with an overhead reel. The rig was the simple paternoster type, with the sinker below and two hooks on droppers tied above. We baited these with whole pilchards.

It didn't take long for the action to start, and I soon caught a nice silver trevally of about two kilograms. Shane Mensforth calls them 'blurters' because of the blurting sound they make with their mouths. They have a tail that is power personified, but these fish were not what we were after. Our target was the nannygai, or red snapper, which is a superb table fish with delicious white flesh. Take care when handling these fish though, as every scale on their body is razor sharp, as are their gill plates. The best way to hold them is by their cavernous, but toothless, mouth. Shane and I eventually did get onto the nannygai, and the best of the day weighed in at 2.5 kilograms. I'm told they are regularly caught up to four kilograms. We ate our nannygai for dinner that night, and it was one of the best I've tasted.

Inshore Opportunities

There is also some tremendous fishing on offer closer to shore off Marion Bay. Along with young gun Paul Worsteling, who was experiencing his first major trip into South Australian waters at the time, we boarded the charter boat *Penguin 3* at Marion Bay jetty and went looking for some inshore whiting action. We were still going to be fishing in what for me is deep water when I'm chasing the 'ol' Chinese fish'. I'm used to fishing for whiting in depths of one to five metres, and we were going to be fishing in water 20–25 metres deep.

At this depth, the fishing can be a lottery. But that's the great thing about fishing, especially in places like Marion Bay – you never know what you'll catch. On this occasion we dropped our baits and the bites come on immediately, but the whiting eluded us as we pulled in a succession of wrasse, parrotfish, barracouta and gurnard. They showed up eventually though, and Paul was the first to land a beauty, weighing in around the 700-gram mark. Before long we were both getting into some huge King George whiting. These kidney slappers are monsters by Victorian standards.

I've also caught some lovely leatherjacket in these waters. The ol' Elvis Presley fish is one of my favourite fish species. We landed three different varieties: the six spine, an unknown variety and the horseshoe. The horseshoe leatherjacket is one of the prettiest fish in the seas; it's like someone has taken a paintbrush and coloured in the blanks. Leatherjacket are also a top table fish.

Conclusion

Our Marion Bay experience started out as a nightmare with Bob's accident, and then turned into a dream fishing spot. The scenery is spectacular, with big beaches and huge cliffs pounded by the might of the Southern Ocean. The whole of the Yorke Peninsula has been kept a bit of a secret from interstate visitors, but the good people of Adelaide know its charms.

Piscatorial Compass

Marion Bay, South Australia

How to get there: Marion Bay is approximately 285 kilometres from Adelaide via Port Wakefield Road, Main Coast Road and eventually Stenhouse Bay Road.

Where to stay: Marion Bay Holiday Villas are fantastic. There is also an excellent caravan park and other holiday unit-style accommodation.

What to catch: King George whiting, snapper, nannygai, blue morwong, silver trevally, snook, garfish, barracouta and various species of leatherjacket and wrasse.

Gear to take: Use light to medium threadline tackle for light reef and inshore work, and medium rods and overhead reels for deepwater reef species.

When to go: Year round.

Guides and charters: Davenport Fishing Charters are great. There are also several other fishing charters operating out of Marion Bay.

Rex reckons: Some of the biggest whiting in South Australia reside here.

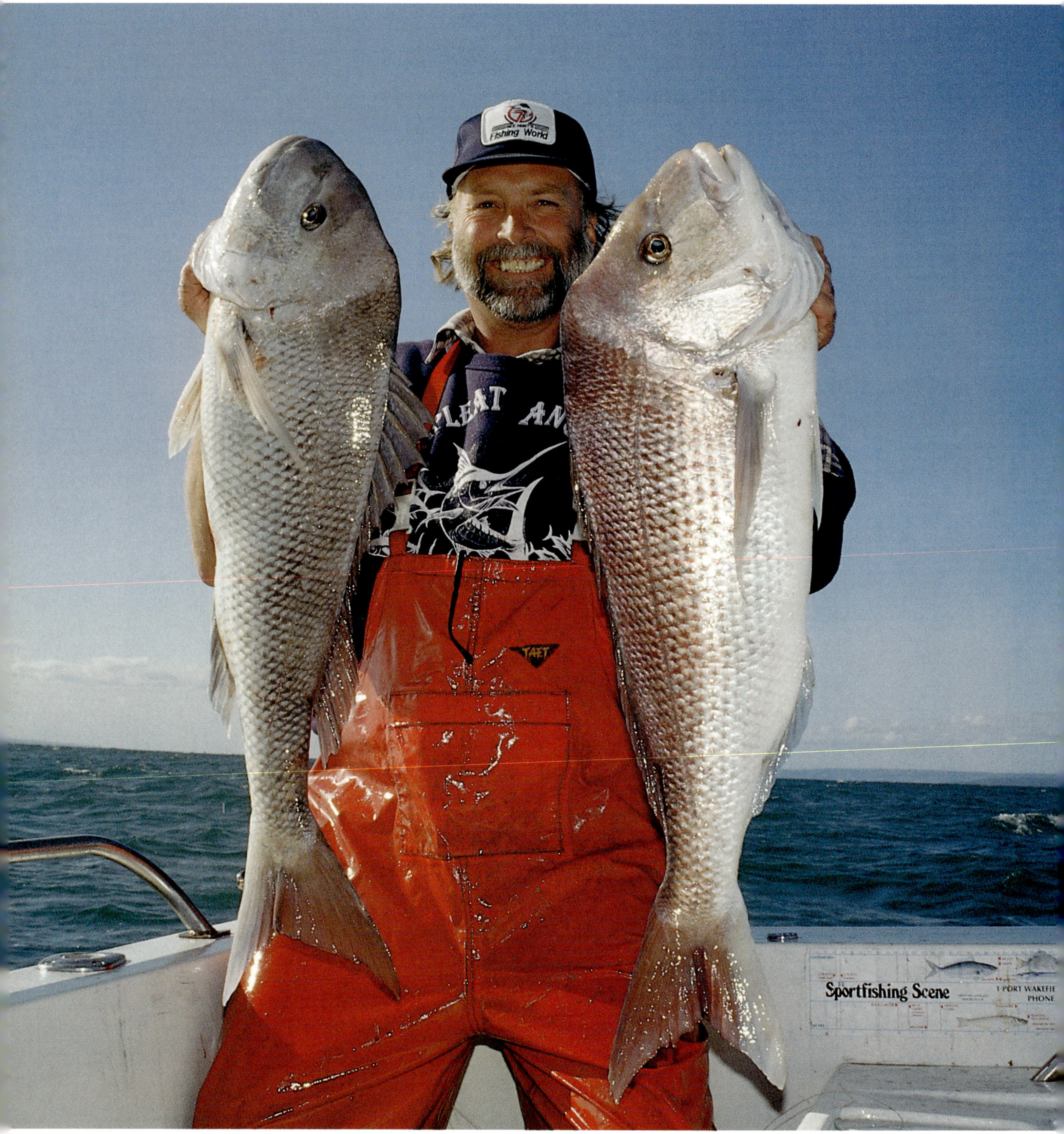
Fishing World
Sportfishing Scene

Whyalla

Whyalla is located on the western coast of upper Spencer Gulf, just south of False Bay. Its reputation as the home of the biggest snapper in Australia is well deserved, with ten-kilogram fish common and fish to 15 kilograms and over possible.

Whyalla was originally named Tummock Hill in 1802 by – you guessed it, folks – Matthew Flinders, during his incredible circumnavigation of Australia. In 1899, the big Australian, BHP, acquired some mining leases in the area and in a few years started to mine iron ore. In 1914, the town was renamed Whyalla and the port established to ship the iron ore.

Today, Whyalla has a population of over 21,000 people and is South Australia's second largest city. While the mining industry still dominates life here, the city has developed other industries such as

OPPOSITE: *Two Whyalla twenty-pounders caught on consecutive casts.*

aquaculture. Tourism, particularly of the piscatorial variety, is also on the increase as anglers from as far away as Melbourne make regular pilgrimages each summer to fish for Whyalla's famous big snapper.

Whyalla's boating facilities for trailer boat fisherman are sensational, with a magnificent marina boasting a four-lane boat ramp with landing jetties, and a massive car park for anglers' cars and trailers. The marina is also home to the Whyalla Sport Fishing Club, who invited us to experience the Whyalla fishing scene in the very early days of the TV show. The club was fantastic, holding what amounted to a civic reception for our arrival. The club members could not do enough to help us, and have a well-known and refreshing reputation for being friendly to visiting anglers. They don't seem to mind putting newcomers onto to some good marks for big red!

ABOVE: *Yours truly with a magnificent blue swimmer crab from Whyalla waters.*

OPPOSITE: *Big yellowtail kings, like this 18-kilogram fish caught by Brett O'Brien, are becoming more common around Whyalla.*

Snapper Fishing in the Spencer Gulf

The snapper fishing out from Whyalla in the Spencer Gulf is almost too good to be true. The Sport Fishing Club gave us some precise marks to fish at the right time in the tide cycle, and I caught

LEFT: *Dene Oehme with a decent Whyalla red. This is the big snapper capital of the Australia.*

my first two nine-kilogram snapper here on consecutive casts. It was unbelievable, after 30 years of fishing Port Phillip Bay for snapper and not getting fish approaching that weight, I had two beauties within twenty minutes. I must say my Whyalla experience spoilt me for a while. It was like a dream – snapper heaven!

To the uneducated, the Spencer Gulf appears as a huge piece of water of which much of the bottom is quite featureless. However for many years the locals have been creating their own artificial reefs or 'drops'. Old car bodies, stripped of their engines and other polluting materials, are taken out and dropped to the bottom to create structure and habitat for the snapper. Many of these 'drops' are not legal, and I'm not endorsing their creation, but nevertheless they exist.

Legal or not, the bonus for anglers has been a snapper fishery which, combined with strict size, bag and boat limits, is second to none in the country. Artificial reefs, with their many nooks and crannies, attract sea growth from sea grasses to barnacles and other shellfish. This in turn attracts bait fish and eventually predators. Like in the movie *The Lion King*, this is the circle of life, err… or should I say the circle of snapper!

Once anchored over these man-made reefs, many local anglers employ a berley bag of crushed fish heads and other smelly stuff which is lowered onto the sea floor. Good baits include fresh squid, Western Australian pilchards and fillets of salmon, tommy ruff or garfish. The prime time to fish is at dawn and dusk, although fishing through the night often produces startling results.

Whyalla also boasts some excellent inshore fishing with whiting, snook and garfish. Yellowtail kingfish are a welcome catch out deep in the Gulf, along with the schools of Australian salmon that turn up from time to time. Whyalla also hosts an annual amateur snapper fishing competition where anglers from all over South Australia and Victoria compete for prizes. The competition is friendly and for Victorian visitors is a taste of what big snapper fishing is all about.

Conclusion

The dream that turned into reality when I caught those two big snapper on that first trip is still with me today. I've been back since, and am still amazed at the abundance of big snapper in the upper Spencer Gulf area. What a fishery, folks.

Piscatorial Compass

Whyalla, South Australia

How to get there: Whyalla is approximately 390 kilometres from Adelaide via Port Wakefield Road and the Princes, Eyre and Lincoln highways.

Where to stay: There is plenty of accommodation with caravan parks, motels, hotels, apartments, holiday units and even an adventure camp.

What to catch: Snapper, King George whiting, yellowtail kingfish, blue swimmer crabs, mullet, garfish and snook.

Gear to take: Use a ten-kilogram medium overhead rod and reel for snapper, and light threadline gear for whiting.

When to go: Year round. Best snapper fishing is in January and February.

Guides and charters: Several charter boats operate out of Whyalla, and many specially target the big snapper.

Rex reckons: It took me a while to get over the size of the snapper I caught at Whyalla. It really spoilt me when I had to come back to the reality of my home-town waters.

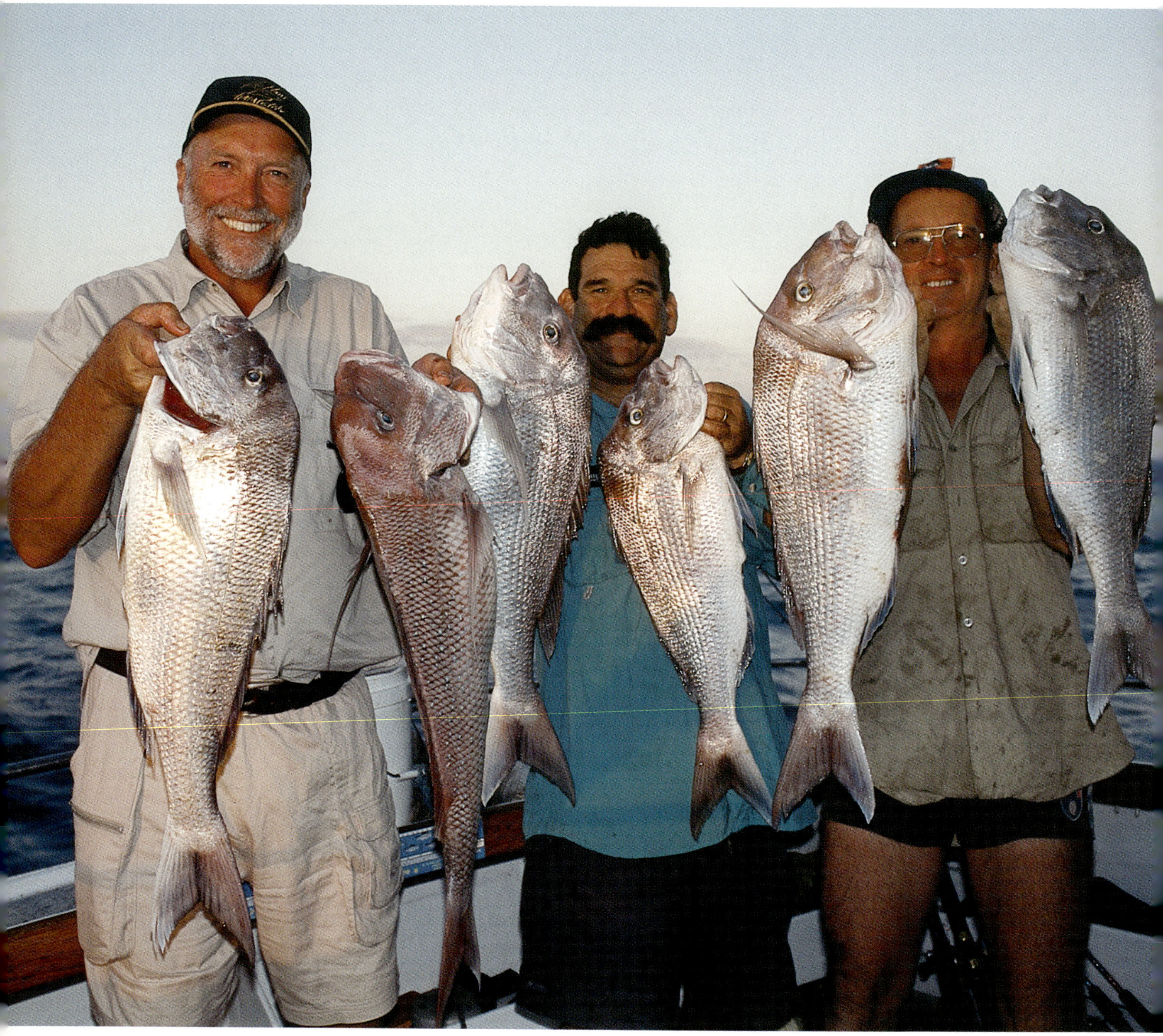

Tumby Bay

A few years ago I was invited by the South Australian Tourism Commission to visit the little seaside town of Tumby Bay about 50 kilometres north of Port Lincoln on the Eyre Peninsula.

Tumby Bay was named by Matthew Flinders in 1802 after the village of Tumby in England. In fact, it was known as Tumby up until the early 1980s before being renamed Tumby Bay. The area was first settled in the 1840s by farmers, but it wasn't until the early 1900s that the town was officially proclaimed. These days it remains an important centre for farming, but it is fishing that has lifted its profile in recent years.

The fishing is varied, with excellent inshore species like tommy ruff, salmon, whiting and garfish available for most of the year. The Sir Joseph Banks group of islands further strengthens the area's fishing credentials with snapper, kingfish, trevally and sweep. As Tumby Bay is located on the eastern side of

OPPOSITE: *Tom 'Tumby' Tierney, Bushy and myself with some lovely snapper taken north of Tumby Bay in the Spencer Gulf.*

the Eyre Peninsula, residents can also fish further out into the vast Spencer Gulf for big snapper and tuna.

The Sir Joseph Banks Group

Discovered in 1802, these twenty-odd islands were named by explorer Matthew Flinders after Captain Cook's famous botanist. The islands are located 12 nautical miles south-east of Tumby Bay and are a declared conservation park to protect breeding populations of seabirds. Many of the islands, such as Reevesby and Roxby, have sheltered bays with sandy areas offering safe anchorage for fishing and boating.

I fished these waters with a couple of old salts – Jeff Woolfood, who runs the local charter boat the *MV Investigator*, and Tom 'Tumby' Tierney, the local whiting guru. At 53, Tom still strips for the local footy side every week and in recent years played in the

ABOVE: *That's me hard at work chasing whiting in Tumby Tom's boat.*

BELOW OPPOSITE: *The big fella with a couple of other big fellas from the Sir Joseph Banks group of islands. Not quite the one-kilogram mark but not far off either.*

ABOVE OPPOSITE: *Tumby Bay jetty attracts plenty of fish and plenty of fishermen. It's a great pier to try with light tackle.*

'seconds' premiership side. Tom runs the local supermarket — well, sort of. His missus runs it when Tom goes fishing, which is a very good deal of the time!

The sand and reef areas in the lee of Reevesby Island, the major island of the group, personify what whiting fishing is all about — crystal-clear water with broken ground and sand channels in conjunction with a new flushing flood tide. We laid anchor at 5 am, and after a little kip and a cuppa we were on deck ready to fish. Tom and I had a ripper session with 37 whiting averaging over 500 grams, with the largest fish weighing in at 890 grams. That's 20 grams short of two pounds in the old scale, if you know what I mean. These were not the magical kilogram whiting we all hear about, but by jingo they were not far off. We also caught some terrific snook up to three kilograms, garfish up to 50 centimetres and any amount of tommy ruff.

ABOVE: Big snapper, like this ten-kilogram speciman caught by Steve Girardi from Tumby Bay, are fun to catch and great to eat.

LEFT: Silver trevally are often found around the islands of the Sir Joseph Banks group, especially near Spilsby Island.

Spencer Gulf

I've enjoyed some fantastic fishing about five hours north of the Sir Joseph Banks group into Spencer Gulf, towards Whyalla. The area is famous for snapper, and Tom, Jeff and I thought we would give them a try. We anchored just off an old prawn trawler wreck and we were immediately into smallish fish. I say smallish, but a 36-centimetre snapper is undersize in South Australia, where the legal limit is 38 centimetres, while in other states it is as low as 27 centimetres.

We were soon to see that there were some serious snapper to be caught in Spencer Gulf. In the next hour we had a hot bite and Bushy and I did some pretty good TV with the snapper action coming thick and fast. We managed to hook, land and then release 16 snapper between 4.5 and eight kilograms. It really was quite amazing that so many big snapper were there and we were the only people fishing.

Conclusion

Tumby Bay and the surrounding area is a fun place. I recall one episode we filmed for the TV show, which commenced with myself on a Harley Davidson whilst poor ol' Bushy was on a 'pushy' – err, bike that is – as we made our way along the main street and onto the jetty before boarding the *MV Investigator* to go fishing.

Tumby Bay has beautiful beaches and is far enough away from Adelaide to escape the madding crowd. As a result the fishing is just superb. There's no doubt I'll be back at Tumby one day.

Piscatorial Compass

Tumby Bay, South Australia

How to get there: Tumby Bay is 600 kilometres from Adelaide via Port Wakefield Road and the Princes, Eyre and Lincoln highways. It is about 50 kilometres north of Port Lincoln via the Lincoln Highway.

Where to stay: For a small town, Tumby Bay is well served with hotels, a caravan park, holiday units, backpacker accommodation and even a Lutheran camp.

What to catch: Snapper, King George whiting, garfish, tommy ruff, snook, mullet, sweep, barracouta, yellowtail kingfish, sharks and silver trevally.

Gear to take: Use light gear for whiting and tommy ruff, and medium-sized tackle for snapper.

When to go: October to April.

Guides and charters: Tumby Bay Charters aboard the **MV Investigator** were fantastic.

Rex reckons: The Sir Joseph Banks group of islands has some great King George whiting spots. Fish in the sand and weed areas and use peeled prawns topped with pipis, locally called cockles.

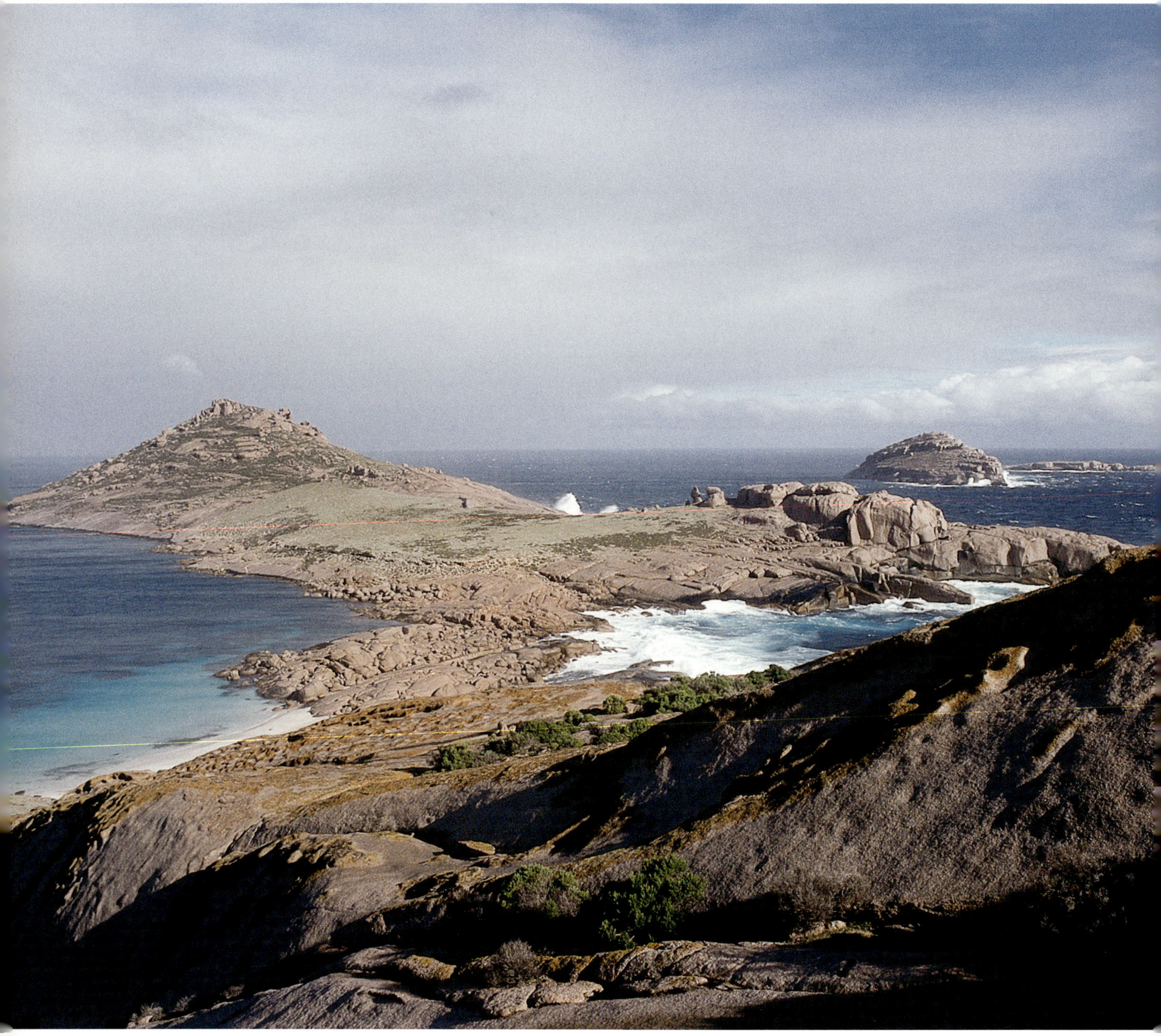

Port Lincoln to Ceduna

This magnificent stretch of coastline along the Eyre Peninsula in South Australia has provided me with many great fishing adventures over the years. It truly is one of my favourite places to fish.

Port Lincoln

Port Lincoln is the largest town on the Eyre Peninsula with a population of around 14,000. As one of the most popular holiday towns on the coast, that population more than doubles at various times of the year, particularly around the Australia Day weekend when the annual Tunarama Festival is held. Now folks, any town that dedicates an entire festival to a fish has got to be good in my book.

The fish is, of course, the southern bluefin tuna, and whilst it roams the wilds of the Southern Ocean attracting game fishermen from all over Australia, Port Lincoln is most famous for its

OPPOSITE: *Pearson Island, off the Eyre Peninsula town of Elliston, is a spectacular place to visit. The fishing is pretty hot too.*

aquaculture farms. These farms use stocks caught in the wild, which are then grown to gigantic proportions before being shipped to Japan, where top-quality tuna is turned into sushi for big money.

The tuna farms are located in Boston Bay and are a giant fish-attracting device, as the feed spreads from the tuna pens out into the open sea, attracting other tuna and some very big yellowtail kingfish and snapper and creating a unique recreational fishery. There are some restrictions on how close you can get to the pens, but opportunities for a piscatorial adventure abound.

Boston Bay is around three times larger than Sydney Harbour and offers good fishing for snapper, tuna, kingfish, trevally, salmon, and whiting, to name a few. One of the best places to try is around Boston Island, particularly along the western shore.

Brennans Wharf is the prime land-based fishing spot. This is where grain is loaded onto ships after the wheat is harvested from the Eyre Peninsula. You can't miss it – it's dominated by huge grain silos almost 50 metres high. The wharf produces good snapper, tommy ruff, salmon and squid.

The beaches on the southern side of the magnificent Lincoln National Park are superb, providing good fishing for whiting and flathead in summer and big salmon in winter.

ABOVE: *This pair of nannygai certainly put up a fight offshore from Port Lincoln.*

Thistle Island

Offshore beyond the Lincoln National Park is Thistle Island. I visited it aboard the mighty sailing ship the *Falie* a few years ago and we had one of the more memorable fishing and filming experiences. Our guide was my good mate Shane Mensforth, and also along for the ride were my son Matthew and Bushy. Folks, you may have heard of the 'Pirates of the Caribbean' – well, we were the 'Pirates of Port Lincoln'.

My producer Bob Grieve decided on a pirates theme for this trip and it worked a treat for the TV cameras. Thankfully the fish cooperated and we caught some lovely snapper, nannygai and blue morwong, also known as queen snapper. Shane also took Matthew

RIGHT: *Queen snapper (also known as blue morwong) abound in the deeper waters off Port Lincoln.*

BELOW: *Patches of sand and weed are some of the best spots to chase King George whiting off Thistle Island.*

and me in a dinghy to fish the shallows around Thistle Island for some famous South Australian King George whiting. The whiting were a little scarce, but we managed a variety of species including a ripper blue-spotted flathead.

Coffin Bay

Located a few kilometres west of Port Lincoln is Coffin Bay. This is a very popular area in summer in spite of its name, which was given to the area by Matthew Flinders in 1802 after Sir Isaac Coffin. A beautiful area with many channels and inlets, the Coffin Bay area also comprises Kellidie Bay, Mount Dutton Bay and Port Douglas.

Coffin Bay has great oysters and silly amounts of garfish and King George whiting. They are relatively small compared with the usual South Australian whiting, but it is a breeding ground. I've also had some excellent fishing for leatherjacket and sweep in the Coffin Bay National Park, which is accessible via a 4WD track. Also, my good friend Geoff Wilson makes regular trips to Coffin Bay from Victoria to fish for the area's huge yellowtail kingfish – some can be up to 40 kilograms. Live garfish is the go for bait.

Just north of Coffin Bay is Convention Beach. This beach is famous for huge catches of Australian salmon. I have fished some of the beaches along this part of the coast with very good results, usually with the aid of a 4WD to get right down onto the beach.

Elliston

Elliston is a little seaside town situated on the beautiful Waterloo Bay. There are a number of excellent surf-fishing beaches in this area, which fish well for whiting, mullet, flathead and trevally along with the usual salmon. The most famous of these beaches is Locks Well, just south of the township.

Elliston has a very long jetty that has been restored, and this offers a great platform for kids to fish for tommy ruff, squid, snook and garfish. The boat ramp at Elliston provides access to Waterloo Bay, which is protected by a reef. Boaters can fish around the bay and, when conditions permit, can venture out to the Investigator group of islands to fish for nannygai, blue groper, snapper and sweep.

TOP: *A lovely blue-spotted flathead taken near Thistle Island.*

ABOVE: *The famous Locks Well Beach near Elliston is renowned as a consistent producer of big salmon.*

Venus Bay

Further west into the Great Australian Bight you'll find the terrific seaside holiday town of Venus Bay. Venus Bay is a quiet and relaxed area with good fishing for whiting, salmon and tommy ruff. The bay is very sheltered and thus ideal for families and anglers with small boats. There are some nice flathead about, and flounder can be caught in the shallows. The town jetty provides good fishing for whiting and mullet.

Streaky Bay

Streaky Bay was one of the very first places the Rex Hunt TV crew visited outside Victoria in the early days. The township of Streaky Bay is located on the southern end of the bay and has a population of around 1000 people. An ideal holiday spot with a few more facilities than the smaller towns along this part of the coast, it provides ample accommodation and has an excellent jetty and boat ramp.

Geoff Wilson was my companion on the first trip, and we fished the bay with local John Brace, who used a tong-like contraption to extract razor fish from the weed beds for use as bait. The razor fish is a bivalve mollusc and the whiting find it irresistible. The best bait was a combination of razor fish and pounded squid, and we managed some lovely King George whiting and a few other species for the TV camera.

Later we fished an area known as 'the Smooth Pool' at the southern end of Corvisart Bay, about 30 kilometres from the Streaky Bay township. The Smooth Pool is a large rock pool big enough to launch a small tinnie in. We fished with lightly weighted baits and caught whiting, silver trevally and a range of colourful wrasse. I remember the sky was exceptionally clear at night in Streaky Bay, showing us the most well-defined Milky Way I have seen anywhere in the world. It was great light-line fishing in a magical environment.

TOP: *A decent 4WD vehicle is indispensable for fishing Ceduna's mulloway and salmon beaches.*

ABOVE: *Hooked up at Convention Beach.*

ABOVE: *A pair of ripper South Aussie salmon off Tuckamore Beach.*

RIGHT: *Big blue groper are easy to find, but hard to land. This one came from Streaky Bay.*

OPPOSITE: *Anglers Camp behind the dunes on a surf beach west of Ceduna – prime mulloway territory.*

Ceduna

With a population of around 4000 people, Ceduna is the last town of any size you reach before you cross the vast Nullarbor Plain. It really is the gateway to the Great Australian Bight, and offers superb seafood such as oysters and whiting, plus a range of other activities. It is one of the best vantage points from which to watch the migration of whales each year.

Shane Mensforth invited me to fish for Australian salmon along the white sands of the Great Australian Bight a few years ago. This is a truly magnificent place. It's a long way from Adelaide – over 1000 kilometres – but the scenery and the fishing action are worth every second of the drive.

Beaches like Tuckamore, Cactus, Yalata and Scotts produce big, black-backed salmon during the cooler months and some of the largest mulloway you'll ever see in the summer. During our day of filming on Tuckamore Beach we caught, kissed and released close to 100 salmon, each averaging just under four kilograms. Some would have gone over the 4.5-kilogram mark and boy, can they pull! I even caught several double-headers and when you get a pair of four-kilogram salmon on the line in a heavy rolling surf, you really know you're fishing!

From its port of Thevenard, Ceduna offers top-notch boat fishing for snapper, mulloway, King George whiting and silver trevally. There are several good boat ramps in the area, in particular at Thevenard and at the caravan park on the foreshore. The jetty at Thevenard is also worthwhile for a variety of species.

Beach access is mainly via 4WD and all beaches in the area fish well depending on fish movements. Smoky Bay, just south of Ceduna, is a prime example with salmon, mulloway, whiting, flathead and tailor on offer.

Conclusion

This whole region offers very good fishing. For newcomers it is probably best to base yourself at Port Lincoln and use the comfort and protection of its facilities. For the more adventurous the whole coast is your oyster. Some of the best remote fishing in Australia awaits, and I for one can't wait to get back.

Piscatorial Compass

Port Lincoln to Ceduna, South Australia

How to get there: Port Lincoln is 650 kilometres from Adelaide via Port Wakefield Road and the Princes, Eyre and Lincoln highways. Ceduna is about 400 kilometres further west of Port Lincoln via the Flinders Highway.

Where to stay: Accommodation is plentiful at Port Lincoln with caravan parks, holiday units and motels. There are caravan parks and motels at Coffin Bay, Elliston, Venus Bay, Streaky Bay and Ceduna. Beach camping with a 4WD is also very popular.

What to catch: Snapper, King George whiting, yellowtail kingfish, sweep, blue groper, a variety of sharks, samson fish, Australian salmon, silver trevally, snook, squid, tommy ruff, garfish, southern bluefin tuna, mulloway, leatherjacket, nannygai, mullet and mackerel.

Gear to take: Use light to medium threadline gear for the smaller species. A ten-kilogram rod and overhead reel are best for snapper and other reef fish. Surf rod and reel for beach fishing.

When to go: Year round.

Guides and charters: Charter boats and boat hire are available at the major towns. Game-fishing charters can be found at Port Lincoln.

Rex reckons: To get the most out of this area, take a 4WD with a dinghy on top.

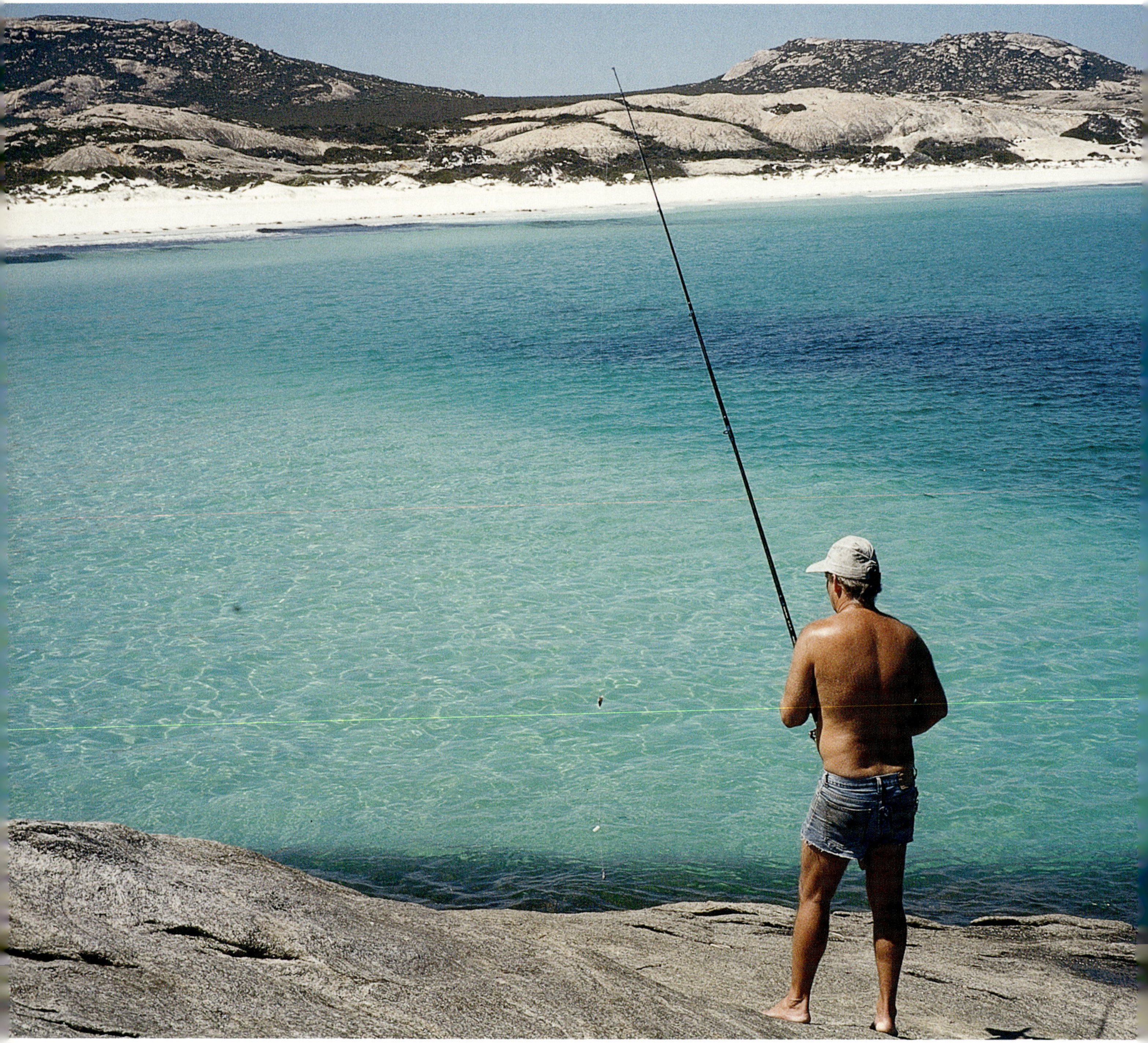

Esperance

Esperance is a bustling town situated on the far south-eastern coast of Western Australia. Any around-Australia adventurer worth their salt would be crazy to bypass Esperance, which is some 200 kilometres south of Norseman and thus off the Eyre Highway, the main route between Adelaide and Perth that crosses the mighty Nullarbor Plain.

Esperance and the 100 or so islands scattered offshore, known as the Archipelago of the Recherche, were named after two French ships that explored the southern part of the Western Australian coast in 1792. The word 'Esperance' is derived from the French word for hope – a pretty good name for a top fishing location, as hope always springs eternal for us anglers.

OPPOSITE: *Esperance personified: aqua-coloured water and white-sand beaches.*

Esperance rapidly developed as the main port to ship the gold discovered in the famous boom town of Kalgoorlie to the north. Today it remains a working port, but it is also the centre of agriculture, commercial fishing and tourism.

I fished Esperance with the film crew a few years ago and it has remained firmly etched in my mind ever since for its rugged beauty, bountiful fishing and untouched wilderness.

ABOVE: *A ripper salmon caught from Eleven Mile Beach just west of Esperance.*

LEFT: *The Cape Arid Yacht Club!*

Beaches

The beaches east of Esperance are as fine and white as any beach I have walked on in the world. I can recall fishing from Squeaky Beach, on Victoria's Wilsons Promontory, many moons ago and thinking that was the whitest and cleanest sand I'd seen. The beaches between Cape Le Grand and Cape Arid, in particular, are so white I had to wear sunglasses to ease the glare from the sun reflecting off the sand, just like it does with snow.

The fishing is simply superb for big Australian salmon, gummy shark, mulloway and silver trevally, tommy ruff and whiting. The salmon, in particular, average five kilograms, with fish up to nine kilograms recorded. Salmon and gummy shark will fall to fresh pilchards rigged on ganged hooks.

Mulloway are nocturnal feeders requiring plenty of patience. The silver trevally, known locally as skipjack, are huge, with fish up to six kilograms a possibility. I fished for them from the rocks as well as the beach. A simple paternoster rig baited with cut pilchards or bluebait was all that was needed.

A 4WD beach safari some 125 kilometres east of Esperance to the Cape Arid National Park was a highlight of my trip to this corner of the Great Australian Bight. We stayed the night at the Cape Arid Yacht Club. It was a small camp, and pretty rough at that. But it was clean and comfy. Some locals came up to greet our party and put on a terrific spread that included fresh abalone and King George whiting. The abalone was from a professional fisherman and he invited us out next day in his Shark Cat to fish for the whiting inside Middle Island.

We didn't get a fish over the magical one-kilogram mark, but neither did we get one under 750 grams. The best bait was abalone gut fished on a long leader with long shank number 4 hooks. The parrotfish and wrasse were a nuisance, but once the whiting moved in it was on for young and old. The following day saw us fishing

TOP: *Deep-sea fishing in the Archipelago of the Recherche yields a wide range of species.*

BELOW: *The magnificent colours of a queen snapper.*

BELOW LEFT: *4WD vehicles are a great way to explore the coast around Esperance.*

from boats around Middle Island and we had one of the best sessions on the silver trevally up to two kilograms that I can recall.

Archipelago of the Recherche

The Archipelago of the Recherche is the large group of islands and underwater sea mounts scattered off the coast from Esperance. The underwater sea mounts, or 'lumps' as they are known, rise from very deep water to just 50 metres or so below the surface. Snapper and other species such as nannygai, queen snapper, break-sea cod, harlequin fish and the monster-size samson fish, which can reach up to 35 kilograms, haunt the top of these lumps.

Charter boats and locals with large trailer boats travel well offshore to find the lumps and simply drift over them with the wind. Rigs are usually hefty, using braided line to eliminate the stretch when fishing deep water.

The nannygai or red snapper, in particular, are a superb eating fish and are found on reefs stretching from Western Australia to the western coast of Victoria. I have encountered these fish many times when fishing offshore in South Australia. They have very sharp scales and should be handled with care.

ABOVE: *Nannygai are a superb eating fish.*

LEFT: *The view of Esperance Harbour looking towards the islands of the Archipelago of the Recherche.*

OPPOSITE: *Snapper are known as 'pink' snapper in the west.*

Species such as queen snapper and harlequin fish have spectacular colours when they first emerge from the water and are also good eating. Samson fish hit like the proverbial underwater freight train and are very hard to stop. These are highly prized by local deep-sea anglers.

Conclusion

Esperance remains one of those destinations that I must visit again very soon. It is a long way from the eastern states and is hardly a weekender even from Perth, at over 700 kilometres; however, it is truly one of the most beautiful parts of Australia that I have ever visited.

Piscatorial Compass

Esperance, Western Australia

How to get there: Perth to Esperance is around 740 kilometres mostly via the Albany, Great Southern and South Coast highways. There are also daily flights available from Perth and other Western Australian regional centres on Skywest Airlines.

Where to stay: There is a variety of accommodation, from caravan parks and holiday units to motels. You can camp on the beaches towards Cape Arid, though some require a permit.

What to catch: Australian salmon, mulloway, silver trevally, gummy shark, tommy ruff, King George whiting, flathead, black bream, nannygai (red snapper), queen snapper, snapper, Samson fish, break-sea cod and harlequin fish.

Gear to take: Take a beach-fishing rod and reel, a medium overhead rod and reel for deep-sea fishing spooled with braided line, and a light threadline for estuary and jetty fishing.

When to go: Year round on the beaches. From March to May is best for deep-sea trips.

Guides and charters: There is a good range of fishing charters operating out of Esperance.

Rex reckons: The beaches east and west of Esperance have some of the biggest salmon, gummy shark and silver trevally on offer.

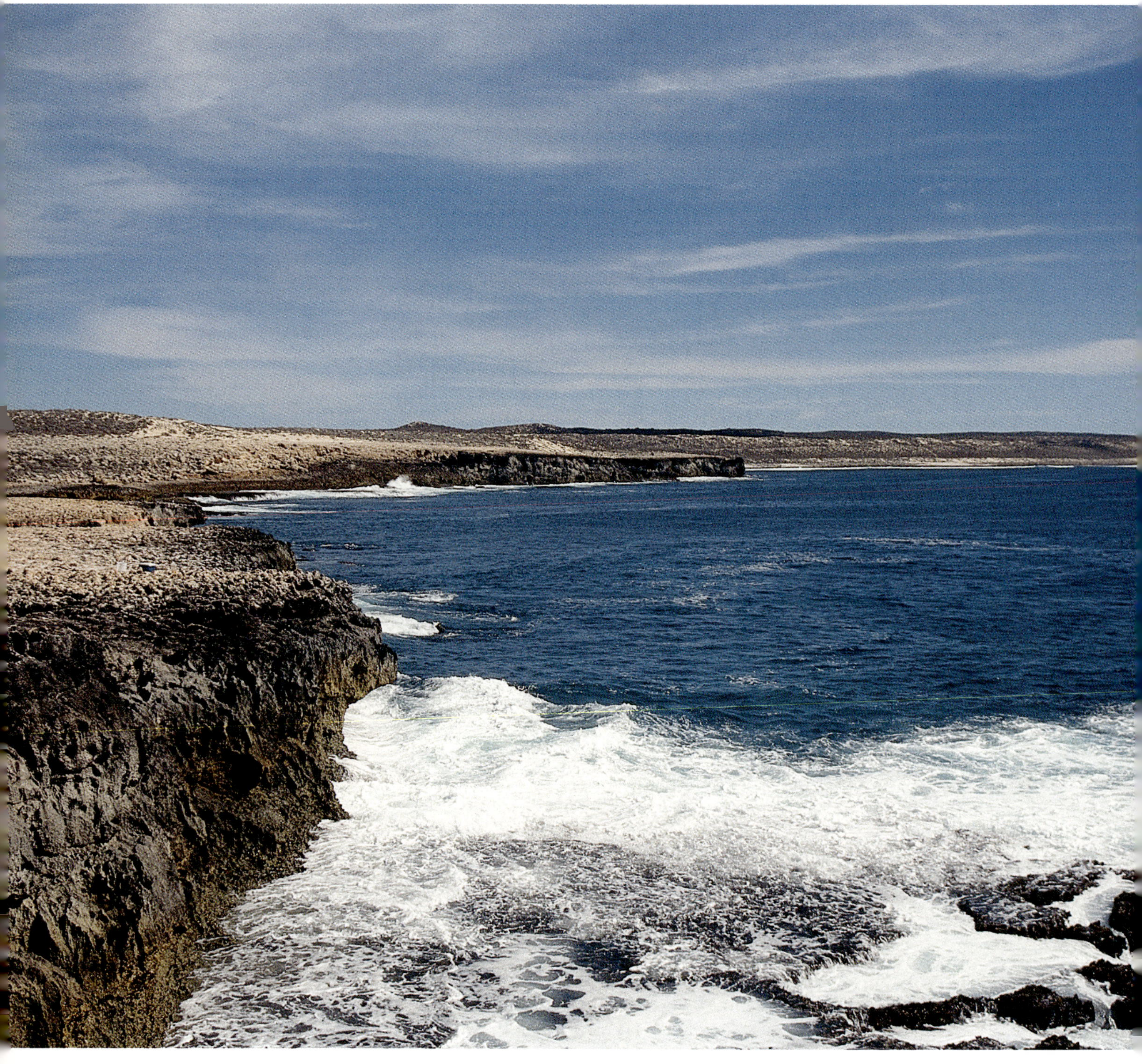

Dirk Hartog Island

Dirk Hartog Island, roughly halfway up the Western Australian coast, is one of my favourite fishing destinations because of its rugged beauty and the variety of fish species. Whenever I am asked to name my favourite fishing destinations in the world, I always include this magical island among the top five. While some other places may have equal or slightly better fishing, I have yet to find a place that is as consistent as Dirk Hartog.

In 1616 the Dutch explorer Dirk Hartog, sailing aboard the *Endracht*, ventured into what is now known as Shark Bay and explored the island that was

OPPOSITE: *The rugged west coast of Dirk Hartog Island.*

eventually named in his honour. Dirk Hartog is a long (around 80 kilometres), narrow (no more than 15 kilometres at its widest) island running north to south, which forms a protective barrier to Shark Bay. This is a wild and remote place that has changed little since European settlement.

The fishing is sensational and reflects the island's remoteness from any population centre. The island offers unspoiled rock and beach fishing plus access to the wilds of the Indian Ocean and its free-roaming pelagics, coupled with the fish-rich waters of Denham Sound in Shark Bay.

The rock fishing – or perhaps I should say cliff fishing – on the western side of Dirk Hartog Island is spectacular, with jagged escarpments that rise high above some very fishy water. The terrain on top of the cliffs is very rugged and uneven. I reckon Neil Armstrong would have been quite at home in this moon-like landscape.

ABOVE: *In contrast to the rugged cliffs in some parts of the island there are also beautiful beaches which are ideal to wade, casting lure or fly.*

OPPOSITE LEFT: *My biggest tailor ever, which I caught off the cliffs at Dirk Hartog Island.*

OPPOSITE RIGHT: *Matt Hunt with a fine bald-chin groper taken whilst fishing off the cliffs. One of the best eating fish in the sea.*

I have vivid memories of the great fishing I have experienced off these cliffs. In a terrific fishing session that we filmed for the TV show, I recall the wind was blowing hard from behind us as we cast our baits into the depths of the Indian Ocean from a rock ledge that was high enough to keep us safe from any ocean swell. The action started almost immediately with the 'Human Broom', Kaj Busch, getting hammered by a big snapper, which eventually busted him off just under the rocks below. I was fishing with 30-pound Laser line with a 50-pound shock leader, wire trace, and ganged hooks rigged with a pilchard.

Eventually, a large long tom took the bait and started to cartwheel across the surface, jumping wildly before I was able to haul him up the cliff for a look. These long toms have teeth like Dick Emery, which fully justified my use of a wire trace. Any creature that is lower down on the proverbial piscatorial food chain should look out; they are probably next on the menu for dinner. I cut off the wire trace, gave it a kiss, and released this fine long tom to fight again another day.

Soon afterwards the reel screamed off again. An unknown fish of considerable weight had attached itself to my line; unfortunately,

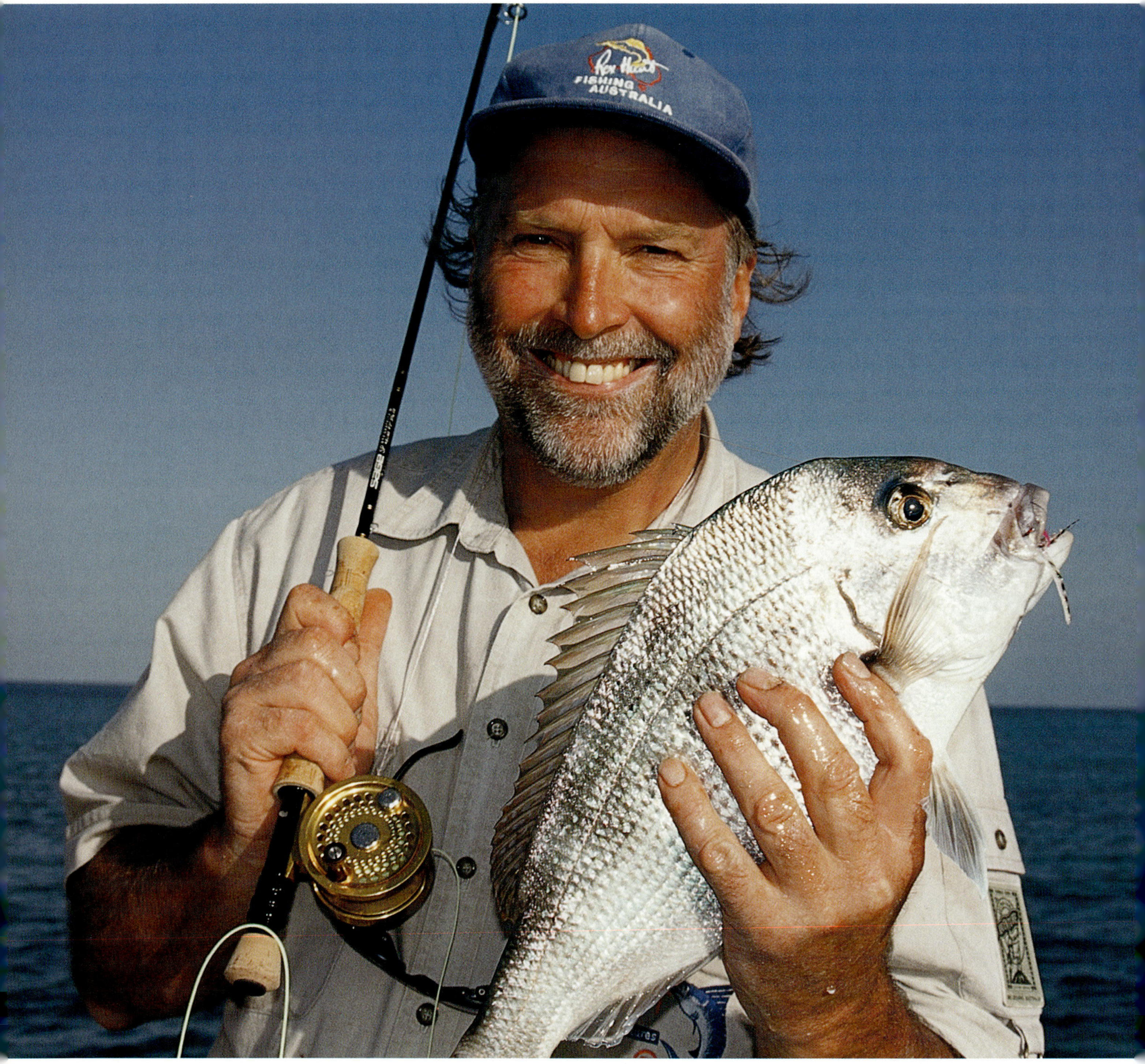
Rex Hunt
FISHING AUSTRALIA

it seemed to be heading for a reef off to the left. Luckily I was able to turn him away from the reef and it wasn't long before we managed to land a gold spot trevally, or turrum, with the use of a highly effective cliff gaff. This fish looked absolutely amazing, folks. All of the species in the trevally family are real street fighters, and this one was a brute weighing over nine kilograms. With the aid of the next big wave I released the big turrum.

It is worth noting that these big fish found in close to the rocks were dining on the abundance of food found in amongst the washes. These environments provide tremendous opportunities for land-based anglers who are willing to get themselves to such remote and uncivilised places. A word of warning, though: high rock platforms aren't any place for young children or inexperienced anglers; you need to have the right footwear and to constantly have your mind on the job.

A massive thump met my bait's return to the water and the rod was fully loaded once again. Eventually a lovely bald-chin groper came to the surface to be gaffed. There was no kissing of this fish, as it was headed straight for the dinner table that night. The bald-chin groper, also known as bluebone, would have to be one of my favourite eating fish. I would put it up there with gummy shark from Victoria's Bass Strait, or the Patagonian toothfish which comes very close for taste.

There are also some huge tailor to be taken here. I took my biggest tailor yet from these cliffs. I reckon it was nearly 14 pounds by the old scale; it took a whole pilchard and was lifted by a cliff gaff to the top. On another occasion, I had hooked a substantial tailor of some four kilograms when a small reef shark attacked the tailor and bit it in half. As the shark came back for the 'left-overs', another larger shark, a bronze whaler, chomped the smaller shark in half before eating it. Such is the law of the sea: eat or be eaten.

The beaches offer some terrific fishing only metres from the island's homestead. I enjoy wading through the shallows on the flood tide over the sandbanks and weed areas casting small lures, flies and soft plastics, and slowly retrieving them. I have taken very

ABOVE: *Shark Bay is renowned for its snapper fishing.*

OPPOSITE: *The snapper are so thick you can even catch them on fly.*

TOP: *A reasonable-sized bar-tailed flathead caught on fly off the beaches.*

ABOVE: *Golden trevally patrol the beaches around Dirk Hartog Island and always put up a tough fight.*

RIGHT: *Matt Hunt and John Rose with a red emperor and Spanish mackerel caught offshore.*

good numbers of bar-tailed flathead here in just a few inches of water. I have also taken sand whiting on a regular basis.

Shark Bay

Shark Bay is a World Heritage Area and is basically divided in half by the Peron Peninsula. The waters of Shark Bay offer some superb snapper fishing. My son Matthew and I once spent an evening fishing from one of the barges on the island.

The area we were to fish was unique as it is near Steep Point, which is separated from Dirk Hartog Island by South Passage. Steep Point is the western-most part of the Australian mainland and where two different currents meet. The cold waters of the Southern Ocean meet here with the warmer currents of the northern waters; this causes an intermingling of the species and it is a truly amazing place to fish. Steep Point is itself part of Australian rock-fishing folklore.

The proprietor of Dirk Hartog Island Homestead, Kieran Wardle, took us out to about 14 metres of water. A two-hour session yielded snapper after snapper weighing between two and six kilograms, all of which were released. At one stage we were feeding cut pilchards out in the current and the snapper were coming up the berley trail in their hundreds, fighting over the feed. Matt is a real hawk-eye; he told me he reckoned there was something else down the trail and thought it was a yellowfin tuna with his name on it. Low and behold, he fed a whole pilchard down the back of the boat and it went off. Twenty minutes later, a 25-kilogram yellowfin came to the side of the boat.

Conclusion

Not only is Dirk Hartog Island one of my favourite fishing holes, it also happens to be one of my favourite feeding destinations as well, especially if you happen to be staying at Dirk Hartog Island Homestead. This homestead-style accommodation is terrific – very homely – and the meals prepared by Kieran and Victoria Wardle are a delight.

There are also many other attractions beyond fishing, including the dolphins at Monkey Mia, which is located on the eastern side of the Peron Peninsula tucked up inside Shark Bay. I must commend to you also a snorkel dive at Surf Point. The clarity of the water is superb and the fish life outstanding.

Piscatorial Compass
Dirk Hartog Island, Western Australia

How to get there: Denham is 820 kilometres from Perth via the Brand and North West Coastal highways and the Denham–Hamelin Road. Skywest Airlines fly four times a week from Perth to Denham, where visitors can either take a ferry or light plane to Dirk Hartog Island.

Where to stay: Dirk Hartog Island Homestead is hosted by the Wardles. It has accommodation for ten to 12 people.

What to catch: Snapper, tailor, bald-chin groper, trevally, yellowfin tuna, red emperor, Spanish mackerel, dolphin fish, cobia, samson fish, wahoo, northern bluefin tuna, flathead, whiting, dart, and spangled emperor.

Gear to take: Use specialist rock-fishing gear with long rods and ten- to 15-kilogram overhead reels. Use an overhead rod and reel for boat fishing, and fly-fishing tackle of six to nine weight for the beaches.

When to go: March to October. Snapper fishing in Shark Bay is subject to strict size and bag limits with a closed season.

Guides and charters: The Wardle family operate fishing, 4WD and Eco tours on the island.

Rex reckons: Use caution on the cliffs on Dirk Hartog, but be prepared to catch just about anything. A cliff gaff is a must.

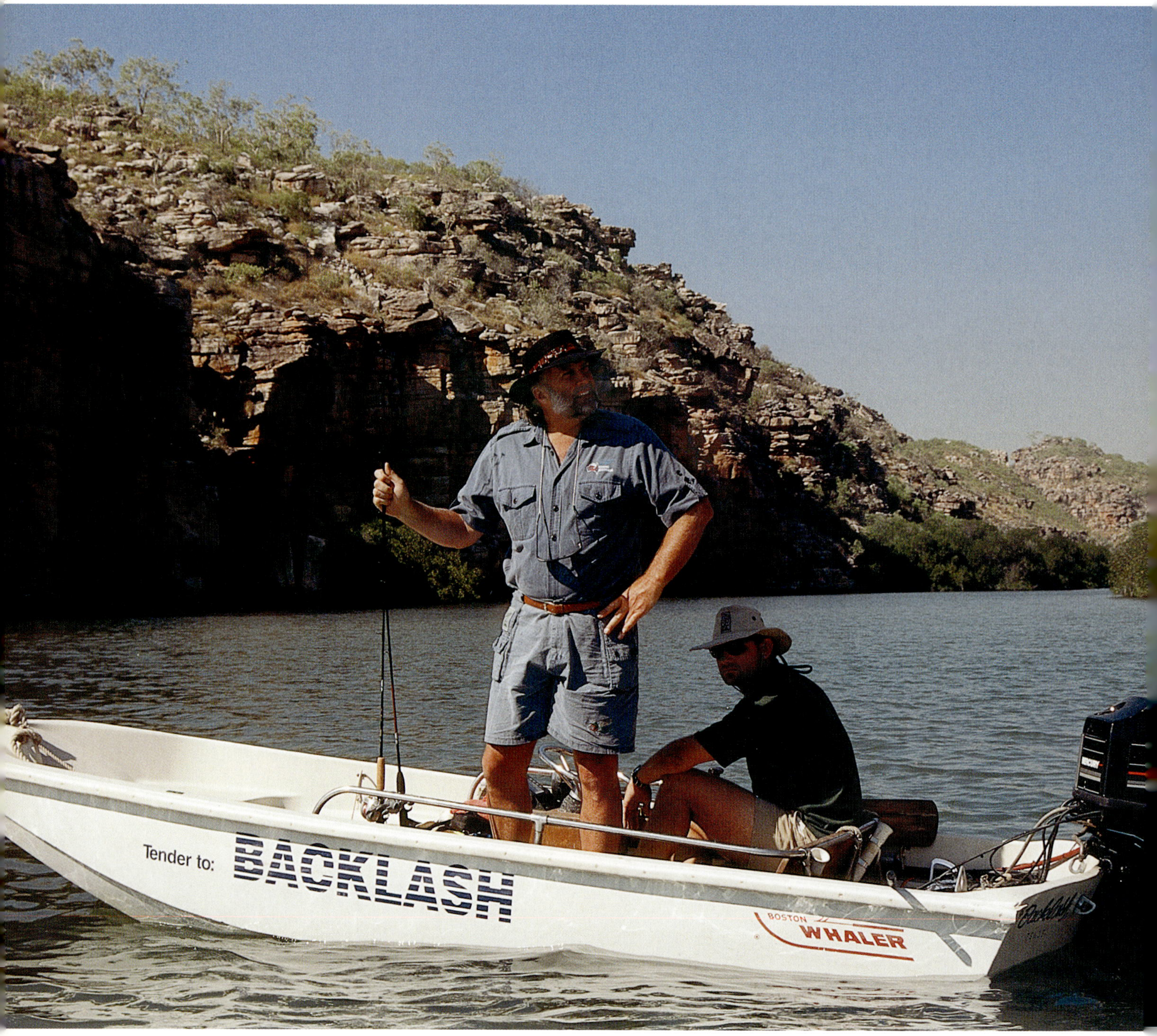
Tender to: BACKLASH
BOSTON WHALER

Kimberley

The Kimberley is an ancient land covering some 421,000 square kilometres in the north-west of Western Australia, stretching from Broome to Wyndham and Kununurra near the Northern Territory border. The landscape is characterised by rugged ranges, pockets of rainforest, gorges and waterfalls, making it a unique environment.

I have been fortunate to have travelled and fished the entire Kimberley region between Broome and Wyndham, both for the TV show and on personal trips. In the early days of the TV show we filmed two separate one-hour specials on Broome and the Kimberley, which is testament to the special place it occupies in people's minds.

OPPOSITE: *Exploring the magnificent gorges of the Kimberley is half the fun.*

Broome

The port of Broome is situated on Roebuck Bay and is home to some of the best fishing Australia has to offer. It is also home to the western pearl fishery. Before the First World War, there were over 400 pearl luggers based in Broome. A town of romantic reputation and colourful history, it has a population of some 12,000 people and draws thousands of tourists each year. Anglers come for the great weather, the magnificent scenery and, of course, the great variety of species that can be caught.

The fishing out of Broome is truly sensational. Sailfish are a huge drawcard in this neck of the woods, and each year hundreds of anglers converge on Broome for the many tournaments that take place. I have found the two most spectacular places in the world for sailfish have been in the Gulf of Thailand and off Broome.

Col Roberts pioneered the fishing publicity for this area and has highlighted its beauty with some of the best photographs I have ever seen. The waters off Broome are full of shallow reef systems, which explains why it is so productive. In one of the earlier TV shows, Col took me offshore from Broome for a lure and bait fishing session.

There was virtually non-stop action as we trolled lures, both

ABOVE: *A typical Kimberley barra.*

LEFT: *Col Roberts holds aloft a solid giant trevally taken on a lure near Vansittart Bay.*

OPPOSITE: *Mangrove jack caught from the King Edward River.*

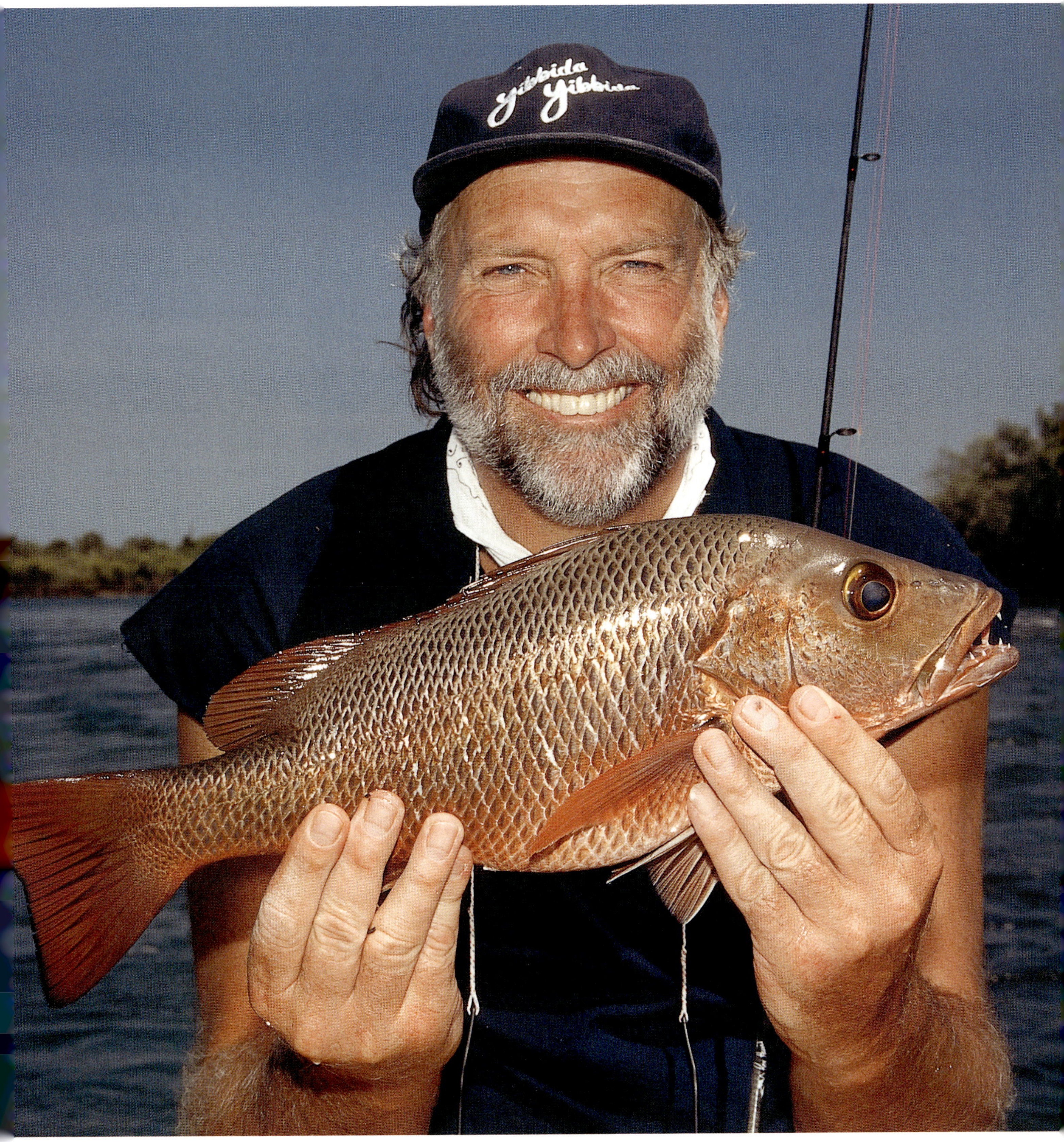

deep divers and skirted varieties, catching giant and golden trevally weighing up to eight kilograms and Spanish mackerel up to ten kilograms. A bait-fishing session in only 29 feet of water, using strips of tuna fed down a berley trail, produced a number of cobia (also known as the black kingfish) hovering around the back of the boat. After I landed my first-ever cobia, weighing about five kilograms, a monster grabbed my line and I eventually landed a fish that weighed 17.5 kilograms for the TV cameras. Col also landed a fish of similar weight.

The waters south of Roebuck Bay were also the subject of a TV show with a young gun lady angler in Jeni Lerch. We anchored above a pinnacle, or small reef, about five kilometres out into the Indian Ocean. We were in for a good session. Almost immediately, both Jeni and I had a double hook-up. My fish was a scarlet sea perch, a magnificent-looking and eating fish. Jeni caught a golden trevally that would have gone seven to eight kilograms; its flanks gleamed in the afternoon sun.

Broome offers surely the greatest variety of species of just about anywhere in Australia. Whether it is trolling, bait fishing, or fly-fishing on the reefs or along the beaches, there is plenty of action on offer at Broome.

Montgomery Reef

The Montgomery reef is a large reef and small island system just out from Talbot Bay and above King Sound, around 280 kilometres north-east of Broome. This is a spectacular part of the coast and very remote.

I fished this area with my wife Lynne and son Matthew, and good friends Rob and Gail Kerr. One evening we were anchored near the reef. It was a falling tide, and in these parts the rise and fall can be anywhere up to eight metres. As the tide neared its ebb, I saw raging torrents, the likes of which I had never seen before. As the water ran from the reef, channels appeared everywhere and the water just cascaded down the channels as it escaped back into the sea. Where these channels met the sea, they created magnificent eddies. It was a fisherman's paradise.

Matthew, Rob and I loaded up our ten-weight fly rods and threw large flies such as Pink Things and deceivers into a school of thumping-big giant trevally mixed with some huge golden trevally as well. It was one of the greatest fishing sessions I have had with Matthew, who managed a golden trevally pushing ten kilograms.

Apart from the fishing, the scenery is stunning. There are many operators who now run trips into this incredible wilderness.

Vansittart Bay

Some 600 kilometres north-east of Broome, near Admiralty Gulf, is Vansittart Bay.

ABOVE: *Matt with a pair of huge mangrove jack from a northern Kimberley river.*
ABOVE OPPOSITE: *My son Matthew Hunt with a thumping giant trevally he caught on fly near Montgomery Reef.*
OPPOSITE: *A lovely trevally and a Kimberley sunset – does it get any better, folks?*

I flew into this area for the TV shoot aboard a Cessna Caravan light plane. One of the biggest single-engine aircraft around, it flew us and our substantial gear into Truscott Airport near Vansittart Bay.

Here we transferred on board the beautiful charter vessel *Backlash*, a state-of-the-art Hatteras some 68 feet long. It was luxury afloat, folks. We spent a week fishing and cruising these magnificent waters. On board were the crew, as well as Col Roberts and Steve Starling. This is a marvellous environment. At low tide you can fossick along the reef edges as well as the fully exposed reefs. Giant clams were plentiful, and many species of sea cucumbers, anemones and sponges abounded.

The barramundi fishing wasn't great, but the mangrove jacks were exceptional. Some of the smaller rivers flowed at over five knots and made for marvellous casting and retrieving. I have always loved casting and retrieving lures on big, fast-flowing rivers. I was in my element. Amongst the mangrove jack were fingermark bream, which took a liking to rattling-style lures.

On the rivers in the region, such as the Mitchell, Prince Regent and King Edward, there was life along the entire length of navigable water that we travelled. Mangrove jack, long tom, trevally and

ABOVE: *One of my fishing show co-hosts, Paul Worsteling, with a fine sailfish he caught off Broome.*

LEFT: *Gun lady angler Jeni Lerch joins the Rex Hunt TV crew for a session off Broome.*

queenfish were plentiful. The best way to catch barra, both here and in all barra areas, is to troll deep-diving lures near rock bars. Find the rock bars and you have found the reason that the barra are there; food and cover.

Trolling around the many islands and quays also yields a large variety of sportsfish. Apart from the queenies and GTs, there are the ever-present barracuda which surely must have saved many a blank day for anglers, including myself.

Wyndham

Wyndham is a major Kimberley town located in the upper reaches of the Cambridge Gulf. This is a huge inlet that is fed mainly by the Chamberlain River that flows through the famous El Questro cattle station, owned by Will and Celia Burrell.

I have fished the lower reaches of the Chamberlain and found very good barramundi up to ten kilograms. I found the lure fishing tough at times, but the best way to go about catching a big barra is by using live mullet fished on a small hook and allowed to swim. I also had some great barra fishing in the waterholes left during the dry season. Many of these are only accessible by helicopter, but the idea is to 'buzz' the hole from 100 feet before landing. This ensures that any feral pigs and freshwater crocs know we are coming in. Will Burrell told me that some very substantial 'salties' (crocodiles) inhabited these waterholes. Suffice it to say, I didn't stray too far when I fished them.

Conclusion

To adequately cover the Kimberley region would require a book of its own. I have attempted to pass on my experiences from my many trips to this area. The Kimberley easily ranks as one of my favourite places to fish.

Piscatorial Compass
Kimberley, Western Australia

How to get there: Qantas flies regularly to Broome from all of the major capital cities. Perth to Broome by road is approximately 2200 kilometres via the Great Northern Highway.

Where to stay: Broome, Derby and Wyndham are the major towns. Broome, in particular, has a massive array of accommodation.

What to catch: Barramundi, mangrove jack, threadfin salmon, fingermark bream, sailfish, cobia, giant trevally, golden trevally, Spanish mackerel, barracuda, red emperor and coral trout are the main targeted species.

Gear to take: You will need a variety of tackle to suit the type of fishing. Steer towards the heavier gear, and take plenty of lures and flies.

When to go: March to October – the dry season.

Guides and charters: The Kimberley is well serviced by fishing charters. Many live-aboard, mothership-style vessels operate here, which I believe is the best way to get the most from the Kimberley.

Rex reckons: Be prepared to tangle with sharks, as these predators soon zone in on a caught fish.

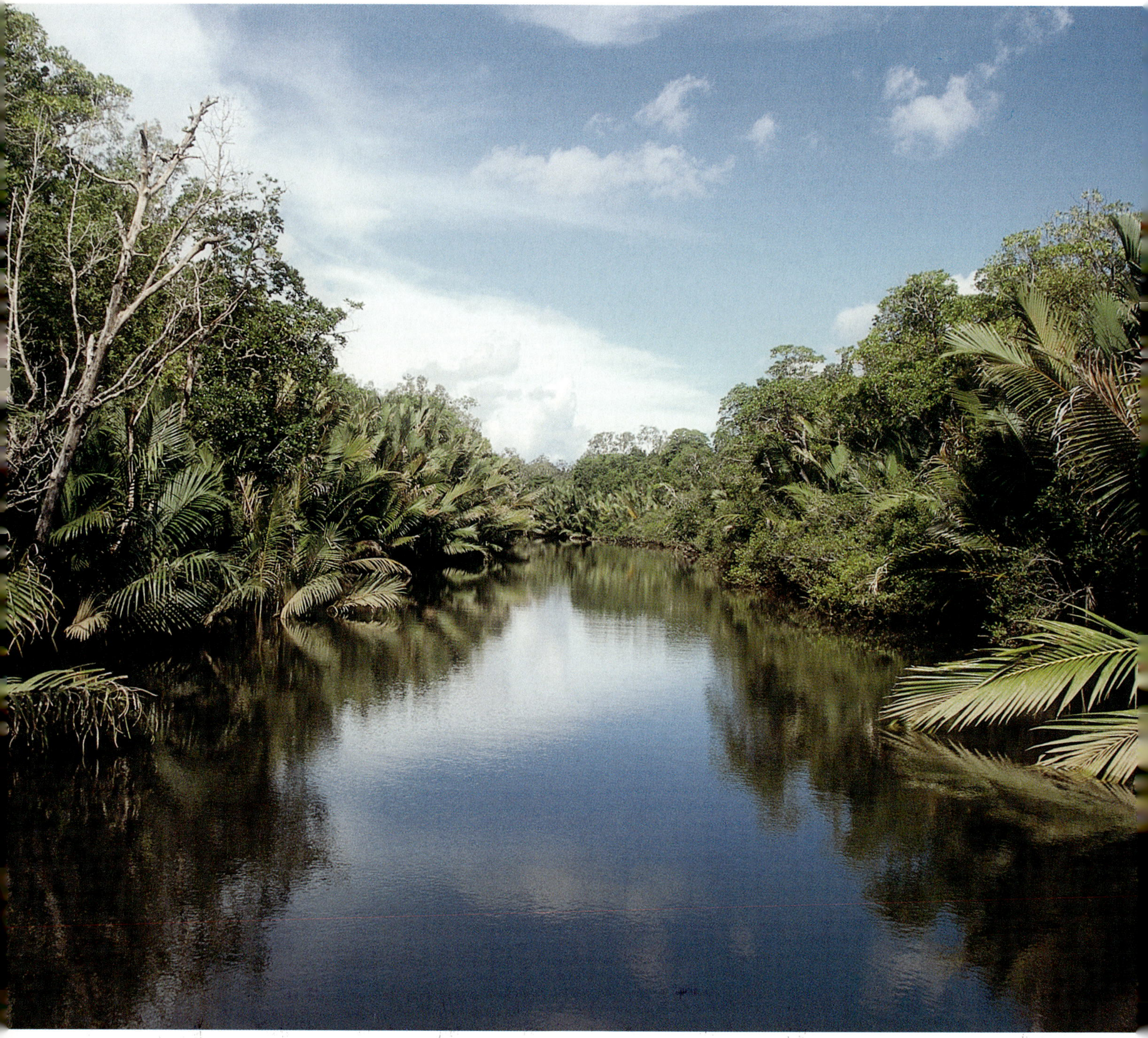

Tiwi Islands

Bathurst and Melville islands, known as the Tiwi Islands, are located in the Timor Sea some 70 kilometres north of Darwin. Named after their traditional owners, the Tiwi people, these islands are two of the biggest off Australia's coast. Melville Island is the largest of the two, about 130 kilometres wide and 70 kilometres deep from north to south.

The Tiwi Islands probably hold the most treasured memories for me in my

OPPOSITE: *The natural beauty of the Tiwi Islands is one of its great attractions.*

barra fishing and tropical sport fishing adventures. Yes folks, they even rate above Kakadu!

I first visited the islands in 1982. Earlier that year Col Roberts, a fine fishing photojournalist and a magistrate from Broome, had visited Melbourne and invited me to come and have a look at this barra fishing wilderness area on a promotional visit.

We travelled to Darwin and then took a light plane to Garden Point. Then we all piled onto a boat, which promptly ran aground. After all stripping to our underwear and pushing the 26-footer through a mud bank, we climbed back on board only to be informed by our Aboriginal guide Neil John, 'There's a lot of big crocs around here, big sharks as well.' Great, we thought!

We arrived at the entrance to Port Hurd on the western shoreline of Bathurst Island and stayed there for a week in tents. It was rough, but this suited the area. We caught a lot of good fish including barramundi, threadfin salmon, mangrove jack, fingermark bream and queenfish by casting or trolling lures or fishing live baits. We also hooked and landed some monster fish off the bank at night on bait. These fish included giant groper, tiger sharks and bronze whalers. When the torch showed us what else was lurking near the beach and

ABOVE: *Yours truly with a threadfin salmon caught in Second Creek at Bathurst Island.*

LEFT: *Sunrise in the Tiwi Islands.*

ABOVE: *A lovely barramundi from Goose Creek, Melville Island.*

RIGHT: *Giant trevally taken on a trolled lure near Port Hurd.*

how close these crocodiles came to our fishing spot, we decided to only fish from the beach in broad daylight.

Bathurst Island

That trip in 1982 was the beginning of a great journey for me and I returned to Port Hurd each year until the pilot strike in the late 1980s. In 1983, 'Barra Base' fishing lodge was built, and that was the start of the islands' phenomenal run as a popular fishing destination. The word got around that Barra Base was THE place to go, and it was booked out year after year. I even became a licensed travel agent and led many trips there with my clients. My records show that in six years I visited Barra Base 27 times, so I became very educated in the habits of the place!

Second Creek, which is the first major river system on the right-hand side of Port Hurd, became the place to catch big fish. My personal best barra from this creek was nearly 14 kilograms, caught on a deep-diving Nilsmaster lure. There was also one season when I caught more threadfin salmon above ten kilograms than under. The 'threadies' seem to follow large schools of mullet and other bait

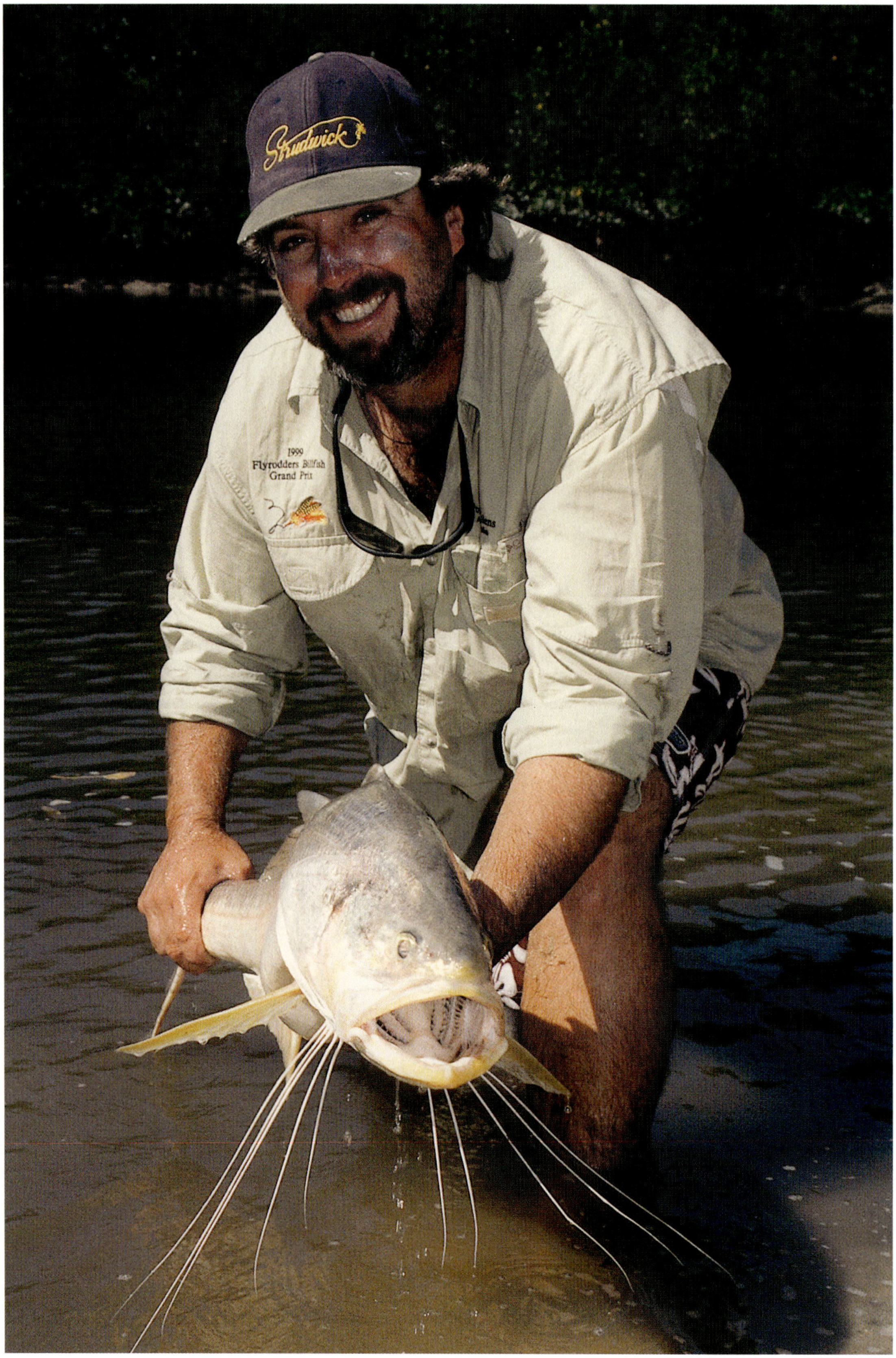
Strudwick
1999
Flyrodders Billfish
Grand Prix

fish into the creek in late May and stay until mid-July.

I also enjoy fishing the flats of Port Hurd itself, which has three main arms with myriad creeks and inlets running off them. I particularly enjoy the middle arm for its vast flats. It was here that I learnt to spot and then cast to cruising big barra and threadfin. My mentor was Graham Williams, who I found to be one of the best tutors in saltwater fly-fishing that I have met.

The lower reaches of the creeks in Port Hurd are spectacular for trolling at the bottom of the tide for barra. During those years that I was leading groups there I acted as a guide. The more I fished the better I became versed in knowing where to go and when.

Rock bars near the mouth of the port are also deadly spots for barra, particularly on high tides late in the evening near dusk. The bottom line is to find the nervous bait and you will find hungry fish.

The other main attraction at Port Hurd is the black jewfish, which is very similar to the mulloway or jewfish found in southern Australian waters. In the middle to top sections of the middle arm at Port Hurd there are reef and rock areas that are the perfect habitat for jewfish and their prey. I have seen some monsters taken from these reefs, and the best bait by far is a strip of whaler shark; I have

OPPOSITE: *Fly-fishing guru Dean Butler with a superb threadfin salmon from Second Creek.*

LEFT: *A small crocodile gets up onto the bank in a small creek.*

BELOW: *A young Matthew Hunt with a 12-kilogram barra from Dudwell Inlet, Bathurst Island.*

never had the success with other baits that I have had on shark.

I wrote in my autobiography, *Rex: My Life*, that when I was at Bathurst Island doing a TV show a magical moment for me was the morning after my mother passed away. I knew that she would want the show to go on, so I was inspired to make the best television that I could. Everything went to plan, and resulted in a black jewfish of over 15 kilograms coming to say 'hi' to the camera.

By far my best results on Bathurst Island have been in the rivers outside Port Hurd. From Gordon Bay just south of Port Hurd is my favourite river, the Parakary. It has a long, strong tidal flow and several major junctions that say 'big fish' to me. I feel that confidence plays a huge part in fishing. I always went there knowing I could fire up sometime in the tide.

I caught a monster in this river with Phil Hall. It was during filming for my first ever series of shows in 1991. While the fish may not have tipped the scales to 40 pounds in the old scale, it came mighty close. We were using live bait and got hit. When I checked the bait it was half gone. I turned around to grab another bait and this big barra ate the half-gone mullet as if there was no tomorrow.

There is some excellent blue-water fishing at Cape Helvetius, Clift Island and Rocky Point, which during neap tides provide very good, clear water conditions on the top of the tide. I have had some wonderful sessions around these structures, trolling lures for giant trevally, golden trevally, Spanish mackerel and queenfish. I have also taken good numbers of wolf herring and giant herring.

As you leave Port Hurd and head north, the two major river

BELOW: *A solid black jewfish caught on an offshore reef near Snake Bay, Melville Island.*

OPPOSITE: *Fishing writer Darren Reid with a whopping Spanish mackerel of 24 kilograms caught on a lure at Cape Helvetius, Bathurst Island.*

systems are Gullala Creek and Dudwell Inlet. Forced to select my favourite, I would have to choose Dudwell. It was here in the mid 1980s that I learnt the value of rattling lures, that is, lures with a ball bearing in them so that when retrieved or jiggled, they make a hell of a racket. My son Matthew and I were on a father-and-son trip one year and were taken to Dudwell by John Fry, who was a very good guide in the area. It was here that Matt took a magnificent barra of over 15 kilograms on a rattling spot lure. Matt and I have returned on many trips since and had very good results. Gullala Creek, by the way, is the better mangrove jack water. Both are difficult to navigate without local knowledge.

Apsley Strait

The Tiwi Islands are divided by a huge tidal channel called Apsley Strait. I have enjoyed some terrific fishing here, and the depth of some areas is amazing. On a recent trip while filming I fished in a hole that was over 90 metres deep. It was full of black jewfish and we landed seven rippers to 12 kilograms on camera. Once again shark was the top bait.

There are many rivers and estuarine systems within easy boating distance and I have found that Munupi Lodge at Garden Point is the ideal base. The rivers off Apsley Strait, whilst not as full of barra as other areas, have enough action to justify some serious casting to the various snags and rock bars and in the deeper, slower regions of the rivers there is an excellent chance of a big barra on a deep trolled lure.

ABOVE: *An early photo of yours truly with my first black jewfish, taken on a lure in the Jessie River, Melville Island.*

Melville Island

Melville Island has seen me visit on six separate occasions. My first trip was into the Jessie River Camp, which, not surprisingly, is on the Jessie River along the northern coast of Melville Island. I found that the lure fishing in both the Jessie and the Johnston was sensational. Barra, jewfish, mangrove jack – plenty of them and big.

One of my all-time favourite places is the now-legendary Jessie

River rock bar. On a recent trip it again showed me why it is one of the most consistent barra structures I have ever fished. In a hot session in front of the cameras I took five barra up to 10 kilograms and a big black jewfish of 15 kilograms, all on deep-diving lures.

I have also fished with my friends 'the Barra Boys' at Snake Bay, or Milikapiti, further west along the northern coast of Melville Island, aboard a mother ship. We accessed the Jessie and Johnston rivers and also had some ace fishing offshore, trolling lures for the pelagics like giant trevally, queenfish and Spanish mackerel. Neap tides were best, with deep-diving lures worked near reef structures the go.

On one occasion, I fished Goose Creek, located on the northern coast of Melville. In the lower reaches the creek is a typical shallow estuary that holds some fine little to medium-sized barra, jacks and threadies. The barra hang around sunken logs and submerged dead tree branches. The water is tannin in colour and you can often see the barra just before they hit your lure. The top reaches of the creek are some of the prettiest waters I have fished – lily pads flowering and barra and saratoga crunching your lures – it does not get much better than that.

Conclusion

Both Melville and Bathurst islands are right up there with my favourite ever fishing destinations. Forced to choose one hotspot from each island, I would say Dudwell Inlet on Bathurst and Jessie River on Melville.

However the hot fishing options certainly don't end there. The Tiwis are free of commercial fishing pressure and this, coupled with the area being so remote and the requirement to obtain permits from the traditional land owners, should ensure that these islands remain one of the hottest fishing destinations in the country for many years to come.

Piscatorial Compass
Tiwi Islands, Northern Territory

HOW TO GET THERE: There are regular flights from Darwin to the Tiwi Islands. Large boats or mother ships also steam overnight across Beagle Gulf and the Timor Sea from Darwin. Special permits are required to land on the Tiwi Islands.

WHERE TO STAY: Specific fishing tent camps are set up by fishing guides, and these locations vary from time to time. You can also stay aboard a mother ship.

WHAT TO CATCH: Barramundi, threadfin and blue salmon, mangrove jack, ox-eye herring (tarpon), fingermark, saratoga, black jewfish, giant and golden trevally, queenfish, Spanish mackerel, northern bluefin tuna and coral trout.

GEAR TO TAKE: Use a baitcaster rod and reel spooled with gelspun line and take plenty of lures, particularly deep-divers. Try fly-fishing outfits from six to nine weight.

WHEN TO GO: March to November; either side of the 'wet' season and throughout the 'dry'.

GUIDES AND CHARTERS: Les Woodbridge's Top End Sportfishing Safaris on Melville Island and Mick Winterton's Fishing Therapy are excellent.

REX RECKONS: The Tiwis offer some of the finest remote fishing available in Australia. The river rock bars are prime structures for barra.

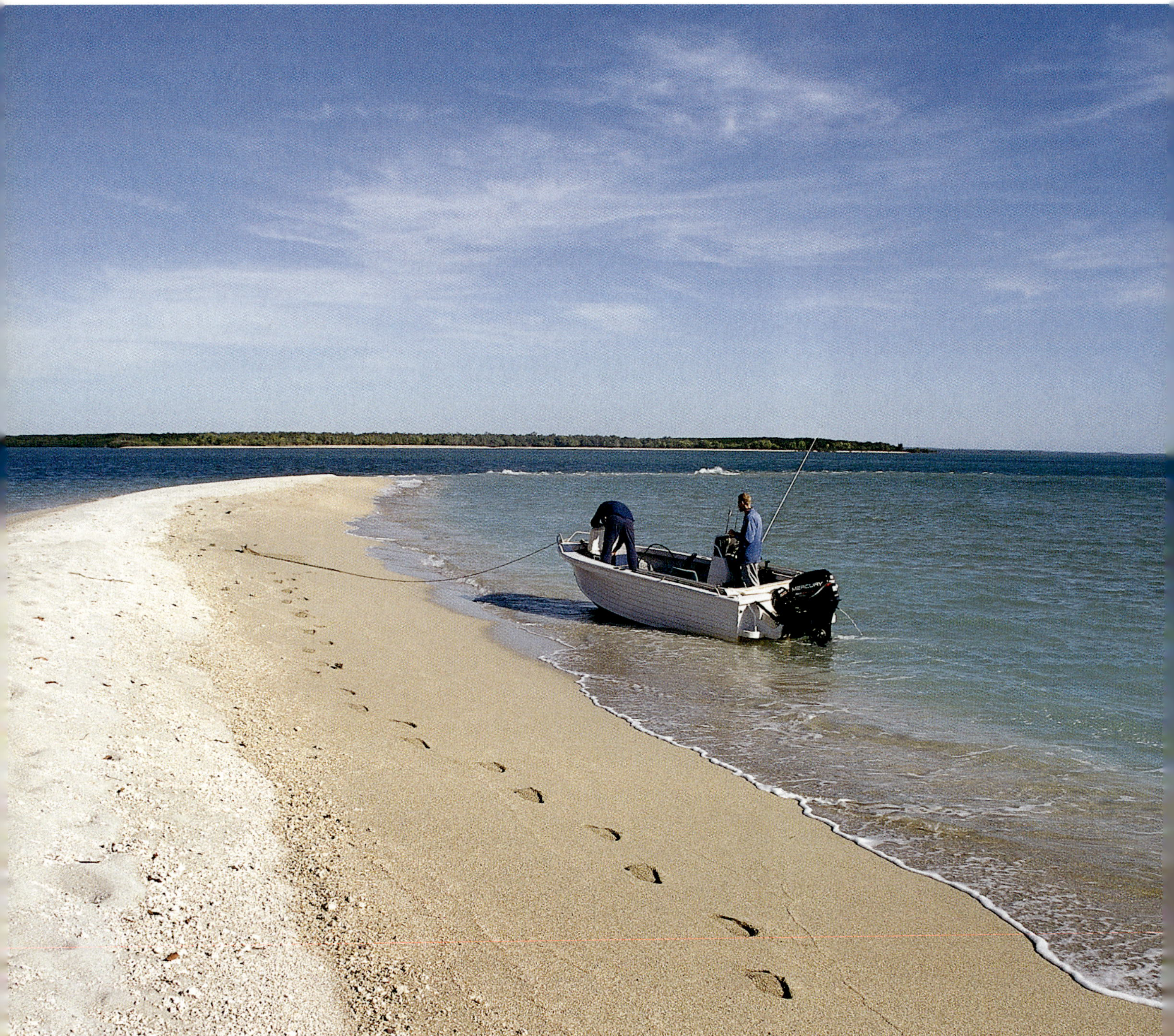
MERCURY

Cape Don

Cape Don is on the western-most tip of the Cobourg Peninsula, which extends off Arnhem Land into the Arafura Sea. This whole area is part of the beautiful Gurig National Park that is jointly managed by the Northern Territory government and the traditional owners. The waters surrounding the peninsula have been declared a marine park, with recreational fishing allowed.

The Cobourg Peninsula is quite different from other parts of the Northern Territory in that it has many sandy beaches, forests

OPPOSITE: *Rex's Cay.*

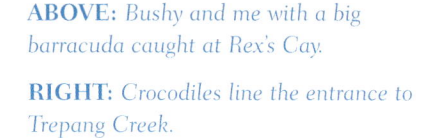

ABOVE: *Bushy and me with a big barracuda caught at Rex's Cay.*

RIGHT: *Crocodiles line the entrance to Trepang Creek.*

and rocky headlands, rather than a coastline dominated by flooded mangroves and mud flats. The scenery is in fact more typical of a national park found in southern Australia, with one major exception: crocodiles! The wildlife is stunning, and it is not unusual to find five or six crocs lying on a sandbank getting a tan.

The actual Cape Don settlement is wonderful and is located right on the northern tip of the cape. It is dominated by the lighthouse, built in 1916, and the old lighthouse keeper's residence, which has been turned into a fishing lodge. Around 50 Australian soldiers were based here during the Second World War, as it was an important early-warning aircraft radar detection station for Darwin.

I have visited and fished the waters off Cape Don on several occasions for television as well as on personal trips with my family. This beautifully rugged area offers spectacular fishing for pelagic species such as giant trevally, queenfish, Spanish mackerel and the like. I have found it disappointing for barramundi, however, mainly because of the lack of major estuarine systems.

The better waters are within easy driving distance of the lodge by sport fishing boat. I have travelled as far as Burford Island, around to the south of the Cobourg Peninsula, and Trepang Bay, along the northern coast.

Dundas Strait

Some of the most rugged water is right off the lighthouse where Cape Don meets Dundas Strait. I have witnessed raging tides of up to eight knots where the monster lure-grabbing giant trevally, estuary cod and Spanish mackerel roam. On the edges of these tides are eddies, which usually are associated with rock ledges and reefs, such as at Hell Rock. There are also quality fingermark bream, mangrove jack and coral trout in this area.

Burford Island

Burford Island is a small island surrounded by reef, which lies around 28 kilometres by boat from Cape Don on the southern shore of the peninsula. Between Cape Don and Burford Island there are many smaller island outcrops and ledges that just seem to come out of the sea. They are covered at flood tide but create nasty navigation problems as the tide recedes. However, it is here that some mighty queenfish can be caught. My son Matthew and I spent a marvellous morning here catching queenies up to nearly ten kilograms, some of which were nearly 1.75 metres in length. I have found that the best lure is the bibless Halco Trembler, which moves fast and rattles plenty. Giant trevally, barracuda and estuary cod are also prevalent here.

TOP: *Queenfish abound in the waters around the Cobourg Peninsula.*

ABOVE: *This mangrove jack was caught within a kilometre of the boat ramp at Cape Don.*

Rex's Cay

There are a few sandy banks literally in the middle of the Arafura Sea. One such place has been dubbed Rex's Cay. The crescent-shaped sand island is off Lingi Point, which is about halfway between Cape Don and Trepang Bay. I have fished here both as a television presenter and a paying guest, and it remains a favourite of mine.

I have caught massive barracuda here, as well as many trevally, queenfish and sharks. The sharks are mainly small whalers, but there are many large hammerheads in the area as well. These captures have been well documented by the TV show and rate amongst the most popular with our viewers.

Trepang Bay

Probably the highest-profile area within range of Cape Don is Trepang Bay, and Trepang Creek in particular. It used to be a favourite spot fished by the guides operating from Seven Spirit Bay in Port Essington. However – for me, anyway – it has failed to impress for barra. I feel the mangrove jack is a much better target than the barramundi.

The scenery in Trepang Bay is fantastic, and low tide in this area is an amazing experience. The place literally drains of water and exposes so much food and cover as to suggest that it should be a fishing paradise. At times it is; but, like any other place, you have to work on it.

Trepang Creek can be fished for barra and jacks, with queenfish and giant trevally at the mouth. The guides at Cape Don will take you into the mangrove forests in search of mud crabs that are caught the traditional way, using a spear. Likely spots are underneath the main roots of a mangrove tree. A few jabs with the spear will soon let you know if a crab is present. That night, you can feast on chilli mud crab that you caught yourself.

If the creeks of Trepang Bay are a bit slow, you can always head

LEFT: *Crocodiles add the 'adventure' to fishing adventures.*

BELOW: *A monster estuary cod taken on a lure near Cape Don.*

OPPOSITE: *View from Dundas Strait of Cape Don Lighthouse. Note the life-encrusted rocks and reef – all prime fishing territory.*

to Vashon Head at the eastern entrance to Trepang Bay from the Arafura Sea. This place is dynamite for pelagics such as trevally, queenfish, Spanish mackerel and other tropical speedsters. Take plenty of large, fast-swimming, minnow-style lures and use a wire trace to avoid bite-offs.

Conclusion

The accommodation at Cape Don is pure luxury compared to many of the Top End's remote fishing locations. This suits the family angler particularly well, especially when combined with the natural beauty of the environment and wildlife such as crocodiles, turtles, dugongs and dolphins to enjoy.

Piscatorial Compass
Cape Don, Northern Territory

How to get there: Access to Cape Don is via light aircraft from Darwin. The flights are usually on a daily basis and are arranged with Cape Don Lodge.

Where to stay: Cape Don Lodge. This homestead was formerly the lighthouse keeper's residence; it has five big rooms and is able to accommodate 12 guests.

What to catch: Barramundi, mangrove jack, threadfin salmon, fingermark bream, giant trevally, queenfish, Spanish mackerel, barracuda, coral trout, red emperor, sweetlips, estuary cod, golden snapper, black jewfish, and whaler, hammerhead, leopard and other species of shark.

Gear to take: You will need a baitcaster rod and reel with plenty of deep-diving and rattling lures and eight to 11 weight fly-fishing tackle.

When to go: March to November.

Guides and charters: Guides are arranged with Cape Don Lodge. Three 4.7-metre sport fishing boats with casting platforms are based at the lodge.

Rex reckons: This is not a barra hotspot; however, it has more than its fair share of sports fishing action, with queenfish, giant trevally and mangrove jacks in abundance.

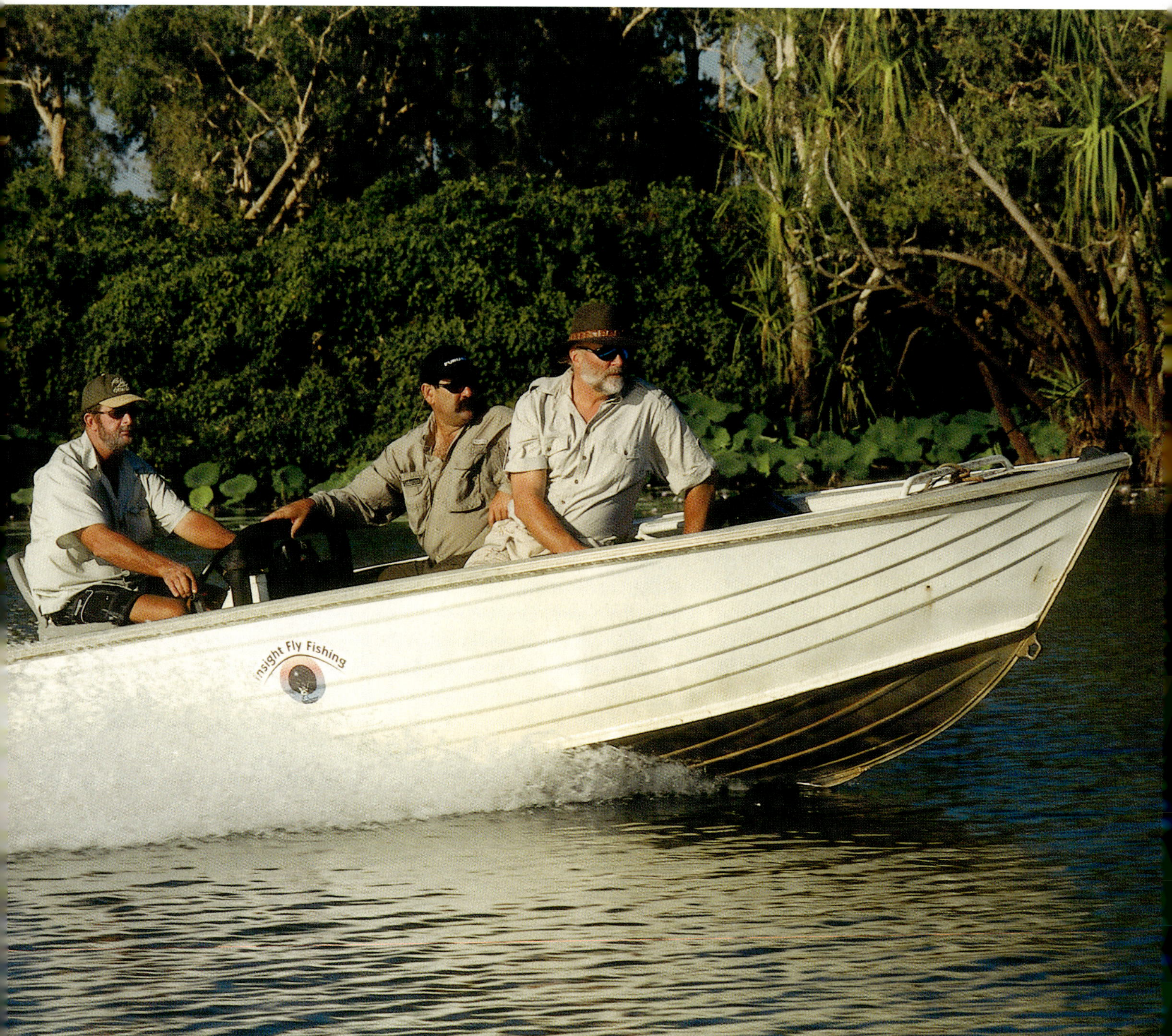
Insight Fly Fishing

Mary River

The Mary River is situated on the edge of magnificent Kakadu National Park east of Darwin. This system is one of the most popular fishing locations close to Darwin. It is an easy drive along the Arnhem Highway, and there are several good roadside cafes with facilities along the way.

The Mary River is fed by a series of rivers, creeks and channels from their source in the Mary River National Park. There is a vast flood plain that leaves a number of lagoons and billabongs in the dry season. The two most prolific are Corroboree Billabong and Shady

OPPOSITE: *On location at Corroboree Billabong.*

BELOW: *Tarpon are prolific throughout the Mary River system and are great fun on light fly-fishing tackle.*

BOTTOM: *Matt Hunt with a threadfin salmon, which are common around the lower reaches of the Mary River.*

Camp Lagoon. Both of these are located upstream of Shady Camp, where there is an artificial rock barrage to impede the flow of salt water into the wetlands during high flood tides.

Corroboree Billabong

The vast wetland and lagoon system is a major part of the Mary River. Filled by the monsoonal rains of the summer wet season, Corroboree Billabong, which is over 20 kilometres long, provides an ideal habitat for water fowl, marsupials, reptiles and, of course, native fish such as barramundi, saratoga, ox-eye herring (also known as tarpon) and catfish. Nature is seen here at its best, with the waterlilies that line the billabong creating a terrific habitat for predatory fish.

Guided by Graeme Williams of Insight Fly Fishing, I filmed one of our best Top End sessions for the TV cameras here a few years ago. Our target was the prehistoric saratoga which lives amongst the lily pads. The saratoga are particularly susceptible to surface-presented flies such as the Dahlberg Diver. The technique is to present the fly on top of the lily pads and rip it back across the surface, often skipping from one lily pad to the next. As the fly drops into the water, the saratoga is often ready and waiting to pounce.

Fishing with Kaj Busch (Bushy), we caught and released several beautiful fish up to two kilograms that simply nailed the green Dahlberg Divers with incredible speed. These fish take some turning, and it is quite a battle at times to get them out from the cover of the lily pads as they can get tangled amongst the thick vegetation.

Another saratoga session followed the next day with Steve Starling; this time we used rubber frogs and rubber mice imitation lures. These brilliant little lures are designed to skip across the surface and avoid snagging with a clever hook position. Casting with baitcaster rods we fished the lily pads for similar results as with fly, although this time our artificial was called a scum frog. Yes, folks – a scum frog!

On other occasions when I have fished Corroboree, tarpon have been prolific in the system. I feel that anyone wanting to learn the correct way to lure or fly-fish would do a lot worse than to catch a few of these silver piscatorial missiles. These fish are highly aggressive and simply never give up.

I have seen some of the biggest crocodiles in my life in the Mary River system. Corroboree Billabong has its share: I have seen a five-metre monster guarding a ten-kilogram barra on the bank. I have also seen a huge Jabiru standing on the back of a huge croc – very brave indeed!

BELOW: *NT fishing guide Mick Winterton with a lovely barramundi taken on a deep-diving lure at Shady Camp Lagoon.*

RIGHT: *Shady Camp Barrage is popular with lure casters who can fish into the fresh upstream or the salt on the downstream side.*

TOP: *Deep-diving lures account for many barra in the Mary River.*

ABOVE: *The Gold Bomber fly is a top taker of barramundi in the Mary River.*

OPPOSITE: *Lily pads in both Corroboree Billabong and Shady Camp Lagoon are great places to fish for saratoga, which will take soft plastic lures and flies.*

Shady Camp

Downstream from Corroboree Billabong is another major lagoon system know as Shady Camp. There are two boat ramps at Shady Camp either side of the barrage, which is designed to inhibit saltwater intrusion into the freshwater wetlands. One boat ramp is used to fish the freshwater section of Shady Camp and the other to fish the saltwater side, where the river is known as Sampan Creek as it heads downstream to Chambers Bay in Van Diemen Gulf.

The barrage has also provided a very good platform for land-based anglers fishing for large barramundi with lures. Without being a killjoy, I am not a big fan of fishing for barra out of the safety of a boat, especially at the barrage where the crocodile population is fairly high. However, plenty of people do it.

There is no commercial netting here and the fishing has improved every year. There are, however, very strict regulations that apply to fishing 100 metres either side of the barrage. There is no bait fishing allowed, and lures can only be used with a single hook attached – that is, no treble hooks.

The fishing from a boat at Shady Camp Lagoon on the freshwater side of the barrage can be fantastic. Large drains or

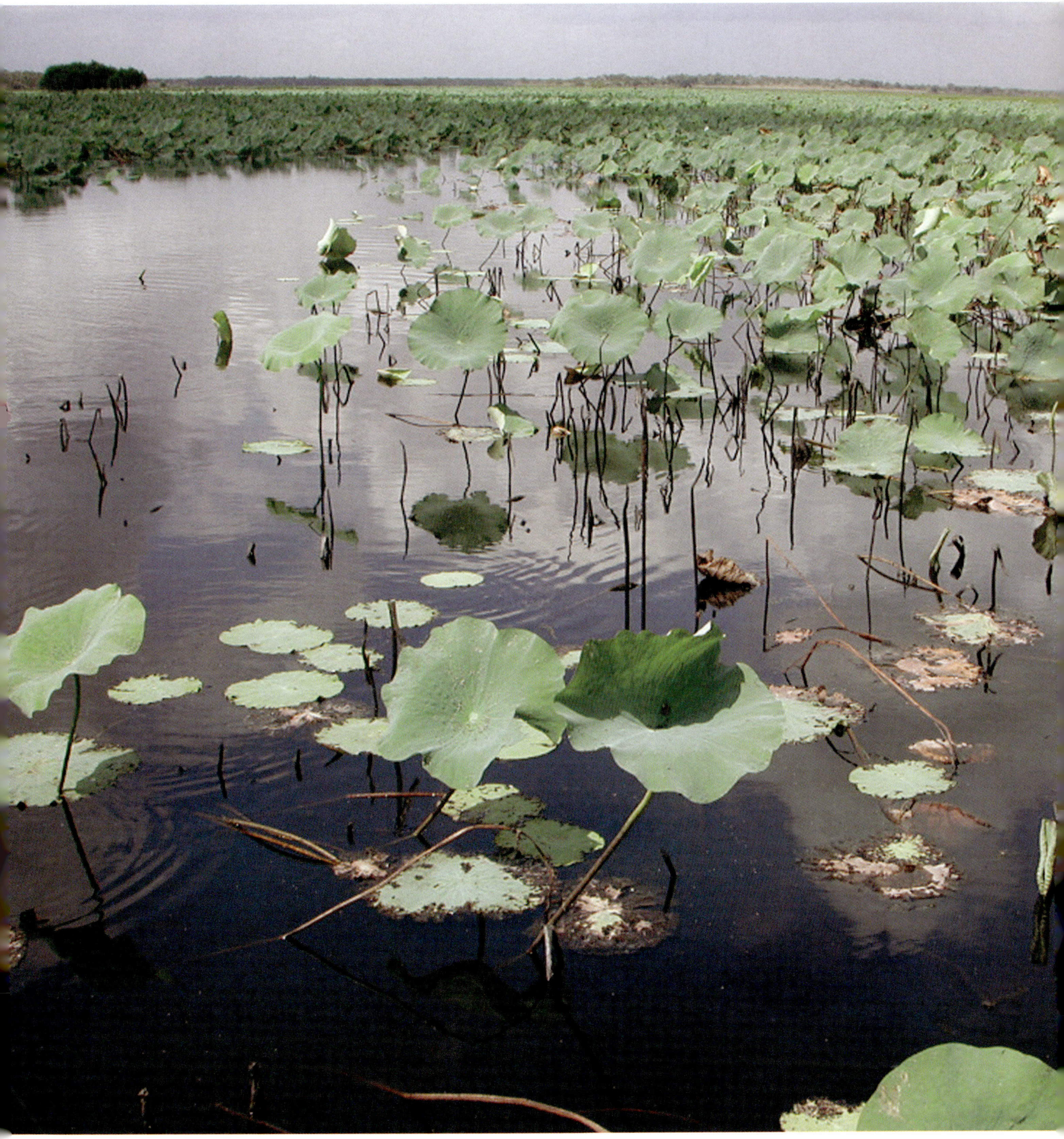

creeks often harbour barramundi, which are best targeted with small deep-diving lures or sinking flies. Amongst them you'll encounter tarpon, catfish and the occasional saratoga. There are also lily pads in Shady Camp which hold saratoga. The fishing here is similar to Corroboree but perhaps not as good.

There is very good fishing, both casting and trolling, downstream from the barrage to the mouth. I have had a couple of very good days in the area known as the 'S bends'.

It's the most popular place on the river around the change of tide, and some mammoth barra are taken from here. Near the mouth as it enters Chambers Bay you can troll for barra, as well as blue and threadfin salmon and other species when conditions are right. The odd black jewfish is also caught in this area.

ABOVE: *Anglers fishing from the Shady Camp Barrage – err... fish at your own risk.*

OPPOSITE: *Say no more!*

Conclusion

The road trip from Darwin to the Mary River system offers a variety of attractions. Howard Springs Nature Park, some 30 kilometres out of Darwin, is a magical place to swim and watch huge barramundi being handfed. The Adelaide River, further down the Arnhem Highway, also has good barra fishing plus huge crocodiles. This is where they teach the crocs to jump for the amusement of the tourists! This is a fascinating part of Australia that everyone should visit at least once.

Piscatorial Compass

Mary River, Northern Territory

How to get there: The Mary River is around 160 kilometres from Darwin via the Stuart and Arnhem highways.

Where to stay: There are houseboats on the Mary River, plus a few wilderness lodges and holiday units, or you can simply stay in Darwin and daytrip.

What to catch: Barramundi, saratoga, ox-eye herring (tarpon), catfish, threadfin and blue salmon, black jewfish.

Gear to take: You will need a bait-caster rod and reel, as well as fly-fishing tackle from six to nine weight.

When to go: April to October. The closed season for barramundi downstream of the barrage is from 1 October to 31 January.

Guides and charters: I would recommend Graeme Williams of Insight Fly Fishing and Mick Winterton's Fishing Therapy.

Rex reckons: This is one of the hottest fishing destinations close to Darwin; consequently, it's a great place for the novice lure and fly anglers to practise on aggressive fish in the form of barramundi, tarpon and saratoga.

188 REX HUNT'S FISHING AUSTRALIA

South Alligator River

The South Alligator River, or the 'South', is a massive system a couple of hundred kilometres east of Darwin and is part of Kakadu National Park. And yes, whether you call them alligators, as one early explorer did, or crocodiles, this water has plenty of them, as does the East Alligator River, which is also part of Kakadu.

The South Alligator River during the wet season is fed from various creeks and rivers high up in the ranges of Kakadu and the surrounding flood plains. For most of the year, though, its upper reaches, south of the Arnhem Highway, form a succession of billabongs that change in size

OPPOSITE: *A bit of sun protection goes a long way in a Kakadu billabong.*

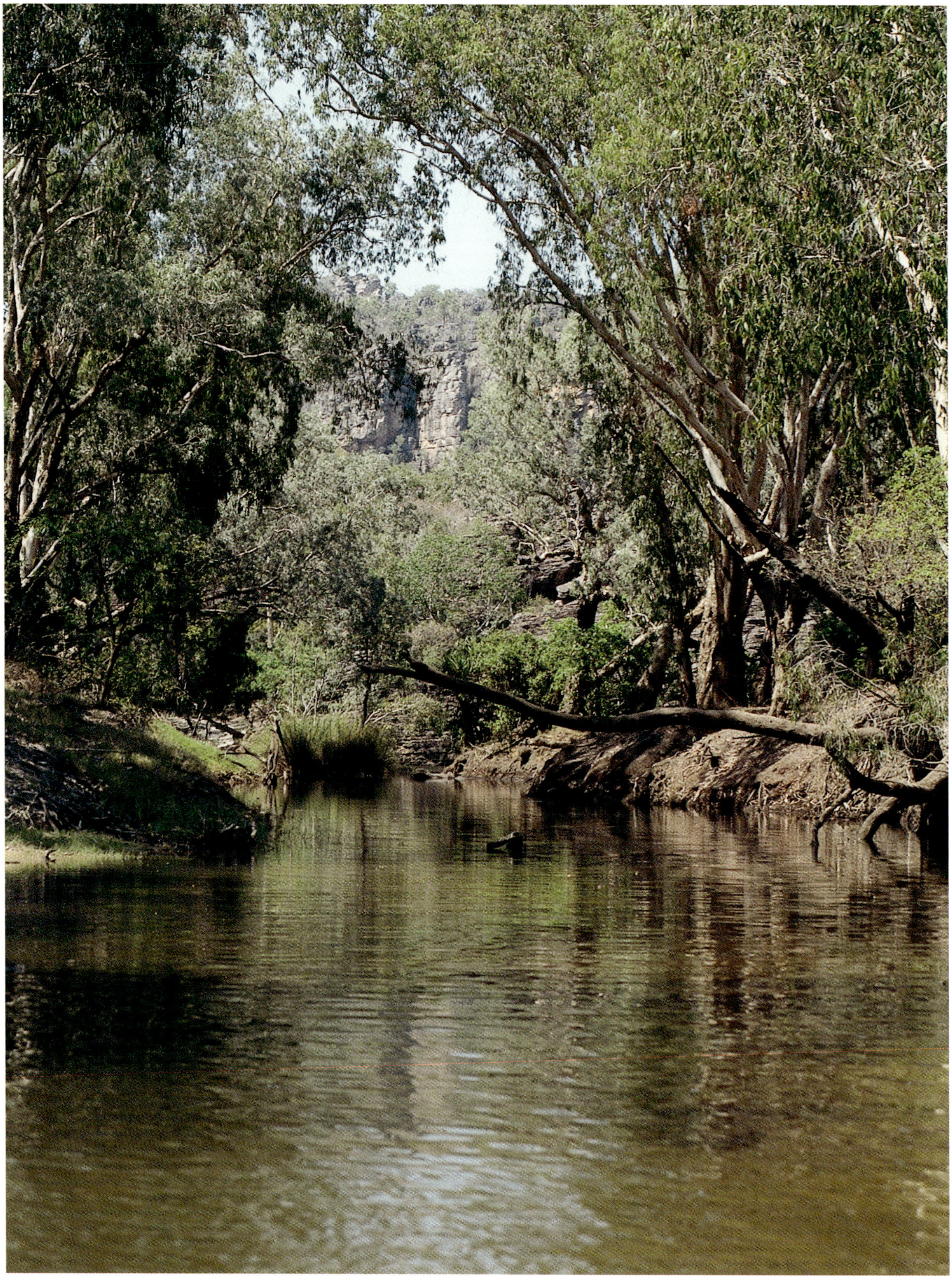

ABOVE: *Lynne Hunt with a fine billabong barramundi taken on a diving lure.*

OPPOSITE: *This is why I fish in Kakadu!*

depending on rainfall from year to year. Below the highway bridge, towards the mouth where the river flows into Van Diemen Gulf, the 'South' widens, presenting some 60 kilometres of navigable water.

Kakadu National Park

Kakadu is Australia's largest national park, stretching from Van Diemen Gulf in the north approximately 210 kilometres to its southern border. To the east it is flanked by Arnhem Land, and to the west by the flood plains and billabongs of the Mary River system. The park is jointly managed by the Aboriginal traditional owners and Parks Australia North, which is part of the Commonwealth government.

Folks, this is one of my favourite places on earth. Kakadu has an incredible abundance of bird and wildlife, with half of Australia's known bird species residing within its magnificent ecosystem. Over 70 species of reptiles, including crocodiles, and an amazing but scary 10,000 insect species call Kakadu home. The landscape is stunning, with high rocky outcrops, flood plains, billabongs, palms and lily pads; it is how the natural world would have looked to prehistoric man.

The fishing is mainly for barramundi, with saratoga and ox-eye herring (tarpon) in the billabongs and upper reaches. As you head north towards the mouth, the number of estuarine species increases, including black jewfish, blue and threadfin salmon, and golden snapper.

Billabongs

Upstream the waters in the dry season are refined to a number of large billabongs. Yellow Waters at Cooinda and Red Lily Billabong are a couple of my favourites and I have taken good barramundi to five kilograms from both. Trolling shallow- to medium-diving lures is best. My son Matthew and I have had good fly-fishing slowly retrieving big bushy flies like Pink Things and Dahlbergs.

On a recent trip my wife Lynne enjoyed excellent fishing, with

ABOVE: *Golden snapper are found throughout the lower reaches of the South Alligator River.*

LEFT: *The fishing is so good in Kakadu you can catch barra with your eyes closed!.*

barramundi and saratoga taking lures such as the Nilsmaster Spearhead fished on four-kilogram line using a threadline outfit. The colour? You guessed it: blue and white. This is a favourite colour of mine; in fact, I caught my first barramundi at Port Hurd on Bathurst Island on a blue and white spearhead.

Nourlangie Creek

Just after the wet, the run-off fishing on the South Alligator River can be spectacular. I had a very hot session where the Nourlangie Creek drains into the 'South' above the Arnhem Highway. Casting large diving lures, Phil Hall from Northern Territories Fisheries and I took a heap of barramundi and fair-sized tarpon in a great session for the TV show.

Lower Reaches

Although the South Alligator is in Kakadu National Park, the waters below the highway bridge are nothing inspiring, but boy, do they have some barramundi. Trolling deep-diving lures is best here. There is a good concrete boat ramp just off the Arnhem Highway.

If you find a hot spot, tie up the boat and cast lures into likely areas. The barramundi respond to a twitching lure that is worked in a jerky fashion, rather than simply retrieving the lure in a straight line back to the boat.

I can recall even catching a small bronze whaler shark on a lure in the 'South' below the highway bridge. That's the beauty of fishing – you never know what will turn up.

The lower reaches of the South Alligator River as they enter Van Diemen Gulf are naturally tidal and can drain out pretty quickly. Don't be put off by the murky water here; the big barramundi are lurking and in good numbers. They will charge at anything when they are hungry.

Conclusion

I have been fortunate to fish the South Alligator and in the waters of beautiful Kakadu on many occasions over the years for both the TV show and on personal trips. I keep coming back, as it is truly one of Australia's natural treasures – and the fishing is pretty good, too!

Piscatorial Compass

South Alligator River, Northern Territory

How to get there: From Darwin to the South Alligator River is around 230 kilometres via the Stuart and Arnhem highways.

Where to stay: The Frontier Kakadu Village is located near the South Alligator River just off the Arnhem Highway. There is also ample accommodation, including camping, at Jabiru in the heart of Kakadu National Park.

What to catch: Barramundi, saratoga, ox-eye herring (tarpon), threadfin and blue salmon, black jewfish and golden snapper.

Gear to take: You will need a baitcaster rod and reel with a good supply of deep-diving and soft plastic lures, as well as six to eight weight fly-fishing gear.

When to go: April to October. This is a dry season only fishery due to road inaccessibility in the wet.

Guides and charters: A range of guides that operate out of Darwin fish the South Alligator.

Rex reckons: The freshwater billabongs are best left until after the wet season. When the roads become accessible, it is action stations for some sensational barramundi fishing.

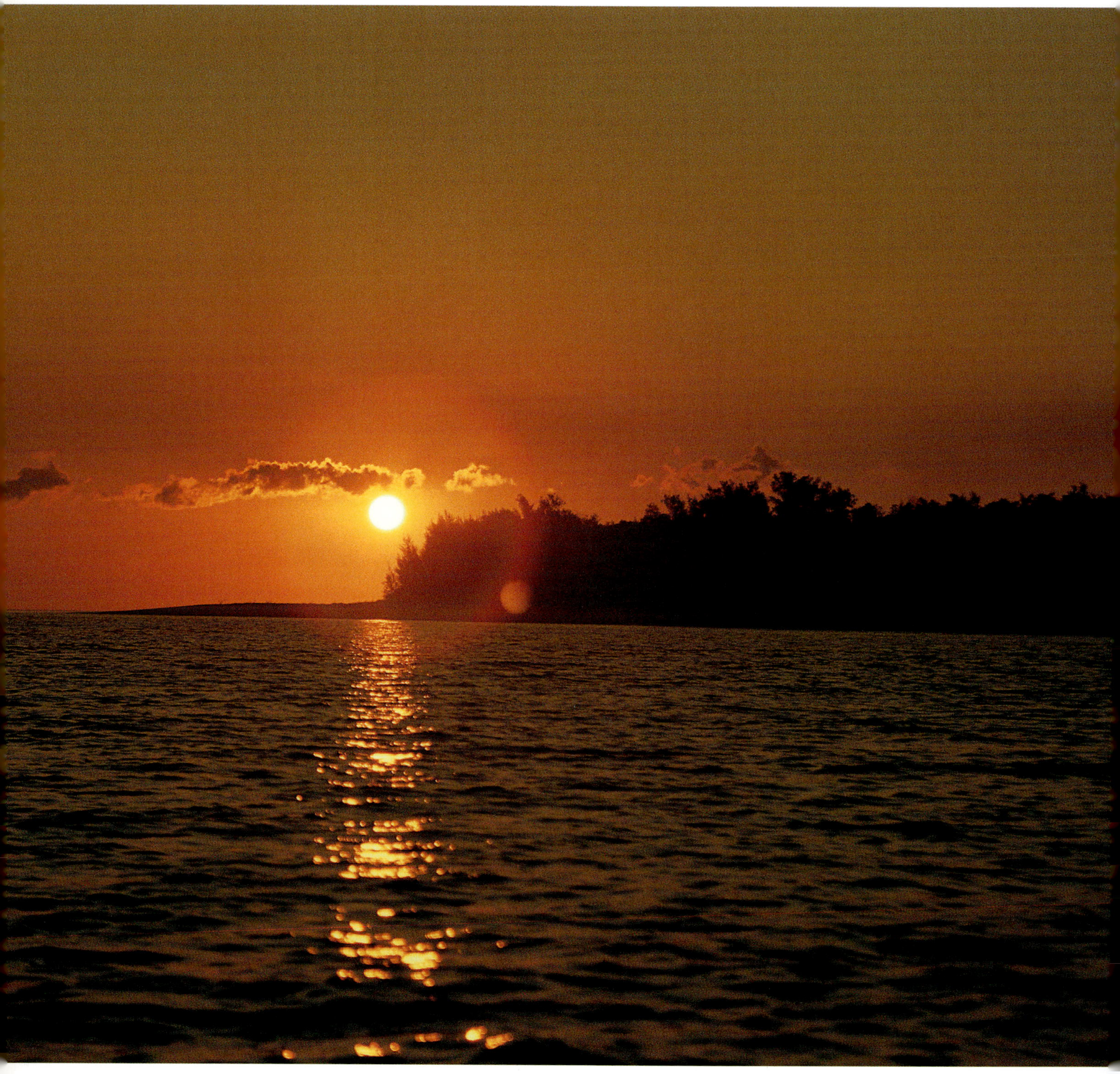

Liverpool River

The Liverpool River and the nearby Aboriginal settlement of Maningrida are located approximately halfway across Arnhem Land. The river begins deep in the ranges of Arnhem Land before descending into the Arafura Sea. Maningrida is a thriving Aboriginal town settled after the Second World War. The traditional landowners are the Kunibidji people, who named this area 'the place where the dreaming changed shape'.

I should explain up front that you cannot just hop on a plane and enter Arnhem Land. Permits are required and at the time of writing it was off limits to fishing, but hopefully this may change soon.

I have been here four times, and already the area is one of my very favourite fishing destinations, as the barramundi fishing is the equal of any I've had. I have caught bigger barramundi more consistently in other areas, but not the

OPPOSITE: *A magical Arnhem Land sunset.*

numbers of frisky small to medium-sized fish that I have encountered here. Fish from two to four kilograms are plentiful and they fight like billyo!

The main system here is the Liverpool River itself, which is a huge system with significant tributaries. One such tributary is the Tomkinson River, which flows into the Liverpool River almost at the mouth. This is a favourite of mine. It has plenty of good snags and drains as well as being quite deep in the lower sections, allowing trolling with deep-diving lures like the Manns 10+. Deep-diving lures often bounce off the bottom of the river, bumping snags and churning up the mud, which attracts the barramundi.

Tomkinson River

One of my all-time best sessions was had at a place right up into the headwaters of the Tomkinson, where there is a small junction with a little 'snaggy' stream. Huge crocodiles live here and some of the slides are immense. Slides are smoothed areas where crocs have slid down the mud bank into the river. I also saw an unbelievable spider's web made by a bird-eating spider that was as big as my hand. It was right out of a horror movie!

This particular day I was with John Dunphy from Shimano and my very dear friend Leo Cisco from Melbourne. Leo and I are part of the group called 'The Barra Boys' and we have been away fishing each year since 1982. Guiding us was Warren 'Wazza' Smith, a very likeable bloke and an ace guide. He was part of the Russell Kenny group NT Barra Fishing Safaris we fish with here. As soon as we anchored and commenced casting it was on – and I mean on. For barely a minute in the two-hour session was there a straight rod.

Cast after cast produced a feeding barrage of hungry barra; we caught and released over 100 in the session. I was using a rattling silver spot-type lure, Leo a Classic Barra and 'Dunph' concentrated on his Magnum Barra lures. It didn't matter what you threw at those fish, it went off.

TOP: *The build-up to the wet season is a good time to fish the Liverpool system.*

ABOVE: *A threadfin salmon taken on fly in the Liverpool River.*

RIGHT: *Small barra typical of the Liverpool are sweet to catch.*

ABOVE: *Matt with a ripper mangrove jack taken on a cast lure.*

BELOW: *Catch, kiss, release – the only way to go.*

Liverpool River

On high tide there are some good areas for trolling at the bottom of the Liverpool River. Once again, deep-diving lures are the go, and I have found that Russell Kenny and his guides are adamant that their client's lures should be bouncing off the bottom to be most effective. You'll get a snagged lure from time to time and sometimes the lure will be lost, but if you're not in the zone you're not in the hunt, err… no pun intended folks! Trolled deep-diving lures will take both barramundi and threadfin salmon; the latter often turn on a better display than the barra. 'Threadies' jump, leap, tail walk, they do the lot.

In some years there are some nice waterholes left after the wet in the upper reaches of the Liverpool. One fine fish I recall was Lynne's 22-pounder (10 kilograms). It was lazing along a billabong until Lynne covered it beautifully with a Nilsmaster Spearhead lure. The fish turned and inhaled the offering. Out of a tiny hole this massive barra was a great catch.

Offshore

Out to sea from the mouth of the Liverpool are Entrance Island and a small atoll. This area offers spectacular fishing for pelagic species like long-tail tuna, giant herring, barracuda, giant trevally, queenfish and golden trevally. Trolling at fast speeds of around eight knots with fast-running minnow-style lures such as Rapalas CD 11 and 13, and surface lures like poppers will produce some amazing action that eventually will leave you sick of catching fish, if that is possible. The trevally species in particular take long runs and will flank you with their wide bodies. They just never give up. Queenfish, which leap in spectacular fashion and make for entertaining fishing, are a very underrated sports fish.

Bottom-bouncing with bait over the reefs will produce good numbers of coral trout and golden snapper. Golden snapper are a bigger version of the fingermark bream found in the estuaries, and are best fished for at night.

Junction Bay

A fair distance to the west from the ramps at Maningrida is Junction Bay. Here two significant estuary systems enter the bay. I have fished both and have found good numbers of barramundi and threadfin salmon, as well as fingermark bream and blue salmon. Although this area is not renowned for mangrove jacks, I have nevertheless caught good-sized jacks in these two creeks. Threadfin salmon are a prime target with the fly, especially on the mud flats in the milky water only a metre deep.

I also had a magical session in the right-hand creek with my friends Leo Cisco and John Dunphy. Once again it was at a junction, and once again the fishing was white hot. The session lasted for over three hours, a non-stop bite of a lifetime. We consumed 14 litres of water that day and counted no less than 142 barramundi caught and released from the one spot. The fish ranged from 1.5 to over ten kilograms. It was as good as it gets for barra, and remains my favourite session with two special friends.

I have fished other areas in this district. The Blyth River to the east is a substantial waterway full of barra, and the water around the Crocodile Islands is terrific. I can recall my wife Lynne and daughter Rachel catching several barra and threadfin salmon here. We also caught some very big and aggressive mud crabs in our pots.

Conclusion

The Liverpool River and surrounding area is not commercially netted for barramundi, and this makes a huge difference. There is tremendous variety with over 40 species on offer, and in particular some of the best barra action I've experienced. I hope to return again one day to Maningrida and the magnificent Liverpool River system.

Piscatorial Compass

Liverpool River, Northern Territory

How to get there: You can fly from Darwin to Maningrida via small aircraft. Maningrida is approximately 530 kilometres from Darwin via road when permits allow.

Where to stay: Since you need a permit to visit this area, most guides or tours will provide your accommodation. We stayed in a safari-style tent camp.

What to catch: Barramundi, threadfin salmon, mangrove jacks, saratoga, giant trevally, golden trevally, queenfish, golden snapper, coral trout and northern bluefin tuna, to name a few.

Gear to take: Guides will provide all gear except for fly-fishing tackle.

When to go: March to November.

Guides and charters: Russel Kenny's NT Barra Fishing Safaris are fantastic. Note that there is currently no access to this part of Arnhem Land.

Rex reckons: Top barramundi fishing in a pristine environment.

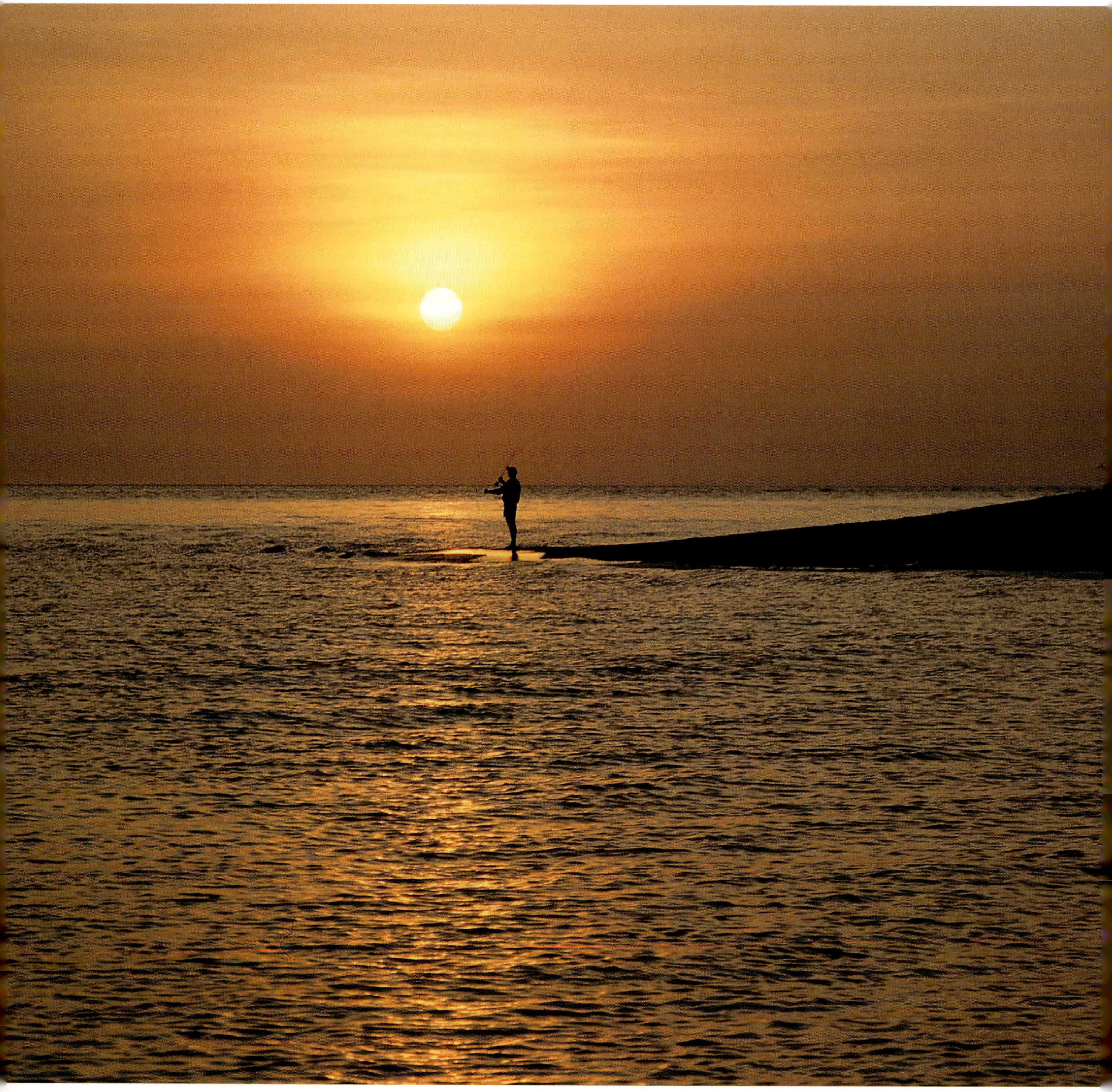

Cape York

Cape York Peninsula is one of the wildest and most remote areas in Australia. Located on the north-eastern tip of Queensland, the cape covers an area of around 130,000 square kilometres. It's the northern-most extremity of mainland Australia, and is only about 150 kilometres from southern Papua New Guinea across the Torres Strait.

Captain James Cook sailed through Torres Strait in 1770 and landed on what is known today as Possession Island. This island is just off Cape York itself. On 27 August 1770, Cook hoisted the English flag there to claim the east coast of Australia for King George III and England. Today the cape is a popular 4WD destination, but only in the dry season when the roads are not flooded.

I was first introduced to this area by Greg Bethune aboard his trusty old boat the *Capricorn Mist*. I was immediately attracted to this rugged and

OPPOSITE: *Fishing at sunset on a Cape York beach.*

beautiful wilderness, but one thing that hit me hard was the rubbish on these remote beaches. I was with the TV crew from my fishing show and made a small piece to camera. I then presented it to the Prime Minister when I met him in Hobart on another matter. I explained that the rubbish was coming across the sea from Indonesian fishing trawlers in the Gulf – this was clear from the foreign writing on the plastic containers. I explained to John Howard that this was a disgrace, and that if he got the opportunity he should mention it. I don't know whether he did or not, but since then I've noticed a considerable drop-off in the rubbish on the beaches.

Doughboy River

Every year myself and a bunch of mates go away on a piscatorial sortie with not a camera to be seen. The venue for one particular year was the west coast of Cape York, where we fished the waters of the Gulf of Carpentaria, utilising again the charter-boat services of Greg and Jennie Bethune of Carpentaria Seafaris. On this trip we

LEFT: *Ol' Rexy with a giant trevally (GT) caught on fly at Cape York.*

BELOW: *Hooked up to a tropical speedster on fly tackle.*

ABOVE OPPOSITE: *A huge groper comes in for a look.*

BELOW OPPOSITE: *My wife Lynne with a superb queenfish she caught on the Skardon River.*

started at Seisia and travelled down as far as the Doughboy River, then made our way back, fishing along the way.

I must say that there is something special about living aboard a mother ship and using small runabout dinghies for fishing, as we did on this trip. The terrific feeling that you get 'at sea' is a real buzz for us city folk. There can be few greater ways to spend a week than with good friends, good food, a few glasses of wine and, of course, the mandatory games of 500 with the odd *open misère* shout!

The fishing in the Doughboy is pretty damn good. Unlike around Darwin, Gulf rivers are not the place for huge barra. However, if you are into catching lure-grabbing or fly-gulping barra from 1.5 to five kilograms, then Cape York is hard to beat. Mangrove jack also make their presence felt, with the trademark dash from snags to ambush a diving Rapala or Nilsmaster lure. I cannot think of a better adversary in the mangroves. Another highlight of the area is the climate. Despite the spring tides, there is little of the whirlpool of mud that is so characteristic of the tidal estuarine systems of the Northern Territory.

Bill Classon of *Freshwater Fishing* magazine was on the trip and made the most of the sight-fishing on the flats. As the water is clear, it is possible to see fish before you cast. Bill sighted, cast to and deceived a giant permit (snub-nosed dart), and on another occasion came across a pair of permit in a metre of water just outside the Doughboy River. The larger of the two surrounded Bill's crab fly and then ate it without hesitation. Bill could not believe his luck, as for two days he and I had tried in vain to get a take. We had cast to plenty and spooked plenty, but they had been too good for us. This time, Bill hooked on the call from Greg Bethune. 'He's got it!' cried Greg. 'Hit him!' and hit him Bill did.

The fish didn't realise what was going on for a while, but then felt the strain of the pressure of the line in its mouth. It then made an express run that saw three lots of line backing hit the water. The fight was on in earnest. It was clear that the four-kilogram tippet was never going to be enough to allow this fish to be brought into an area where it could be controlled and then subsequently landed.

LEFT: *Two young lads hooked up on northern bluefin tuna off Cape York.*

LEFT OPPOSITE: *Fishing writer Leeann Payne with a solid barra she caught on fly.*

RIGHT OPPOSITE: *A couple of nice threadfin salmon.*

BELOW OPPOSITE: *Paul Worsteling with a northern bluefin tuna he caught on a recent film trip to Cape York.*

After about 25 minutes of struggle the line gave way. A closer examination revealed a solid cut through the leader. The fish had obviously turned and the flukes on his tail had severed the thick leader like a hot knife slices butter. Fish size estimates ranged from seven to eight kilograms, but whatever the size it was clear that this was serious stuff in water only a metre deep. To have hooked the fish in the first place was the act of a master angler.

This adventure will make us come back and go harder next time – it's what fishing is all about. Anticipation, the thrill of the hunt, heart pumping high on adrenaline as the cast is made. I think to really get the most out of anything you have to experience losses and tough times so that you can recognise and savour the good times. Wouldn't it be a boring old world if everything was perfect?

Gulf Waters

Although I have fished the entire west coast of the Gulf of Carpentaria from Weipa to Seisia, my favourite area is south of Seisia as far as the Skardon River. I have also fished the Macdonald and Jackson Rivers. While I have caught some nice barra in these rivers, it is mainly for the pelagic species that I go to these waters.

In my travels around the world, I have not yet found better fishing for queenfish and golden trevally than that which exists here. Greg Bethune's records show that over 50 species have been caught by his clients on his trips. Just recently Greg and Jennie took possession of a lovely new motor yacht that I describe as a floating fishing lodge. We experienced it during a filming trip and we enjoyed all the comforts of home. You can also stay at Seisia or Weipa and do daytrips from these ports, but this restricts the distance you can travel and therefore the areas you can fish. The best thing to do is to hire one of the live-aboard vessels in these areas. Using small boats you can then explore these fish-rich places better. I particularly like boating close to the beach, where I have seen some massive fish in the shallows and watched first-hand some of the biggest manta rays I have ever seen.

The offshore reefs in the Gulf hold a variety of reef species from desirable table fish like coral trout, red emperor and golden snapper, to a host of whaler sharks, as you may have seen on episodes of the TV show.

Cape York Beaches

Beach fishing is very relaxing. I like to walk for miles sight-fishing for trevally, queenfish, giant herring and other fish. I have cast several times to permit (snub-nosed dart) but as yet have not connected to one. Bill Classon came close in the Doughboy River, but Pat Levy destroyed the holy grail fly-fishing myth that permit were uncatchable by trolling up a seven-kilogram fish on a Stumpjumper lure!

I have had many highlights in this part of the world. Two beach-fishing moments stand out. I was sight-fishing a beach south of Weipa with Peter Morse, TV presenter and fishing writer. Peter sighted a massive cobia (black kingfish) and I threw a beautifully tied half pilchard in front of it. The take was awesome and the fight a long one. After 45 minutes of chasing and fighting this fish I landed my best cobia to date, of around 24 kilograms. It was a real thrill.

ABOVE: *4WD vehicles are mandatory to access Cape York*

BELOW: *The fish are hungry at Cape York – here's the business end of a golden trevally with the lure firmly stuck in its gob!*

The other highlight was a classic. As the camera was running on me doing what we call a stand-up piece, my fly was taken by a golden trevally, the likes of which I have never had before. The first run took me to the second backing and I estimate that over 200 metres of line ran off the spool before I gained control and eventually landed the fish.

Greg Bethune and I also had a memorable session for the TV cameras casting to feeding queenfish working a small eddy off one of the beaches as the tide started to flood in. We caught and released several beautiful fish of between two and three kilograms on fly tackle using pink Clousers and anchovy imitations.

One thing to watch when wading on a Cape York beach, folks, or any tropical beach for that matter, is the ever-present threat of box jellyfish. Greg and I came across an ugly specimen whilst filming and this is why we always carry a bottle of vinegar. A dash of this stuff can relieve the extreme pain of a jellyfish sting. Apparently north-westerly winds blow these dangerous critters onto the west coast of Cape York beaches, and many young Aboriginal kids have been stung whilst swimming and tragically have died. If their tentacles drape across your chest you're in real trouble.

Conclusion

The western coast of Cape York is one of my favourite places to fish. Its remoteness, coupled with the luxury of a mother-ship operation, is hard to resist. I'll keep coming back as long as the fast-swimming pelagics of the cape beckon me.

Piscatorial Compass
Cape York, Queensland

How to get there: By road (4WD only) from Cairns it is almost 1000 kilometres to Seisia. It is far easier to fly from Cairns to the airfield at Bamaga, where it is only a half-hour drive to Seisia.

Where to stay: Accommodation is available at Seisia and Bamaga. Weipa further south is a large town with a wide range of accommodation. Of course, when using a mother-ship operation you stay on board the boat.

What to catch: Barramundi, threadfin salmon, mangrove jack, queenfish, giant herring, giant and golden trevally, Spanish mackerel and a variety of reef species.

Gear to take: Use a Baitcaster rod and reel with a swag of lures. Fly-fishing tackle from seven to eleven weight is best depending on the fish being targeted; eight to nine weight is ideal for beach-casting.

When to go: March to November.

Guides and charters: Greg and Jenny Bethune of Carpentaria Seafaris are a great choice. Check out www.seafaris.com. There are many other guides and charter boats operating out of Cape York.

Rex reckons: Take a good camera, as you'll being catching, kissing and releasing more fish that you can poke a stick at!

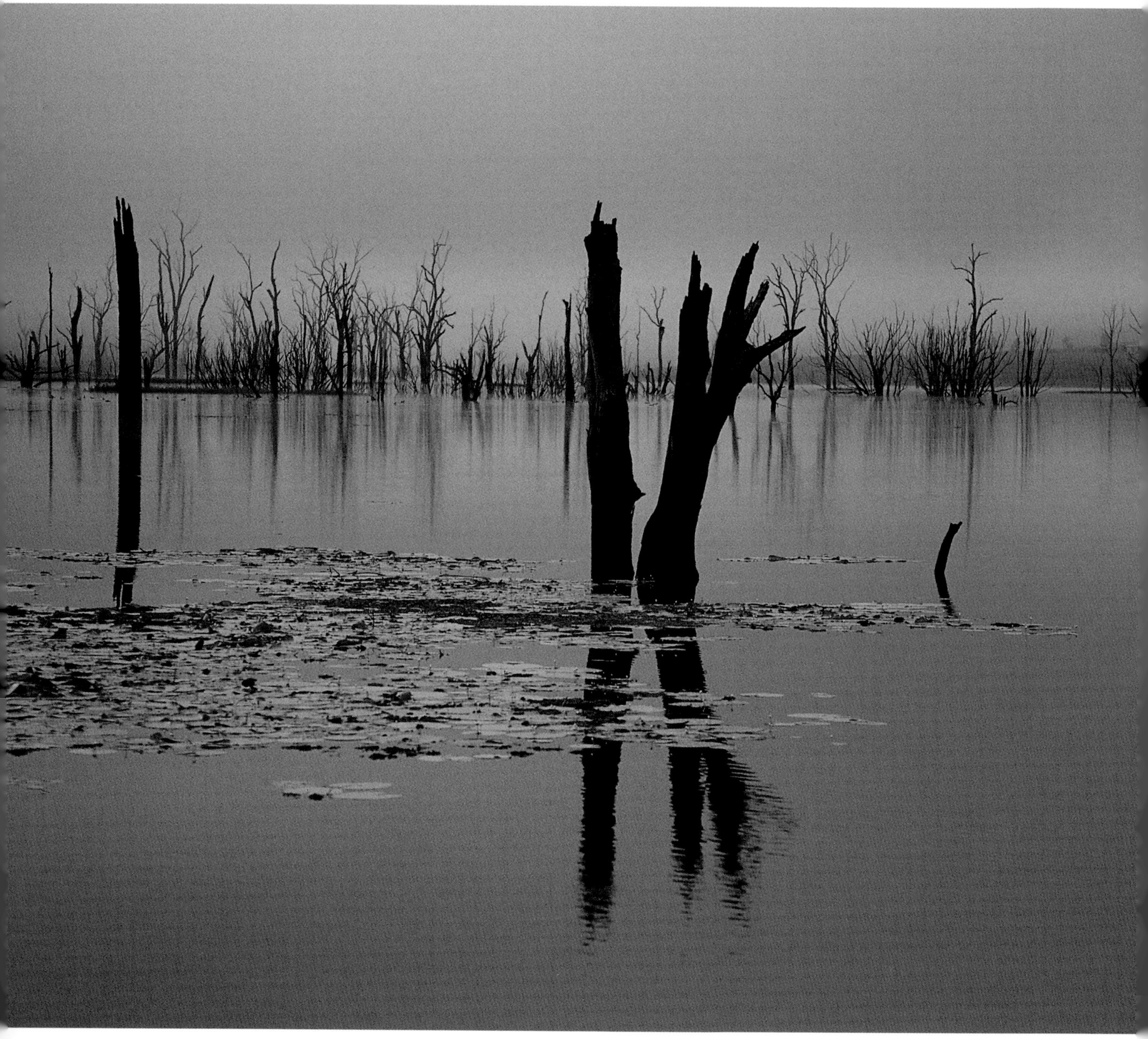

Lake Tinaroo

Lake Tinaroo, in northern Queensland, was formed when the Barron River was dammed in the mid-1950s. This massive lake, some 670 metres above sea level on the Atherton Tablelands, has a shoreline in excess of 200 kilometres and is the third biggest impoundment in the Sunshine State. Lake Tinaroo is renowned for its scenic beauty and prolific birdlife.

The Atherton Tablelands are west of Cairns and offer a cooler alternative to the tropical heat of the coast. They are named after an early gold miner, John Atherton, who in the late 1800s explored the area and found tin in a creek, subsequently naming it Tinaroo Creek.

These days, mention the word 'Tinaroo' and immediately anglers think monster barramundi. Fish over 80 pounds (35 kilograms) in

OPPOSITE: *A perfect barramundi haunt just after dawn. Tinaroo barra bite best in dark conditions.*

the old scale have been taken in Tinaroo. The biggest on record, 37.85 kilograms, was caught by Dave Powell only a few weeks before I visited Tinaroo. Even the average barra are big at around 12 to 15 kilograms.

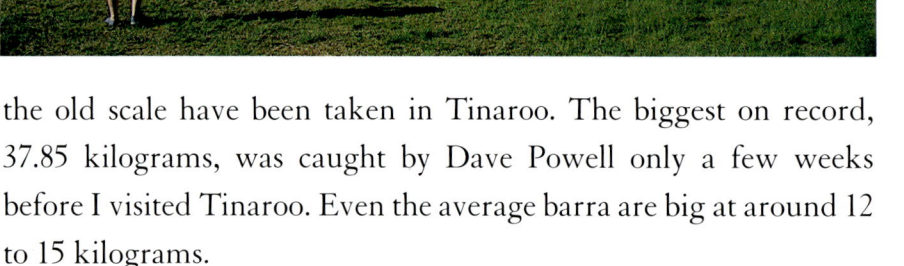

I visited and fished Lake Tinaroo in late 1999 with legendary fishing writer and photographer John Mondora. Mondora has fished all over the world but in particular in the Top End of Australia. He raved about Tinaroo, and for good reason – it truly is barra heaven.

The environmental make-up of the lake is very good and perfectly suits the barramundi. There are a number of bays and inlets lined with lily pads, and there are other areas of the lake that have superb structure, including plenty of submerged timber. The dam wall is a prime spot, as it is very deep and often holds some huge barramundi.

The reason for the high growth rate is found in the abundance of the food supply. The food chain consists of red claw, a freshwater crayfish, plus, in particular, two small fish species known as mouth almighty and bony bream.

Stocking of barramundi into Lake Tinaroo commenced in 1986

ABOVE: *Yours truly with a 20-kilogram Tinaroo barramundi that was 'electro-fished' by Queensland Fisheries to check its weight and growth patterns. The fish was released unharmed.*

LEFT: *The spillway of Tinaroo dam in flood.*

OPPOSITE TOP: *Need I say more about this place, folks.*

OPPOSITE: *A fine Tinaroo barra caught by fishing writer John Mondora. It weighed over 60 pounds in the old scale.*

OPPOSITE RIGHT: *This is the world-record barramundi at 37.85 kilograms caught by Dave Powell in Lake Tinaroo.*

and has been a remarkable success story. Fingerlings bought from fundraising are released by the Tableland Fish Stocking Society each year. I did a TV show on releasing the barra fingerlings with children from the nearby Yungaburra Primary School.

The secret to the barramundi of Tinaroo is to study the moon.

Both the new and full moon are very good, with slow-trolling lures the best method in the dark of night. Barra lures that are usually successful at other locations will work at Tinaroo provided they can dive down to between four and eight metres plus.

Although my trip filming wasn't overly successful, we did manage a good barra of around 12 kilograms on a trolled lure just on dark in a small inlet. During our three-day trip we saw several 20-kilogram fish caught. We were also privy to seeing a fish over 25 kilograms taken by freshwater fishing writer Neil Schultz, who is recognised as a gun angler for the Tinaroo barra.

One segment we filmed was with Alf Hogan, the senior fisheries biologist of the Northern Fisheries Centre based in Cairns. Aboard the Fisheries boat we electro-fished an area to sample the existing

ABOVE: *Myself and a couple of kids from the local school prepare to release some barramundi fingerlings into Tinaroo.*

OPPOSITE: *A feed of magnificent red claw crayfish.*

barramundi stocks. This technique does no harm to the fish and after a short while they happily swim away. I was truly amazed at the amount and the size of the barra that were electro-fished, measured, weighed and then returned to the water. I had my photo taken with one of the fish, and its colour and condition were unbelievable.

There are also sooty grunter in the lake, which take lures trolled or cast around sunken trees and logs. Pots set by amateurs trap the red claw crayfish and there is some concern that over-fishing is occurring. As an important food source for the barramundi in the lake, there may need to be restrictions put in place in the future. They are, however, a superb eating crustacean.

Conclusion

Tinaroo is barra heaven, for sure. The fishing isn't easy, though, and anglers need to put in considerable hours and be prepared to fish at night, often trolling for a considerable period of time before success comes your way. However, when a huge barra engulfs your lure, the hard work pays off in spades.

Piscatorial Compass

Lake Tinaroo, Queensland

How to get there: Tinaroo is around 90 kilometres south-west of Cairns via the Bruce Highway and the Gordonvale–Atherton Road.

Where to stay: Leighton's Home Style Lodge, plus there are some motels in Tinaroo and a holiday park.

What to catch: Barramundi, sooty grunter and red claw crayfish.

Gear to take: You will need a medium bait-caster rod and reel suitable for trolling and casting deep-diving lures.

When to go: October to March is best. Barra are available year round, though, as there is no closed season for barramundi in Tinaroo. However, any barra caught in the closed season of 1 November to 1 February must be taken to an approved tagging station for tagging, and fish over 120 centimetres caught at any time must be tagged at an approved station.

Guides and charters: I would recommend local guide Jack Leighton.

Rex reckons: The barra are very big but can be hard work. The prime time to fish is dusk going well into dark.

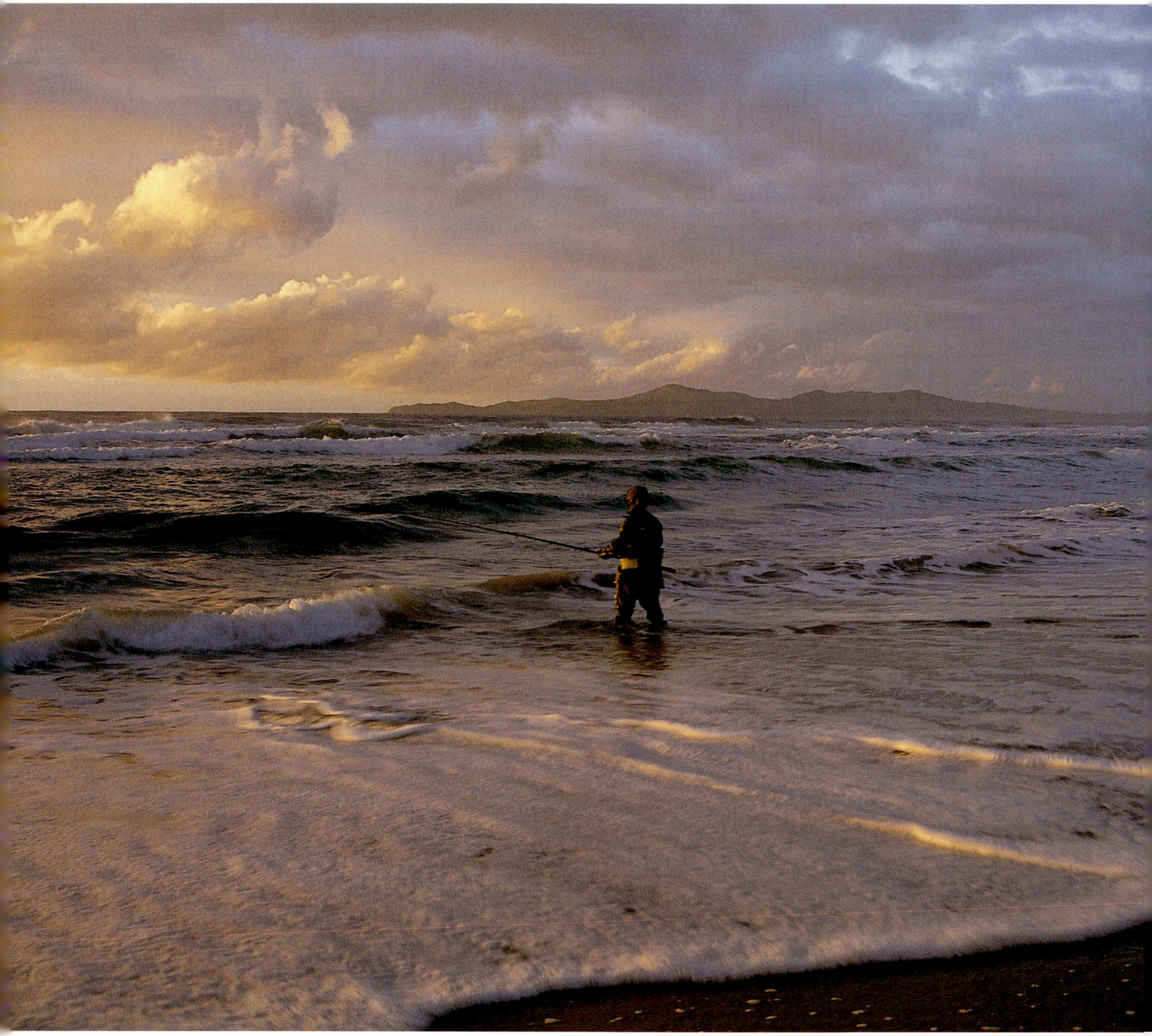

Noosa

Noosa, on Queensland's Sunshine Coast north of Brisbane, is a truly beautiful place. Superb beaches, a year-round warm climate and tremendous fishing – what more could an angler want in a destination?

Similar to the Gold Coast, this has been the holiday playground of Brisbane-based families for many years, although these days visitors from interstate

OPPOSITE: *Early morning during winter is a prime time to catch tailor along Noosa's beaches.*

probably outnumber the native Queenslanders during holiday times. Just about every second person you meet comes from either Victoria or New South Wales.

I have visited and fished Noosa several times over the years for both the TV show and on breaks during the winter from calling the football on radio in Melbourne. For me the variety of fishing, from the beaches and offshore to the magnificent Noosa River, is what sets Noosa apart from many other destinations. The light-line estuarine fishing, in particular, is good for sand whiting, yellowfin bream, a wide variety of trevallies and Australian bass in the upper reaches.

Noosa River

The yellowfin bream in the river can be quite small in size if you use soft baits such as beach worms or peeled prawns. If you fish with harder baits such as crab or a large unpeeled prawn, then you will do well. The bream will also respond to soft plastics bounced along the bottom with the tide.

There are many shore-based opportunities along the foreshore at Noosaville just where Davo's Bait & Tackle is located. Large flathead are also in the estuary and are best fished for at first light with live bait or rubber tail lures.

There are some excellent sand whiting to be caught on a year-round basis. I have had some nice whiting catches in the fast water just inside the entrance. The best time is the last of the ebb tide, and the best bait is locally pumped nippers. An effective berley to attract the whiting can be created by pumping up the nippers in the shallows and allowing the scent to drift with the tide. Some of the best areas to fish are barely a metre deep.

In the stretch that flows past the Sheraton Hotel there are several good spots for large bream, as well as a broad piece of water that holds tailor and giant trevally that can be targeted using lures and flies. A top fly for the small giant trevallies is a chartreuse-coloured clouser. Also, most houses that back onto the estuary have a jetty and a resident school of hungry bream.

In the upper reaches of the Noosa River is a beautiful area known as the Everglades. I caught some small Australian bass here in the mid-1990s on surface poppers. Access is difficult now, as powerboats are restricted in the upper reaches; however, it is still possible to fish from a canoe or boat fitted with an electric motor, albeit it's a long haul to the best fishing.

RIGHT: *View of Noosa Heads and the beaches stretching north.*

OPPOSITE LEFT: *Filming a segment on sand whiting in the Noosa River.*

OPPOSITE: *Blackfish or luderick are a most sought-after species on the breakwall at Noosa Heads.*

Noosa Heads

The rock breakwall where the Noosa River enters the Coral Sea is a prime place to catch blackfish, or luderick as they are called in the southern states. I fished with local guru John Cobb, who uses a finely balanced outfit rigged with a stick float and light line. We caught blackfish to one kilogram from the breakwall using cabbage weed for bait. These are vegetarian fish that feed midstream in the water column, especially on an incoming tide.

Other species encountered along the breakwall include jewfish, sharks, tailor and bream. Knowledge of the best tides and wind direction to fish is paramount to success here.

BELOW: *A nice catch of bream and tarwhine caught off the beach.*

OPPOSITE: *The Noosa Blue Water charter boat enters the Noosa River after fishing offshore for snapper, cobia, coral trout and mackerel tuna.*

Beaches

Beach fishing can be good, with tailor and sand whiting the main species. Mullet, bream, tarwhine and dart are also taken regularly. 4WD vehicles are allowed on the beach and it is a very interesting drive right through to Rainbow Beach. The best fishing spots include North Shore Beach, the mouth of the Noosa River, and anywhere along Teewah Beach where there are deep gutters or holes.

Offshore

Offshore fishing on reefs such as Chardons, Sunshine, Halls and North Reef, along with the Barwon Banks and the Jew Shoal, can be highly productive. Snapper, cobia, red emperor, mackerel tuna, coral trout and some huge cod can be caught. I have fished with Noosa Bluewater Charters for the TV show and had a memorable session with a massive cod of well over 40 kilograms that came up from over 30 metres. The charter skipper skilfully popped the fish's swim bladder, which allowed it to swim away, hopefully not too worse for wear for the experience.

ABOVE: *My daughter Rachel with a fine Australian bass she caught on a soft plastic lure in Lake Macdonald during a segment for the TV show.*

LEFT: *Dusky flathead are a prime target in all of south-east Queensland's estuaries – the Noosa River is no exception.*

Lake Macdonald

This man-made impoundment near Cooroy is Noosa's main water supply. Queensland fisheries have stocked the lake with Australian bass fry and they have absolutely thrived in this environment. Lake Macdonald is a 'put and take' fishery where the bass have reached legal size within two to three years.

We filmed a couple of episodes for the TV show and caught bass from one to 2.5 kilograms on soft plastic lures called Sliders worked slowly along the lake bed. One of the sessions was extra special for me, as my daughter Rachel made her first appearance on the show and duly showed me up by catching a fantastic bass that measured 48 centimetres to the fork!

Conclusion

A great place to escape the cooler winters of the southern states, particularly my home state of Victoria. Any time of year, though, is worth a visit to this very popular holiday location on Australia's Sunshine Coast.

Piscatorial Compass

Noosa, Queensland

How to get there: Noosa is around 140 kilometres north of Brisbane via the Bruce Highway, Sunshine Motorway, Mountain Aerial Road and Noosa Road.

Where to stay: Noosa has a huge range of holiday units and apartments, caravan parks and motels. Book early, as this is an extremely popular holiday location.

What to catch: Yellowfin bream, blackfish, tailor, sand whiting, dusky flathead, Australian bass, dart, tarwhine, mullet, giant trevally, big eye trevally, golden trevally, snapper, pearl perch, coral trout, sweetlip emperor, reef cod, cobia, maori cod, mackerel tuna and northern bluefin tuna.

Gear to take: Take a light threadline reel for the estuary, overhead gear for offshore, and a beach-fishing rod and reel.

When to go: All year round; even the winter months offer tremendous fishing options.

Guides and charters: Talk to Davo's Bait & Tackle in Noosa to hook up with various charters and guides.

Rex reckons: Take plenty of sun cream and a hat when fishing; they don't call this the Sunshine Coast for nothing.

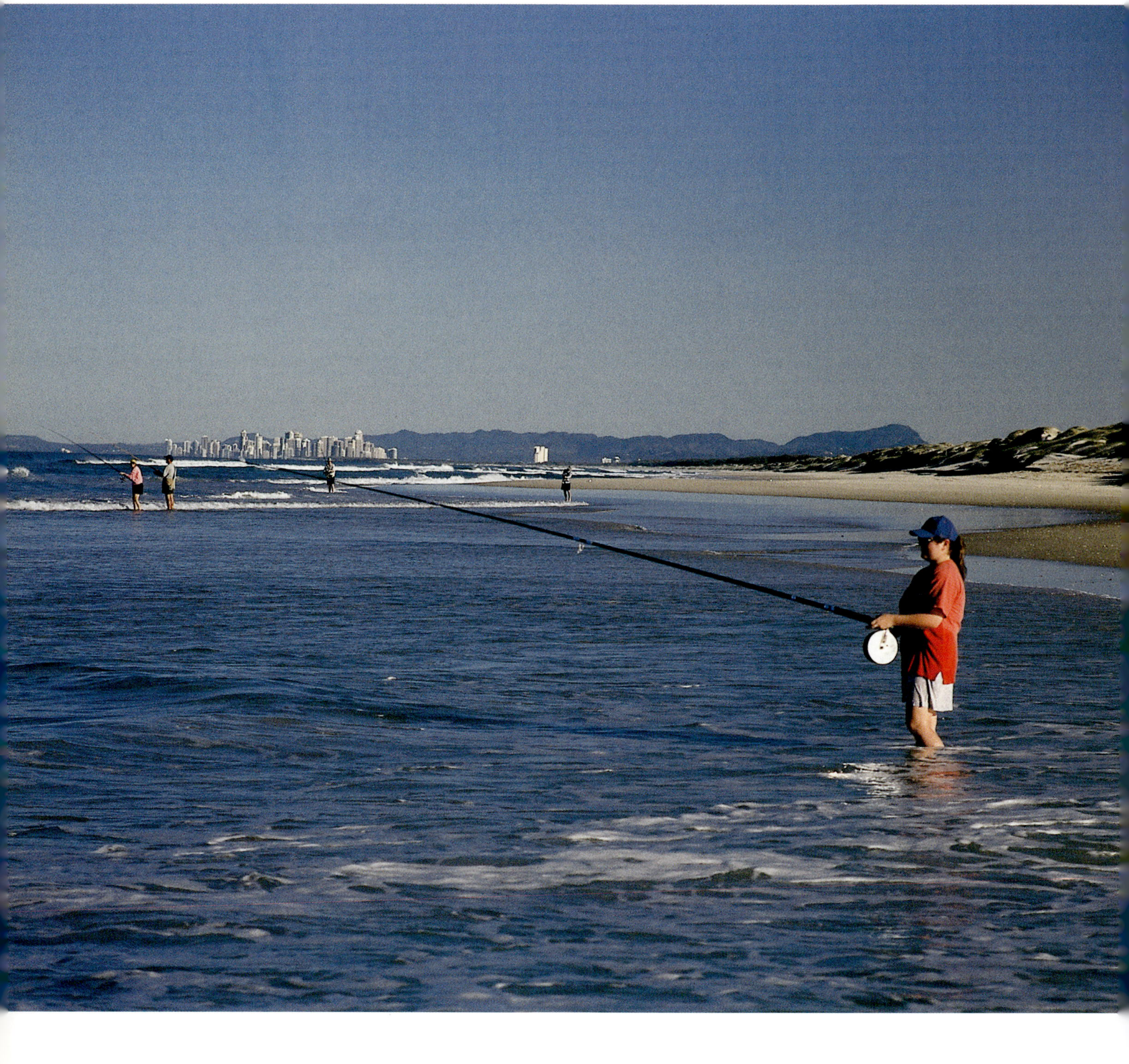

Gold Coast

The Gold Coast is now far more than just Surfers Paradise. It has become an international playground, with long, sandy beaches, towering apartment buildings, Indy cars and theme parks. Originally a beach holiday escape for Brisbane families in the 1950s and 1960s, the Gold Coast has grown to become a city of around 250,000 people that is literally expanding by the day.

I have been lucky enough to have fished here since the early 1980s when my wife and I visited every September school holidays. Always on hand were the fishing rods. I still regularly visit the Gold Coast with the TV show or on personal trips each year.

OPPOSITE: *Beach fishing on South Stradbroke Island with the Gold Coast skyline in the background.*

Beaches

The beaches of the Gold Coast are, of course, superb and surprisingly productive considering the activity that goes on. As a family we have fished off the beach in front of Cavill Avenue, in the very heart of Surfers Paradise. I can remember collecting pipis from the surf beach, which the kids and I then used for bait to catch yellowfin bream, sand whiting, sand flathead and dart. We rarely missed out. Some days we were even fishing amongst the swimmers. All of the beaches from Coolangatta, Burleigh Heads and Broadbeach through to South Stradbroke Island will produce fish.

ABOVE: *The Broadwater is a very popular boating and fishing spot for families.*

OPPOSITE: *Anglers 'pull' beach worms for bait off a Gold Coast beach.*

Nerang River

The Nerang River flows into the Broadwater at Southport. The fishing for sand whiting here can be very good using marine worms for bait. I have found that a worm bait will out-fish any other bait three to one. Worms can be gathered on the surf beaches or pumped along the sandbanks or bought from the bait shop. Bream, flathead, small giant trevally and mangrove jack are also caught in the Nerang River. The giant trevally hang around man-made structures, particularly in the canals. They are best targeted with lures cast into the structure and slowly retrieved. They are easily spooked, and usually if one is caught the others will become very lure shy.

Broadwater

The Broadwater is a long, slender body of water stretching from Southport to Jumpinpin. This very popular waterway is totally protected from the ocean swell by the land isthmus known as the Southport Spit (the home of Seaworld) and South Stradbroke Island. It is fed by the Nerang and Coomera rivers.

Big dusky flathead are the go here and can be caught right throughout the system by trolling deep-diving lures, casting soft plastics or flies, or with a live mullet fished unweighted. Much of the bottom is weedy and thus lures will get snagged up fairly regularly; however, if the lure isn't nudging the bottom or close to it, it isn't in the flathead's strike zone.

Several tag-and-release competitions are held in this area each year. There has been a real effort to conserve the large female breeding stock. The Broadwater, though, is still commercially netted despite tourism angling creating millions of dollars for the economy.

Jumpinpin

Mention marvellous bream water and, for me, Jumpinpin, which is the body of water separating the northern tip of South Stradbroke Island from North Stradbroke Island, springs to mind. This is some of the best fast-water 'breaming' around. Dave Bateman, the local

RIGHT: *Fishing writer Leeann Payne with a fine sand whiting she caught in the Nerang River.*

ABOVE OPPOSITE: *Small black marlin can be prolific in the cobalt-coloured currents off the Gold Coast.*

OPPOSITE: *The Gold Coast Seaway is an excellent fishing platform for tailor, mulloway, bream and sharks.*

champion angler, introduced me to the area and taught me the fine skills of hooking and catching speedy fish in even speedier water using light line. It's a totally specialist way of catching bream, and with the soft-action long rods with ultra-light line and pink nippers as bait, I found out why the 'Pin' has such a fine reputation.

The Gold Coast Seaway is the entrance to the Broadwater from

LEFT: *The islands in the Broadwater are a good haven for big dusky flathead. This one took a trolled lure.*

TOP: *Mangrove jack are found in surprisingly good numbers in Gold Coast estuaries.*

ABOVE: *A ripper sand flathead caught off the beach at South Stradbroke Island near Jumpinpin.*

the Coral Sea. It can be quite dangerous at times, but, like all bars, a little experience and common sense goes a long way. I have caught some whopping flathead from the rock walls here, as well as having some very busy sessions on the tailor.

Wave Break Island, which faces the entrance at the Gold Coast Seaway, is a very reliable spot for chopper tailor and other species that venture into the estuary from outside, such as mulloway, sharks and kingfish.

Offshore

Offshore fishing can be sensational. I am fortunate that local anglers and fishing writers David Green and Peter Pakula have always pointed me in the right direction. At times the small to medium-sized black marlin fishing can be superb. Trolling skirted lures, using the depth sounder to locate bait balls that are being herded by the ravenous marlin, is the way to go.

The reefs offshore, some of which are only two or three kilometres out from the Seaway, produce a range of species such as pearl perch and small snapper, which are locally called squire. Baits should be fished on the bottom, with fresh squid and strips of fish fillet or pilchards the best option. Trolling lures and live baits around these areas will produce Spanish mackerel, cobia and yellowtail kingfish. There is also some excellent fishing for big snapper using a berley of pilchard cubes and then casting an unweighted bait into the cube trail.

Conclusion

The Gold Coast has the great advantage over fishing environments further south of higher water temperatures. This brings a wide range of species on a year-round basis and also ensures that fish are actively chasing food. The beaches are still mostly in pristine condition, which is remarkable considering the development that has occurred.

Piscatorial Compass
Gold Coast, Queensland

How to get there: The Gold Coast is 80 kilometres from Brisbane via the South East Freeway and Pacific Motorway, taking the Gold Coast exit. You can fly directly into Coolangatta (on the southern Gold Coast) from any capital city with either Qantas or Virgin Blue.

Where to stay: The Gold Coast has a huge range of holiday accommodation. There are caravan parks all along the coast and thousands of holiday apartments. It is best to book early.

What to catch: Dusky flathead, mangrove jack, giant trevally, tailor, yellowfin bream, sand whiting, dart, sand flathead, mulloway, snapper, Spanish and spotted mackerel, yellowtail kingfish, cobia, teraglin, black marlin and various reef species.

Gear to take: You'll want light to medium threadline gear for fishing the estuary and breakwall, a ten-kilogram overhead rod and reel for trolling and reef species, plus a beach-fishing outfit.

When to go: Year round.

Guides and charters: There are many charter boats that fish offshore from the Gold Coast, as well as a few guides that fish the rivers and Broadwater.

Rex reckons: A top place to take the family fishing, the Gold Coast usually has great weather and a good variety of species to catch.

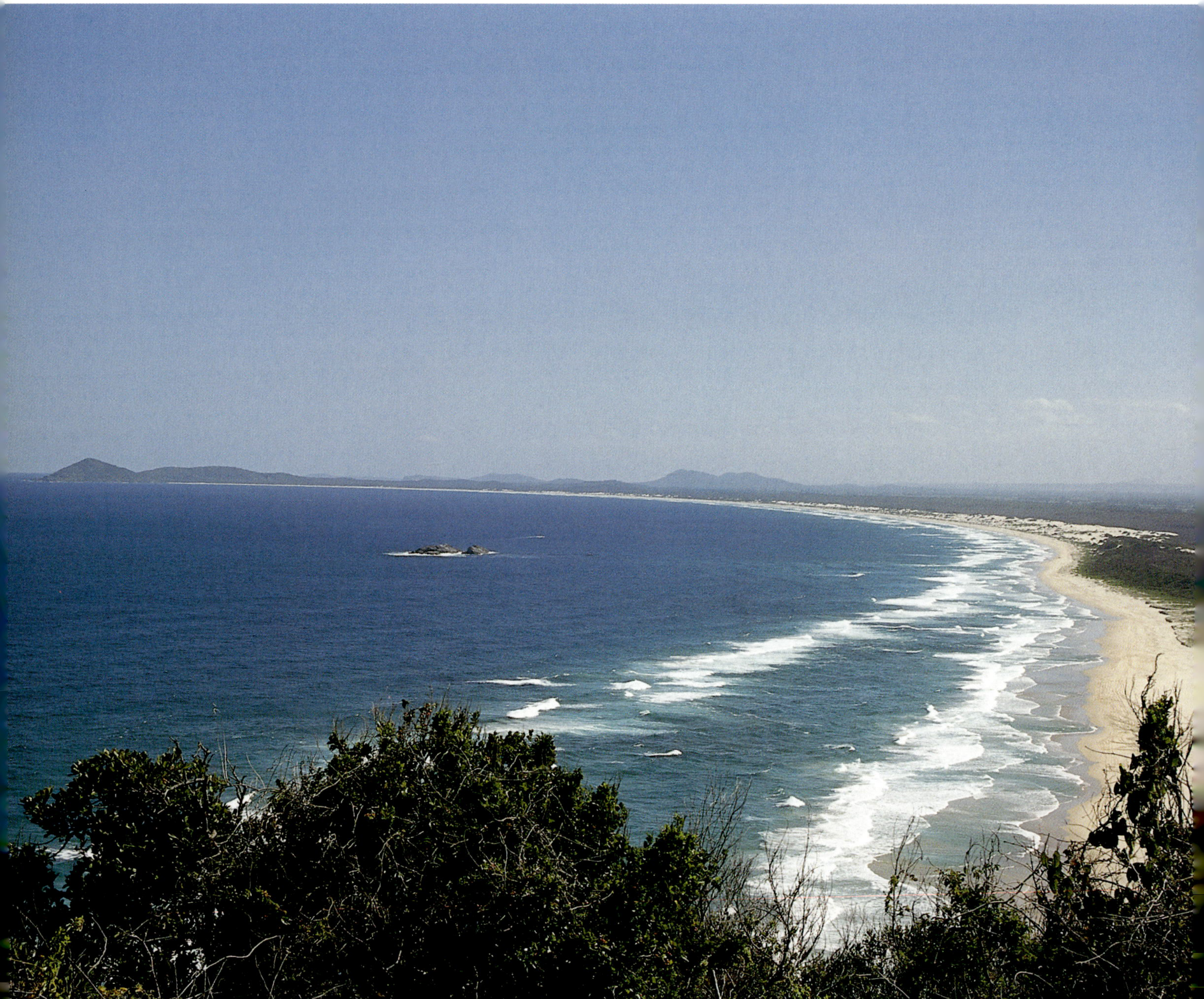

South West Rocks

Situated on the north coast of New South Wales between Coffs Harbour and Port Macquarie, this lovely little town is a favourite of mine. I've been there several times now and was hosted on each occasion by Lawrie and Julie McEnally, photojournalists and husband and wife charter boat team.

South West Rocks is tucked inside Trial Bay, just north of Hat Head National Park. Trial Bay has quite a bit of history behind it. The brig *Trial* ran aground here after being hijacked by a group of escaped convicts in 1816. They were headed for south-east Asia but fell a little short, folks. Ironically some 60 years later in the 1870s a gaol was constructed on top of the hill at Trial Bay. It was eventually closed and then reopened in 1915 to intern German citizens during World War One. Today, it is a museum and a very interesting place to visit.

The coastline in this part of the country is

OPPOSITE: *The view from the Smoky Bay lighthouse looking south towards Hat Head – just magnificent.*

ABOVE: *The magnificent Fish Rock offshore from South West Rocks — one of the fishiest places I've visited.*

LEFT: *Lisa Wantuch with her superb yellowtail kingfish caught at Fish Rock.*

OPPOSITE TOP: *A black marlin takes to the air just offshore from South West Rocks. Even small boats can get amongst the marlin action.*

OPPOSITE BELOW: *Big dusky flathead are worth chasing in the Macleay River. They can be targeted on all methods: bait, lure and fly.*

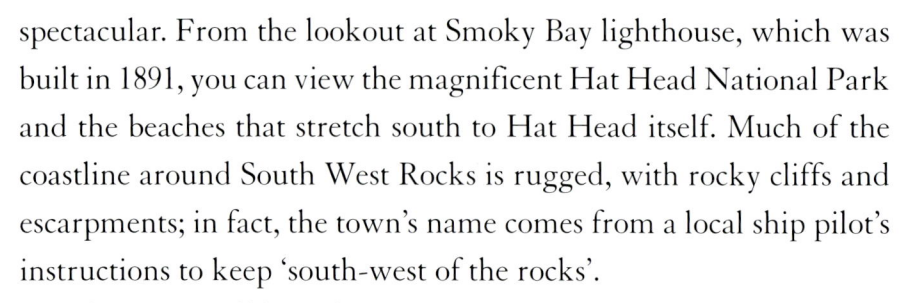

spectacular. From the lookout at Smoky Bay lighthouse, which was built in 1891, you can view the magnificent Hat Head National Park and the beaches that stretch south to Hat Head itself. Much of the coastline around South West Rocks is rugged, with rocky cliffs and escarpments; in fact, the town's name comes from a local ship pilot's instructions to keep 'south-west of the rocks'.

The waters offshore from South West Rocks are fairly deep close to the coast. Unlike much of the Australian east coast, the 'blue water' is found virtually as soon as you head out beyond Trial Bay; you can see game boats and small trailer boats trolling for marlin from the hilltop at Trial Bay. This 'blue water' sets South West Rocks apart from virtually any other fishing destination on this side of the continent.

Adding further to the piscatorial environment at South West Rocks is the magnificent Macleay River. The Macleay is a vast estuarine system that meanders down to the coast at South West Rocks before entering the Tasman Sea at Trial Bay. Quite deep in parts, the river has man-made breakwalls lining both sides in its lower reaches. Upstream it is characterised by sand banks, small islands, and channels, along with several tributaries that provide great interest for the angler.

There is a smorgasbord of species to be caught at South West Rocks. As the area is subtropical it gets a mix of both southern and northern species. Offshore there are black marlin, dolphin fish, yellowfin tuna, Spanish mackerel, cobia and yellowtail kingfish. Reef fish like pearl perch, snapper and sweetlip are also caught at times. Off the beaches there are dart, yellowfin bream, sand whiting, luderick, tailor and mulloway, and in the river you'll find big dusky flathead, mulloway, luderick, bream and whiting.

Offshore

Offshore from South West Rocks is dynamite, mainly because of the excellent deep water available close to shore. I once did battle with a 100-kilogram black marlin just three kilometres from the coast. The fish got away, but that's the luck of fishing. Black marlin are regular visitors to South West Rocks and many anglers don't bother with big expensive game boats – they get out there on good days in a half-cabin boat and troll for marlin with the best of them. The optimum times are between December and February.

There are good FADS (Fish Attracting Devices) out wide that have been placed there by New South Wales Fisheries and my mate Lawrie. The dolphin fish are very thick and we've caught fish to nearly 15 kilograms on slimy mackerel and sliced metal lures. I've also had a very good session here with Bushy, taking the dolphin fish on fly. These fish are great sport and terrific on the table.

On one trip we managed to get into some large cobia, also known as black kingfish. These chocolate and cream coloured fish are very good fighters, and may be mistaken for a shark when first sighted. They take very long and strong runs and it is best to underplay them early, as this is when they can do you big time on the reef and bust your line. Baits can be fished on the surface or on the bottom, and in my experience a fillet of fresh bonito is the most prized bait. The best time to fish for cobia is during the autumn months.

Fish Rock

Fish Rock is a marvellous fishery located just south of Smoky Cape. An underwater cave found here is a famous diving place, and as the current runs fast past the area it is also one of the fishiest spots at South West Rocks. This is the place where local lady angler Lisa Wantuch played and landed a massive yellowtail kingfish of nearly 15 kilograms a few years ago. It took a popper and was caught magnificently for the Channel 7 TV camera.

Bushy and I have also had some great success here free-swimming live slimy mackerel into the current flowing around Fish Rock, which were devoured by the ravenous kings. One king of about 12 kilograms took my bait literally at the back of the boat as I was winding in to check it after a few 'enquiries'. The best times to catch kingfish are from July to December.

Beaches and Rocks

Along the shore there are several rock washes where an early-morning unweighted pilchard will be hammered by some very big tailor, particularly in the winter months.

The beaches around the area are very good at times and I have had some wonderful sessions on sand whiting, bream and dart. The best bait to use is beachworms, which can be gathered on the spot.

Macleay River

The Macleay River has a very good population of fish, both from resident schools and from those that visit the river from the ocean. On one trip I saw several dolphins chasing baitfish well up the river near the boat ramp. I also saw some very large luderick working the south wall near the entrance. Yellowfin bream and mullet are plentiful and can be caught on nippers, which can be pumped upstream on the flats at low tide.

Mulloway, or jewfish, are also found in the river in good numbers. The larger fish seem to stay downstream along the wall

TOP: *Anglers pump for nippers upstream on the Macleay River.*

ABOVE: *A wahoo caught offshore from South West Rocks.*

OPPOSITE: *Fishing writer Phil Bennett with a lovely sailfish. These predators are occasional visitors to South West Rocks.*

and in deeper holes, while the smaller school fish are taken well up the river. The Jerseyville Bridge is a very popular place for the locals to chase the jewies.

Some giant dusky flathead are also taken from this river. Live mullet, herring or yakkas are very good baits, and the new soft plastic lures are taking their share of fish. Deeper holes or drop-offs found with the aid of a depth sounder are the best places to try along the length of the river. The duskies are best targeted from late spring through summer.

Conclusion

The local people welcome fishing tourists to the area, and in my experience they are very friendly and will help you at all times. As South West Rocks is a good five-hour drive from either Sydney or Brisbane, it remains something of a hideaway from the crowds of summer tourists.

Piscatorial Compass

South West Rocks, New South Wales

How to get there: South West Rocks is around 460 kilometres north of Sydney via the Pacific Highway, turning off the highway at Kempsey. It is approximately 500 kilometres south of Brisbane via the Pacific Highway.

Where to stay: Accommodation is plentiful, from the beautiful caravan park located on Horseshoe Bay beach through to holiday units, flats and private house rentals.

What to catch: Black marlin, yellowtail kingfish, cobia, yellowfin tuna, dolphin fish, Spanish mackerel, wahoo, mulloway, snapper, dart, dusky flathead, yellowfin bream, sand whiting, tailor and luderick.

Gear to take: Use light to medium threadline tackle for the river, and medium to heavy overhead gear for offshore.

When to go: Year round. There is always something on the bite at South West Rocks.

Guides and charters: Lawrie and Julie McEnally run Splashdown Charters.

Rex reckons: Fast-moving currents and a natural ambush point for predators make Fish Rock just offshore from South West Rocks one of the fishiest places I've visited.

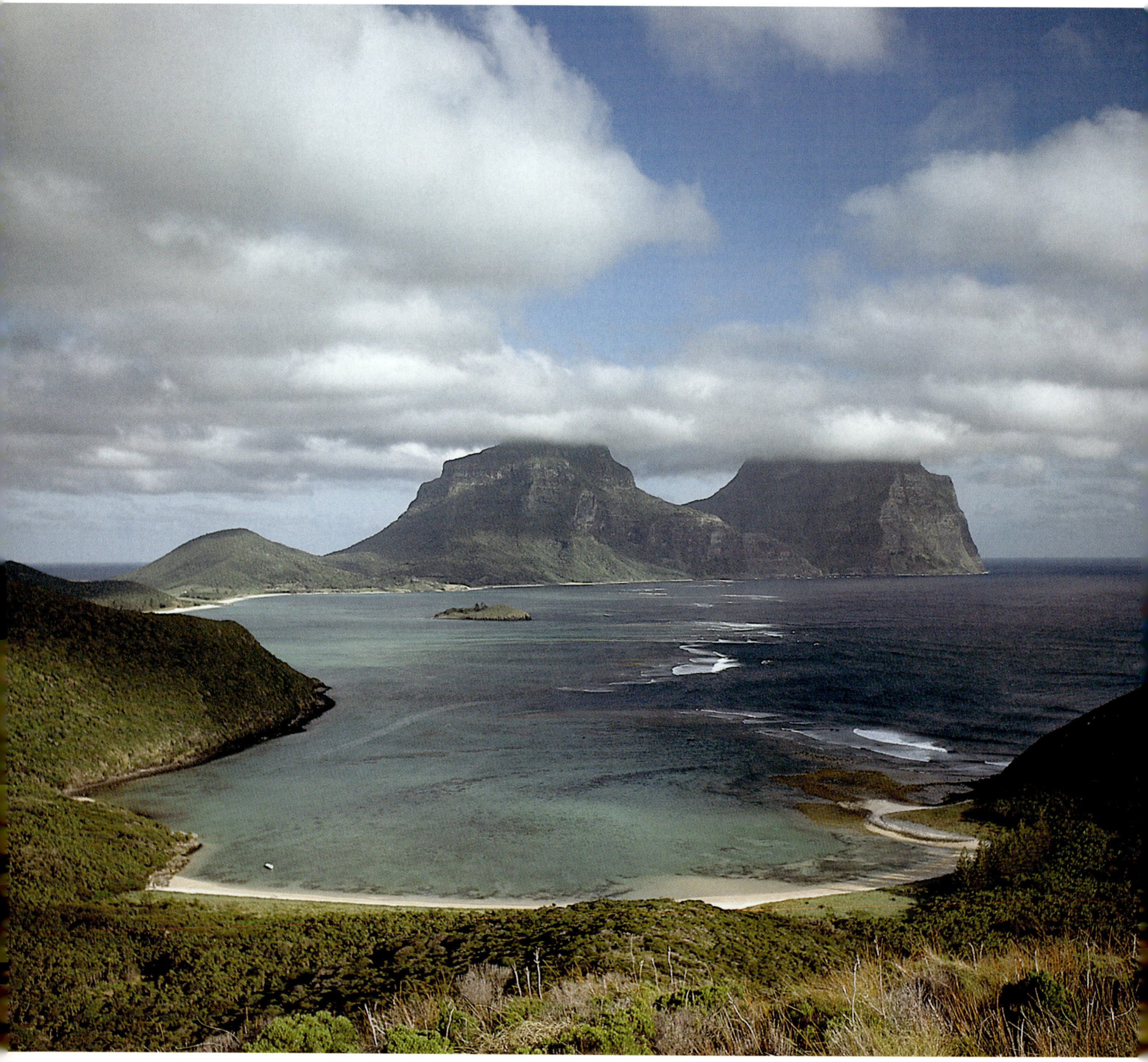

Lord Howe Island

If I had to be shipwrecked somewhere in the world, then Lord Howe Island would be right at the top of my list, folks. This beautiful island paradise is not way up in the tropics as you might expect, but about 700 kilometres off the New South Wales mid-north coast in the South Pacific ocean. In fact, Lord Howe can lay claim to having the southern-most coral reef in the world.

Lord Howe Island was discovered in 1788 by Lieutenant Henry Lidgbird Ball on Her Majesty's ship the HMS *Supply*. He was heading to Norfolk Island from the newly settled Sydney town when he spotted the towering peaks of the island, which are now named Mount Lidgbird and Mount Gower.

Many years later, whaling ships would work the waters around Lord Howe and the

OPPOSITE: *Spectacular Lord Howe Island.*

island was eventually settled by New Zealanders in the mid 1830s. Settlers from the Australian mainland also arrived, purchased land and set up various businesses. Today the island relies heavily on tourism, as commercial forms of fishing have been virtually eliminated to protect surrounding seas from exploitation.

The island was World Heritage listed in 1982 for its unique flora, as there are literally dozens of plants there not found anywhere else in the world. The bird life is both prolific and spectacular, with thousands of birds calling Lord Howe home. To preserve the natural beauty of Lord Howe, there is a restriction of 400 on the number of tourists allowed to visit at any one time.

The fishing around Lord Howe can be magnificent. I have been to this magical place three times. Each time I stayed at the Pinetrees

Guest House and was hosted by local fishing legend Gary Crombie. Gary runs the bakery with his wife and they know a great deal about the fishing on the island.

Inshore and Offshore

There are a few species that fascinate me when I'm on Lord Howe. One of them is the bluefish. It stands out like a beacon when found, and it is just a matter of throwing some berley (Gary's bread of course), attracting the fish, getting its attention and then fly-fishing with bread flies, which are simply flies tied with fur and wool to imitate a small piece of bread. The fishing is fun and easy, as it should be. I have done two very good television stories on these fish.

Whilst fishing the lee side (Australian mainland side) of the island I have also noticed some very big Australian salmon. While not in the South Australian or Western Australian class of fish, I have caught salmon up to nearly four kilograms on light fly gear (seven or eight weight). I've also had some great fun casting small silver lures to salmon in the three-kilogram class.

I have come across huge yellowtail kingfish, some of which

BELOW: *A ripper trevally caught offshore from Lord Howe.*

RIGHT: *There are several deepwater areas quite close to the island that offer a variety of pelagic species to chase on lure or fly.*

OPPOSITE: *Hooked up in the aqua-coloured inshore waters of Lord Howe.*

ABOVE: *Even small kingfish make great targets on fly tackle.*

LEFT: *This is what Lord Howe is all about – big kingfish and great scenery. That's Balls Pyramid behind the angler.*

OPPOSITE: *Yours truly puckering up to the unusual 'double-header' or hump-headed wrasse.*

would weigh over 30 kilograms, and have seen many sharks including small whalers, black-tip reef sharks and even a small hammerhead. Tusk fish of around four kilograms are also present.

Balls Pyramid to the south of the island is a massive fish-attracting structure that rises out of the ocean. Kingfish are common here, and will test any angler's mettle and tackle.

The three main species of marlin – black, blue and striped – plus yellowfin tuna and other game fish such as wahoo are caught around the island, mostly by trolling lures. The best time of year is from summer to autumn. Note that the wind can be a hazard for keen game fisherman in the South Pacific, but suitable days do present fairly frequently.

Land-based opportunities

The jetty in the sheltered lagoon on the eastern side of the island is a very busy place, with charter boats and supply boats constantly berthing and casting off. In between, though, there are some great fish to be taken. For light-line enthusiasts the garfish here are as good as anywhere, and there are plenty of them. Some very big specimens have been taken and garfish are relatively easy to catch.

Although there is no fishing at Ned's Beach, it is essential that you visit at fish-feeding time. Every afternoon a local identity takes down a bin full of fish scraps from the local restaurants and feeds the fish. It is amazing to see most of the people on the island gravitate to the beach late in the afternoon for this event.

The variety and size of the fish that are attracted to this area are mind-boggling. I am told that a majority of the fish just 'hang around' Ned's because they know that they will get a good feed each day at that time.

Conclusion

Visiting the tropical lagoons is a delightful way to observe fish thriving in their natural environment. My measure of any place is if I can go home and say to my wife Lynne that we will go back as paying tourists. Lord Howe is one such place. I describe it as a jewel in the middle of the ocean, and a must-see destination.

Piscatorial Compass

Lord Howe Island, New South Wales

How to get there: Lord Howe is approximately 700 kilometres north-east of Sydney. Qantas fly regularly to the island via Sydney and Coffs Harbour.

Where to stay: Pinetrees Guest House is wonderful.

What to catch: Yellowtail kingfish, bluefish, Australian salmon, hump-headed wrasse (double-header), garfish, tusk fish, yellowfin tuna, black, blue and striped marlin, wahoo, sharks and various species of trevally.

Gear to take: Use a medium ten-kilogram overhead rod and reel. Fly-fishing outfits from six to nine weight are ideal.

When to go: Year round.

Guides and charters: Gary Crombie was excellent.

Rex reckons: Some of the kingfish are huge. If you don't get control early, it's good night! For a real piscatorial and scenic thrill take a trip to Balls Pyramid.

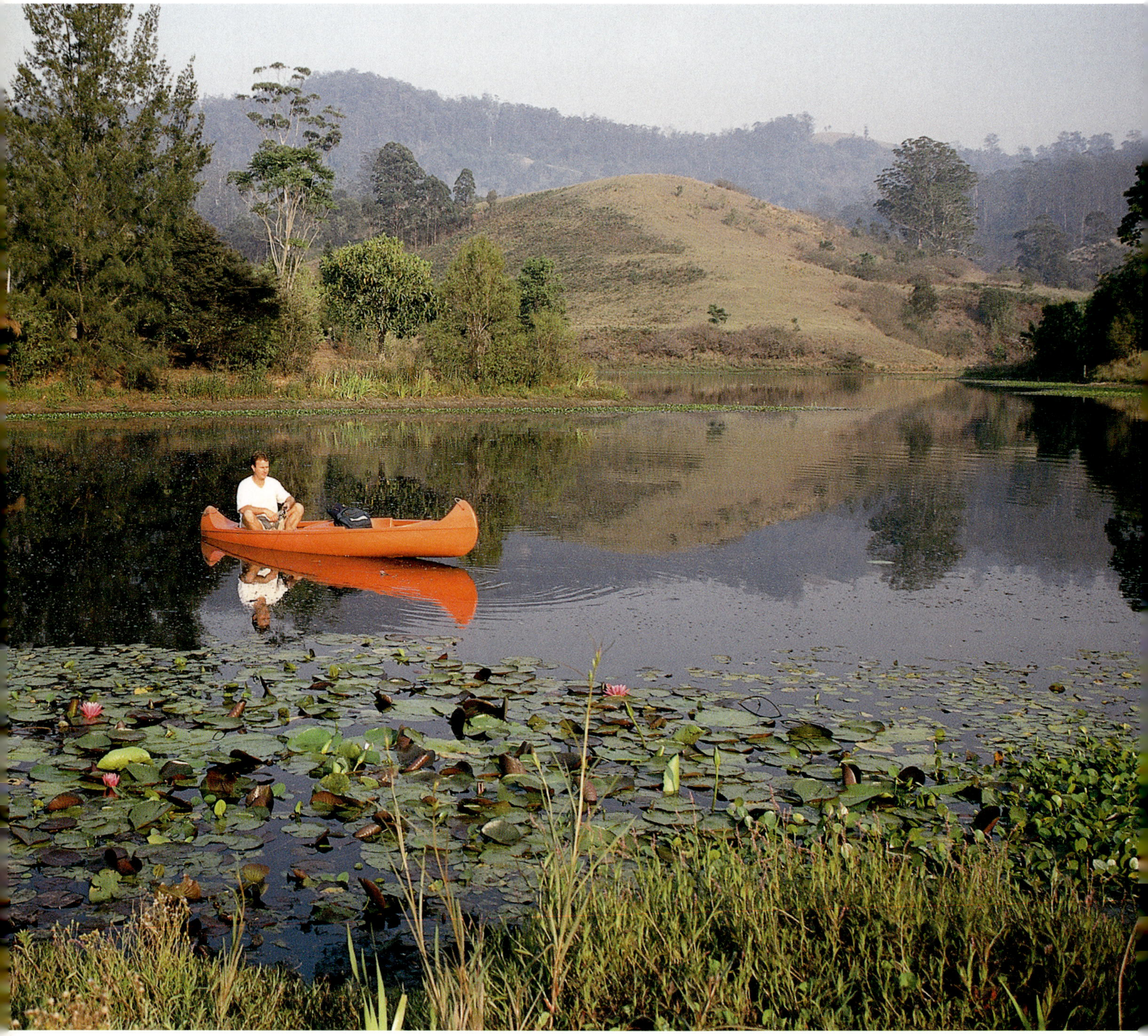

Hawkesbury River

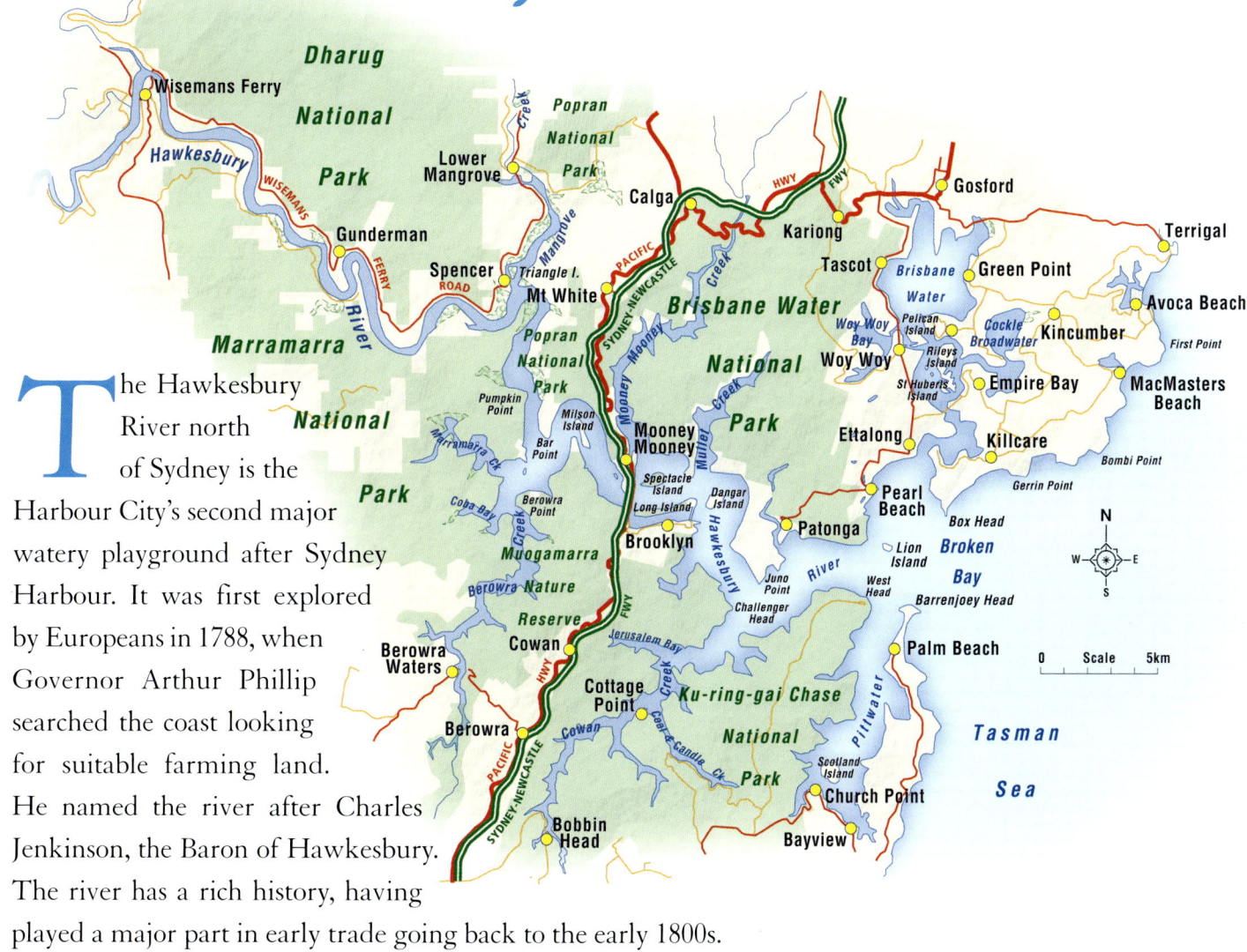

The Hawkesbury River north of Sydney is the Harbour City's second major watery playground after Sydney Harbour. It was first explored by Europeans in 1788, when Governor Arthur Phillip searched the coast looking for suitable farming land. He named the river after Charles Jenkinson, the Baron of Hawkesbury. The river has a rich history, having played a major part in early trade going back to the early 1800s.

OPPOSITE: *The upper reaches of the Hawkesbury River offer some great lure and fly-fishing for Australian bass.*

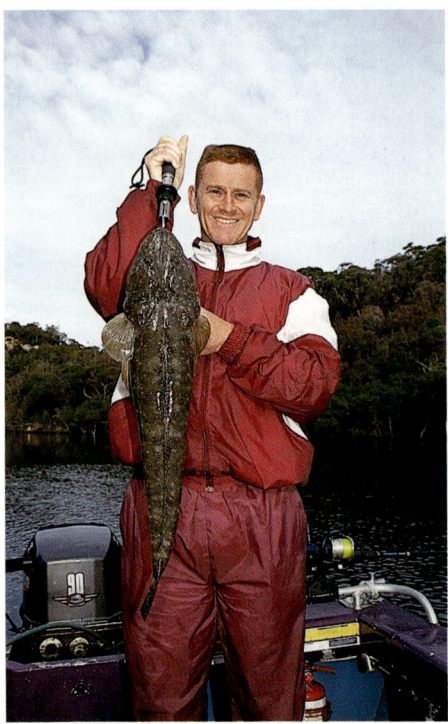

The Hawkesbury is a huge system comprising the upper freshwater reaches of Cowan Waters, Broken Bay and Pittwater. It holds an immense volume of water, which begins as small creeks and run-offs that run many kilometres upstream to form the main river. In the lower reaches there are myriad arms and branches, which together form one of the most impressive and popular waterways in this country.

LEFT: *Yours truly and David Lockwood with our catch of Hawkesbury hairtail.*

ABOVE: *The Hawkesbury is renowned as a producer of big dusky flathead.*

OPPOSITE: *A beautiful Hawkesbury jewfish taken on a soft plastic lure.*

The River

I have fished areas throughout this system, including well upstream around Wisemans Ferry, which except on extreme tides is mainly fresh water. In the early 1990s I fished there with John Bethune, who is recognised as a top bass angler. We had a very good session and caught some quality bass over a two-day period. Not to be confused with the bass is the estuary perch; while they look similar, they are two different species. Some excellent perch also hold around the snags in this river and the best method is a soft plastic lure allowed to sink and slowly raised up and off the bottom.

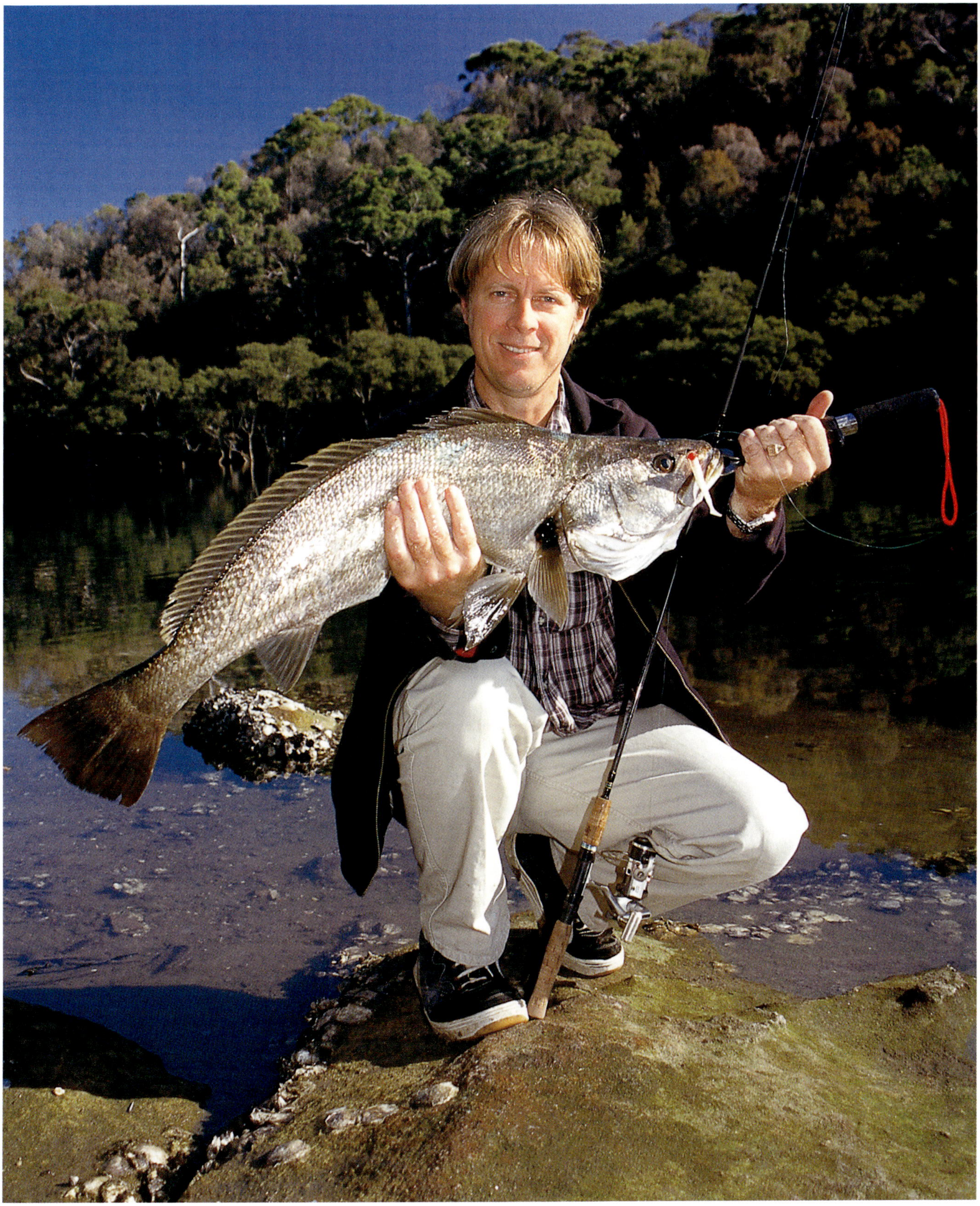

Below the fresh water in the tidal reaches, the Hawkesbury is a lovely estuarine system offering many terrific fishing areas. Quality catches of bream and dusky flathead, mullet and some sand whiting can be taken here. The best baits in my experience are cut pilchards, beach worms, peeled prawns and pipis.

There are plenty of structures like rock walls, snags, sand flats, oyster racks and bridge pylons in the river. Huge jewfish, or mulloway as they are called in the south, inhabit these areas, as well as big schools of smaller jew known as 'soapies' or 'schoolies'. Serious jewfish anglers fish large dead or live baits, often through the night.

I have also fished the Hawkesbury successfully for that amazing fish, the hairtail. Quite a few years ago, fishing and boating writer David Lockwood took me out at night on the Hawkesbury in search of these ferocious-looking predators. Hairtails are silvery fish with fangs like a barracouta, and they inhabit areas like Akuna Bay, Jerusalem Bay and Coal Creek during the cold winter months. They are mainly taken at night, and it looks like fairyland when all the floats are lit up and the lights from the boats are on. Ganged hooks and wire traces are the only way to go as the hairtail will make short work of anything else.

Broken Bay

The river eventually widens into Broken Bay, which when weather permits turns on some remarkable fishing. Large schools of Australian salmon, yellowtail kingfish and tailor, as well as striped tuna and bonito, come in regularly enough to offer some exciting fishing around Barrenjoey Head. The birds working the various schools of fish will soon divulge where you must throw in your line.

A couple of years ago I fished with Greg Joyes of Calm Water Fishing Charters off Woy Woy in the channel that flows from the Brisbane Waters system into Broken Bay. Unfortunately a huge southerly was blowing the tops off the waves in this normally serene and beautiful area, and this, combined with some huge tidal currents, made fishing difficult.

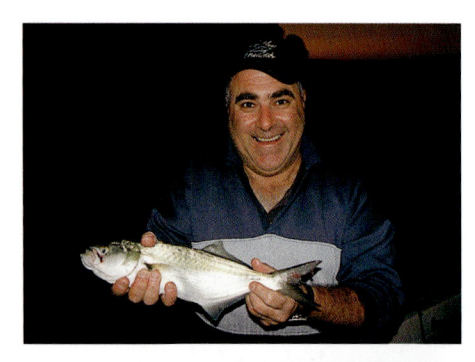

TOP: *Fishing writer Colin Buckley with a tailor caught on a lure in Broken Bay.*

ABOVE: *Jewfish are the jewel in the crown of Hawkesbury River fishing.*

Our target was a big jewfish. I've always had a soft spot for these magnificent fish, elusive predators that have to be matched by a skilled angler as they don't simply jump onto the end of your line. Jewies require patience, persistence, a willingness to find the right bait and the ability to put in the hours.

As I've said many times on my fishing show, preparation is the key to success; very rarely do rewards come from just turning up and throwing in a line. The best bait for the jewies is the pike, and so before we started we trolled a few up on lures to use as live bait.

We used rather substantial light game-fishing gear on the charter, because we knew that if a big jewie came along, landing it in the fast current would be a challenge. The depth of water was around three metres right in the middle of the channel, however there were several deep holes that many smaller fish hold up in. Jewies wait in ambush around these holes.

Although we missed out on the big jewie that time, we got a couple of juvenile 'soapies', and we also managed to catch a lovely 4.5-kilogram flathead and some nice bream on camera, thanks to Greg's expertise and persistence.

Pittwater, which runs from inside Barrenjoey Head and all the way behind Sydney's northern beaches, is a popular harbour for yachts and game boats. I have fished here and caught yellowfin bream and sand whiting. Being so close to the entrance to the ocean, Pittwater regularly gets a flush of species and bait fish from the open water. It seemed that that every wharf or jetty I went to had large bream lurking around every pylon.

Conclusion

The Hawkesbury is a remarkable fishery, folks. I love the wilderness feel, and the fishing can be sensational. They need to get rid of the prawn trawlers though, as these commercial operators take too many juvenile species as bycatch. They are a very powerful lobby group but hopefully Fisheries will see the light. The Hawkesbury could only get better as a result.

Piscatorial Compass

Hawkesbury River, New South Wales

How to get there: From the centre of Sydney to Palm Beach on the northern beaches, and access to Broken Bay, is around 40 kilometres via the Pittwater and Barrenjoey roads. The Hawkesbury River is crossed via the freeway from Sydney to Newcastle when exiting Sydney via Hornsby.

Where to stay: There is ample accommodation around the Hawkesbury and Brisbane Waters area. Day-tripping from Sydney is also practical.

What to catch: Jewfish (mulloway), dusky flathead, yellowfin bream, mullet, sand whiting, luderick, Australian salmon, tailor, Australian bass and estuary perch.

Gear to take: Try a ten-kilogram medium overhead rod and reel for jewie and flathead fishing, and light threadline and spinning gear for other estuarine species.

When to go: Year round.

Guides and charters: Greg Joyes of Calm Water Fishing Charters and Craig McGill of Fishabout Tours are the best guides in this area.

Rex reckons: The Hawkesbury offers some of the best fishing close to a major city in the world. When fishing there you feel like you're a million miles from civilisation.

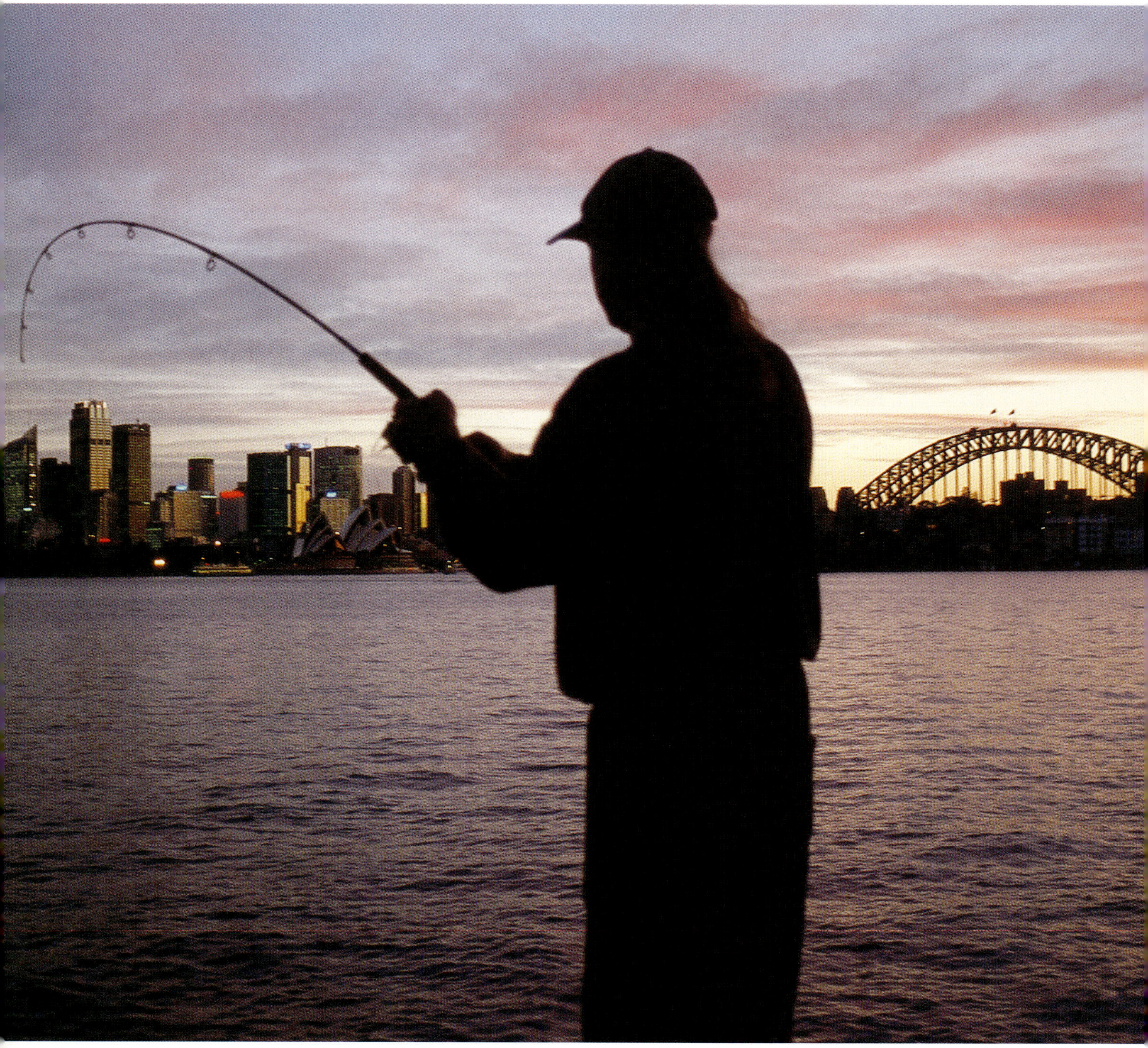

Sydney

Sydney is Australia's largest city, and with its famous harbour and beaches it is a very fishy place. One thing is for sure folks, no one in the First Fleet would have gone hungry if there was a fisherman or two amongst them when they arrived in 1788!

For most of the year Sydney has a warm climate, which means higher water temperatures and an increase in fish activity compared to the area further south. Positioned right on the edge of the eastern coast of Australia, ocean currents from the north literally glide right past Sydney Harbour, bringing with them all manner of species from marlin and yellowfin tuna to subtropical species such as dolphin fish and spotted mackerel.

The harbour itself, along with Botany Bay and Port Hacking, offer some excellent estuary fishing in spite of the fact that four million people live on their doorstep in metropolitan Sydney. The most common species are flathead, bream, mullet,

OPPOSITE: *An early-morning fish on Sydney's spectacular harbour – what a time to be on the water.*

tailor, bonito, small snapper, Australian salmon, silver trevally, yellowtail kingfish, calamari squid and leatherjacket.

Offshore there is trolling for black and striped marlin and yellowfin tuna, and snapper, morwong, John Dory, ocean perch and kingfish are also common reef and deep-sea species found here. The beaches and rocks offer bream, sand whiting, jewfish, drummer, blackfish (luderick), bonito, striped tuna and squid, to name a few.

ABOVE: *Sydney Harbour offers many fine fishing spots with access to deep water and ocean currents.*

ABOVE OPPOSITE: *Big bream from a big capital city.*

BELOW OPPOSITE: *Bonito are one of the most common species caught offshore from Sydney, particularly when trolling lures near rocky headlands.*

Sydney Harbour

Sydney Harbour is undoubtedly one of the most beautiful waterways in the world. Tourists flock to see it and the fantastic attractions on its foreshores, notably the Harbour Bridge and the Opera House. Visitors and locals alike can catch a ferry to locations all around the harbour and take in the spectacular scenery.

I have enjoyed some very good fishing in the harbour and have fond memories of fishing with Craig McGill, taking some very good Australian salmon and bonito around the heads. I've also fished along the rocks and washes of North Head and caught very good-sized bream in the white water. On another occasion I had a ball hooking tailor to two kilograms on unweighted pilchards cast from a drifting boat. Bait-fish profile lures also work a treat on the tailor and salmon.

Good areas to fish inside the harbour include the fashionable Sydney beachside suburbs of Rose Bay, Watsons Bay, Double Bay and Vaucluse, which is renowned for its bream.

Further into the harbour, from the area around Darling Point on one side to Mosman Bay on the other, there are good catches of bream, mulloway and leatherjacket, among other species. Then, under the Harbour Bridge and to the west towards the Parramatta River, there are excellent areas for flathead, bream, jewfish and tailor. The area off Manns Point can be productive, with the channels near both the Parramatta River and the Lane Cove River worth a try.

There are many vantage points around the harbour for the shore-based angler, too. Soft plastics and hard-bodied lures are used regularly around structures like bridge pylons, wharves and jetties. In the lower reaches between Watsons Bay and the heads I've also done very well on large flathead taken casting lures or using live mullet or yellowtail scad.

There are areas that hold good numbers of yellowtail kingfish, and I took a nice one of six kilograms early one morning fishing near the structure known as 'the Wedding Cake', which is a shipping channel marker in the middle of the harbour. Fresh squid and long soft plastic lures called Sluggos will take quality kings here. Craig McGill is the master at catching kings in this area.

Jewfish are prolific in the system, and at prime times of first and last light, or during the full moon, there have been several very good fish taken especially near the main Sydney Harbour Bridge.

I can also recommend fishing with either bloodworms or peeled

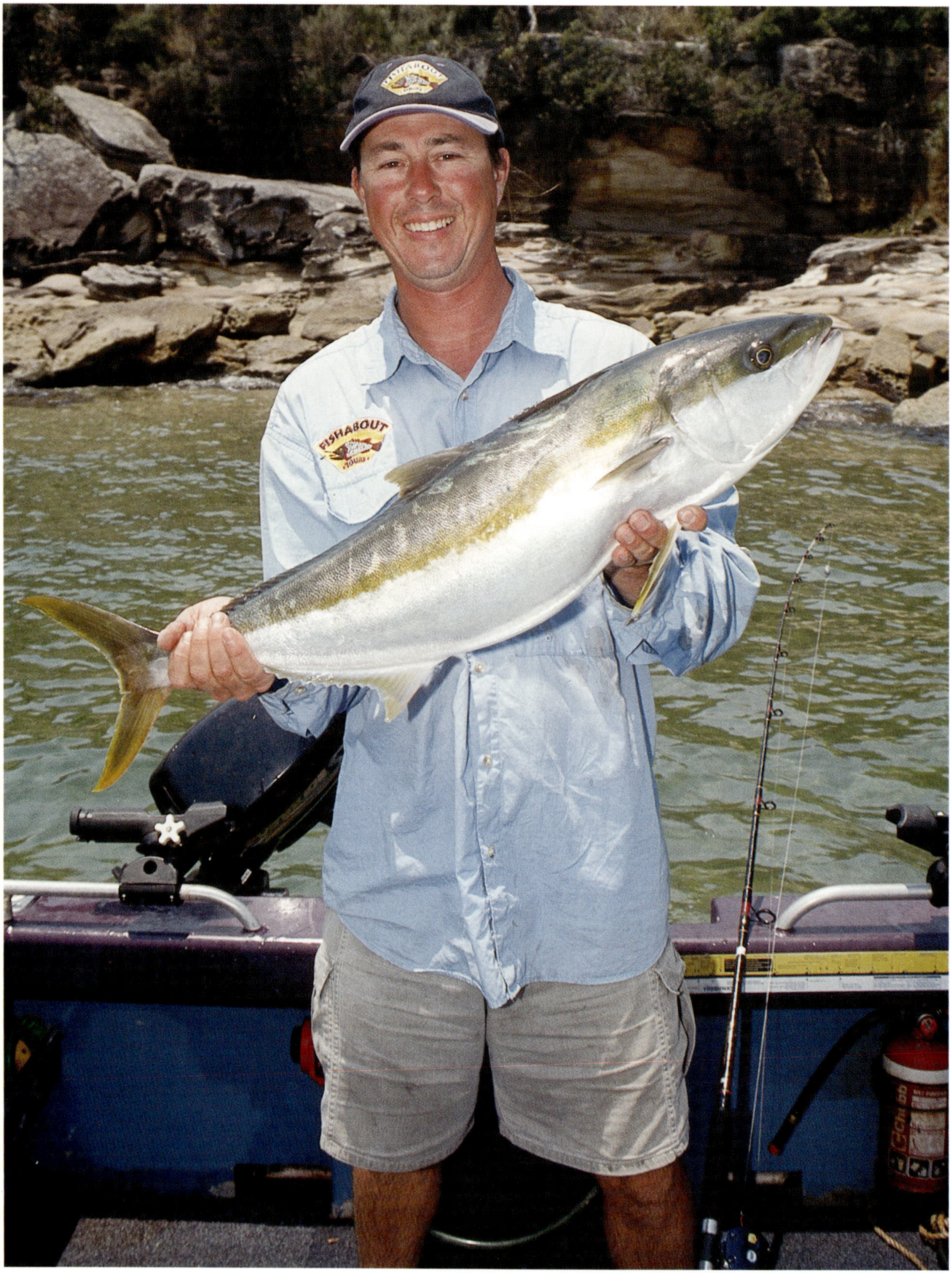

prawns for yellowfin whiting in the Manly area. I have had a couple of good mornings in the sand areas there. The aquarium at Manly is also well worth a look.

In Middle Harbour, to the north of Port Jackson, there are some tremendous land-based fishing areas. Bream are plentiful at times from the rocky outcrops, and flathead and mulloway are present in good numbers. Freshly caught squid is a prime bait here. I am also very impressed with the leatherjacket population in Middle Harbour; they are very good to eat in spite of their appearance and the fiddly process you have to go through to clean them.

The North Harbour, to the east of Middle Harbour, is also excellent for rock fishing. Although this area does not fish as well as Middle Harbour, there are usually good catches of bream, snapper, trevally, kingfish and flathead to be had.

Botany Bay

Botany Bay is not quite as productive as Sydney Harbour and is often more difficult to fish, being open and subject to large waves in windy conditions. Nevertheless, it has recently benefited from being designated a 'recreational fishing only' zone, which means it is now completely free of commercial netting. The result is that in the last couple of years there has been an explosion in estuarine fish populations there, from small snapper to tailor, salmon, dusky flathead, bream and yellowtail scad.

I witnessed first hand the improvement in Botany Bay when fishing aboard Scotty Lyon's charter boat with various guests on the TV show. These guests included young tenor Jason Weston, country singer Adam Brand and dual Olympic gold-medalist Michael Diamond.

Each trip onto Botany Bay produced an amazing array of species. I fished near the oil refinery, which is a huge structure for fish. With the aid of a little berley we got some fantastic action, nothing huge, but good quantities of fish including bream, yellowtail scad, tailor and flathead. It showed me that the future of this fishery is virtually

TOP: *Tailor are one of the most common species caught in Sydney Harbour and Botany Bay.*

ABOVE: *John Dory are caught both within the harbour and offshore.*

OPPOSITE: *Master Sydney angler Craig McGill with a superb Sydney kingfish.*

assured, as the all-important juvenile fish are now allowed to grow and won't end up in a net.

Port Hacking

Port Hacking is south of Botany Bay and provides some of the best fishing in and around Sydney. It is very shallow, and vast sandbanks are exposed at low tide. The main species found here are yellowfin bream, mullet, dusky flathead, and sand whiting. The extensive sandbanks hold good numbers of pink nippers, which are very good bait in the system.

The water runs quite fast on the tide in this area and a boat is an advantage, however there are several fine shore-based spots to catch a decent fish. One session I had resulted in good numbers of bream and flathead, and some huge six-spined leatherjacket. The best bait that day was small pieces of striped tuna.

Land-based fishing is quite limited however, so you'd be better off hovering with a boat so you can explore the sand flats and deep channels that exist throughout the estuary. A good variety of species is encountered, from large dusky flathead on the flats to bream and silver trevally around the jetties and wharves.

ABOVE: *A lovely dusky flathead caught in Sydney Harbour.*

OPPOSITE: *Andrew Ettinghausen (ET) with a fine sand whiting he caught in his home water of Port Hacking.*

Conclusion

I've made countless trips to film various segments in Sydney over the years, from an early show when Steve Starling and myself caught John Dory and perch out wide, to terrific trips on the harbour with Craig McGill fishing with a wide variety of people. Every time I visit Sydney I marvel at its shining harbour, which exists in pristine splendour with a huge cosmopolitan city around it, and yet still offers very good fishing.

Piscatorial Compass

Sydney, New South Wales

How to get there: Sydney is located on the south-eastern coast of Australia, approximately halfway between Melbourne via the Hume Highway and Brisbane via the Pacific Highway. Flights from all capital cities are numerous.

Where to stay: Accommodation is generally fairly expensive in Sydney, particularly close to the waterways. It is best to stay in the outer suburbs and commute.

What to catch: Snapper, morwong, yellowtail kingfish, John Dory, yellowfin bream, sand whiting, jewfish (mulloway), dusky flathead, mullet, calamari squid, silver trevally, tailor, Australian salmon, bonito, drummer, blackfish, leatherjacket, black and striped marlin, yellowfin tuna and sharks.

Gear to take: Use a light threadline rod and reel for bait fishing and spinning with lures for estuarine species. Try a ten-kilogram medium overhead rod and reel for reef species, and game-fishing tackle for pelagics.

When to go: Year round. Best variety in October to May.

Guides and charters: Craig McGill of Fishabout Tours is a winner on Sydney Harbour as is Scott Lyons for Botany Bay. There are many offshore and game-fishing charters available.

Rex reckons: First light on Sydney Harbour is something to behold.

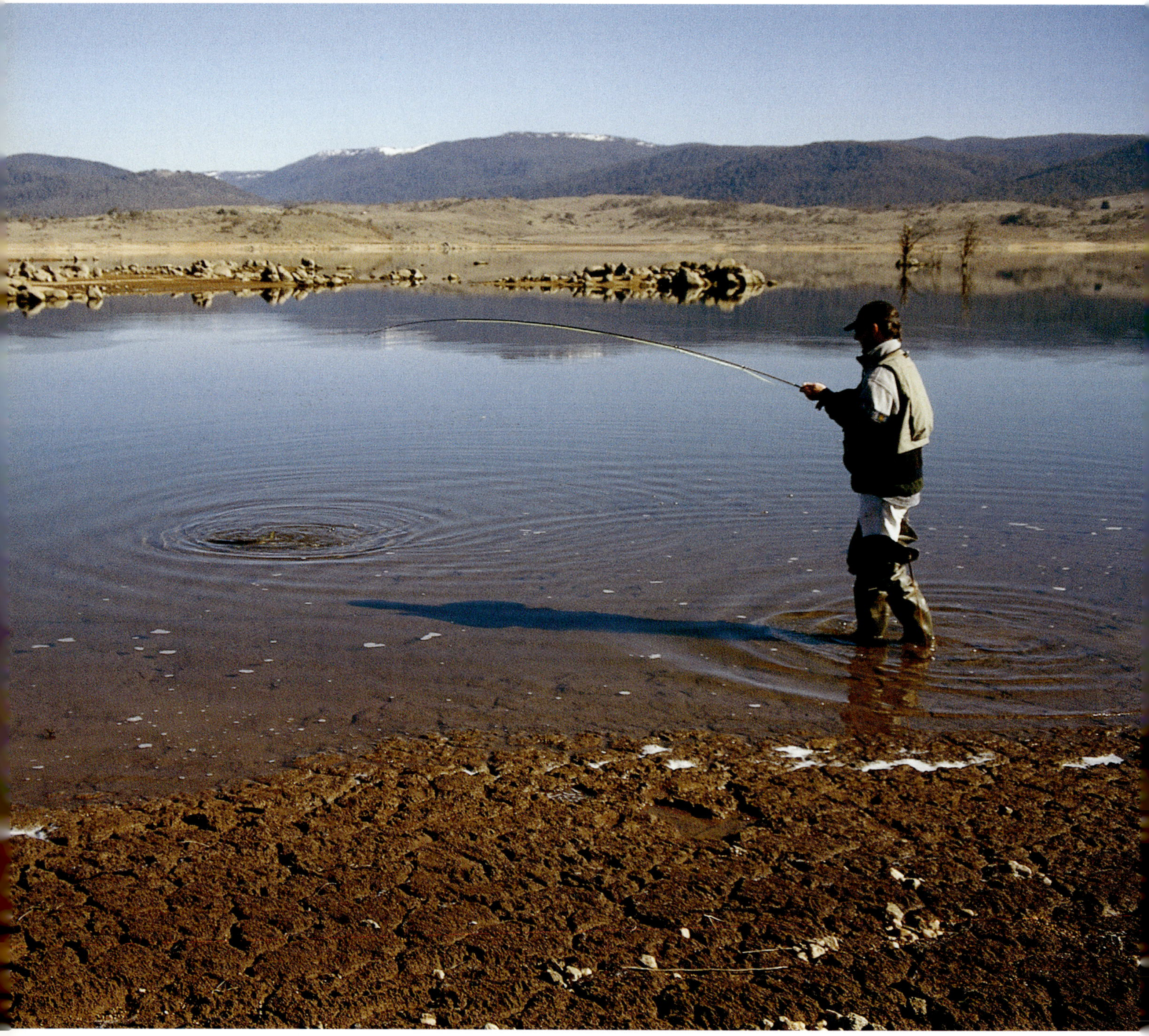

Snowy Mountains

The Snowy Mountains are located about six hours' drive south-west of Sydney in southern New South Wales, near the border with Victoria. The Snowies are most famous for the hydroelectricity power scheme that took almost two decades to build, Kosciusko National Park and snowfields such as Thredbo and Perisher Valley. This area is also the main trout-fishing destination on the Australian mainland. There are several fine storages that hold very good populations of salmonids, and despite years of drought, there are enough streams to keep any angler happy.

OPPOSITE: *Fly-fishing on Lake Jindabyne on a windless day – magical.*

Lake Eucumbene

Lake Eucumbene was created as part of the hydroelectric scheme with the damming of the Eucumbene River. Completed in 1958, it is the largest lake in the Snowy Mountains region, and has been well stocked with brown and rainbow trout since its creation.

I first fished here in 1972, which was the year of my marriage to my wife Lynne. I thought I would do the right thing and take her to a luxurious place – the Providence Portal Lodge, which in those days was an old army hut. Despite the single beds and almost freezing conditions, we managed to battle on, and this year celebrated our 32nd wedding anniversary.

One of the first places we fished on the lake was the Providence Portal Arm in the north-western section. We were trolling in this area just prior to the closing of the trout season. The brown trout had commenced their spawning run into the portal, preparing for their annual run up the Eucumbene River. Lynne would keep a watch out for a fish rising and I would steer the boat so that our trolled lures would go straight over where the rise was. Most times it was bingo.

That trip I saw the amazing sight of wall-to-wall trout moving

LEFT: *Trolling is a very effective way to catch trout on Lake Eucumbene.*

BELOW: *Thumping brown trout caught on a lure in Jindabyne.*

ABOVE OPPOSITE: *A lovely Snowy Mountains trout swims off after bring released.*

BELOW OPPOSITE: *There are many picturesque little streams like this one to fish in the Snowies.*

up the river to spawn. One morning I walked to a spot they called the Suicide Hole, and saw several anglers carrying sackloads of ripe fish out of the gorge. I have never fished for spawning fish and was pretty shocked.

The Providence Portal area, even out of spawning time, is a very good fish-producing arm of Eucumbene. I have had some fine sessions in the area where the water comes out of the Portal from Tantangara Dam. The constant flow of this water offers good cover and food opportunities for trout. I have successfully fished here with a slow-sinking fly line, using a green or a red and black Matuka Longtail fly. I have also taken some very good trout on unweighted scrubworms allowed to run and then sink as the current allows. Come to think of it, there are not many trout that will refuse an unweighted juicy scrubby, properly presented.

Although I have never used a mudeye in this part of the lake, I have in plenty of other areas, and I am told the bug mudeye is very good in November and December fished under a float against the drop-offs to some of the deeper sections of the Portal arm.

On another occasion, I had a great afternoon fishing with the wind at my back. It was February and the grasshoppers were big and plentiful. The trout were on the grasshoppers in their droves on the lee bank. The gusts of the westerly shot many of the unsuspecting hoppers into the water and some seriously big browns and smaller rainbows had decided to have a hopper feast.

I only had my spinning gear with me but I improvised. Using a small piece of stick for a casting weight, I tied a dropper about 50 centimetres under the stick. I then fished out onto the edge with a large single hopper. The fish went ape droppings, folks. My two-hour session reaped 11 trout, mainly small rainbows of about 750 grams, but included two magnificent browns of over two kilograms. It was a matter of me being in the right place at the right time.

Anglers Reach further down the Providence Portal Arm is also a very popular area. I have had good success there trolling flat line, with lures such as Tassie Devils, Super Duper, Deep-Diving Rapalas, and

ABOVE: *A nice rainbow trout caught whilst trolling with attractors.*

RIGHT: *A nice brown caught on fly from the Eucumbene River.*

OPPOSITE: *Brrrrr... it gets cold when trout-fishing in the Snowies!*

believe it or not, Longtail flies weighted with a barrel sinker. I have fine memories of this area as it was the base for the late John West.

He was a local legend who gave fishing reports every Saturday morning on my fishing program on radio 3DB in Melbourne.

Another area where I have had success is the 'Seven Gates'. This fronts onto the north-east shore of Frying Pan Arm. I usually fish here before Christmas as the snow melt causes the lake to rise over new ground of sprouting grass. A humble bunch of worms or a single scrubworm will always get some response.

Similarly, an excellent spot is right into the top of Frying Pan Arm. Early in my television days around 1993 I did a segment on bait-fishing from the bank with hand-picked flat-tail earthworms. Using long, soft taper rods rigged with light line and a running sinker rig with an extra long trace of up to a metre, I had one of my hottest sessions between sunrise and midmorning. Fish after fish, mainly browns, fell to that method.

The Buckenderra Arm in the south of the lake is another popular place. In the late 1980s, when I was trying to find my way towards making a living, I used to run bus fishing trips all the way from Melbourne, a nine- to ten-hour trip. I found this area ideal, and the bank-fishing stretched for miles. In the five years we ran the trips, the biggest fish taken was a brown trout of over four kilograms. Yes, you guessed it, taken on a single scrubworm fished on the bottom.

The other favourite spot of mine is the water around the main dam wall. I have had a couple of sessions there and both times I have had success late in the season casting and retrieving deep-diving lures around the steep drop-offs and also the sunken timber that is found along the edges of the coves. The Rapala Rainbow Trout pattern lure is deadly here.

Lake Eucumbene remains one of my favourite freshwater impoundments. Although the fishing may have been more spectacular in the early days when the dam was first filling, it remains one of the most popular and consistent trout-producing waters in Australia.

Lake Jindabyne

Lake Jindabyne was also constructed as part of the massive hydroelectric scheme, and was another of the areas I first fished in 1972. I can remember flat-line trolling wobblers with Longtail fly droppers in the area known as Creel Bay. Once again it was spawning time and the brown trout had commenced their movement to Creel Bay in preparation to move into the Thredbo River to spawn.

It is in the lower reaches of the Thredbo River that the Gaden Trout Hatchery is located. Here millions of trout are produced each year for liberation into New South Wales lakes and streams. There is a fish trap near the hatchery and they capture wild brown and rainbow trout, and strip them of their eggs and milt. The fish produced from the stripped eggs are artificially reared in the complex.

In Creel Bay, it is possible to hook some monster trout and Atlantic salmon. Downrigging is very popular and I have found that

TOP: *Lee Rayner with a whopping brown caught in Lake Jindabyne.*

ABOVE: *Little rainbows are plentiful in Lake Eucumbene as the lake is constantly topped up with stocked trout.*

it does not matter which lure you use as long as you get it to the depth where the fish are feeding. I don't understand a lot about water temperature thermoclynes, but I do know that with the assistance of a depth sounder you can actually see the fish and work out at what depth they are.

It is also in Creel Bay and nearby Huon Bay that I learnt how to troll ford-fender attractors baited with mudeyes. This is a deadly method at certain times of the year; October and November were good for me. There is some criticism about the difficulty of retrieving a fish with cow bells, fenders and the like on the line. I never worry about that because the prize, beautiful big lake trout, is always worth it.

I have had some good shore-fishing at Kalkite Point in the northern section of Jindabyne, as well as the eastern shoreline of Kalkite waters. In October and November, when the snow melt increases the level of the lake, scrubworms or earthworms fished on a running sinker rig are always successful.

In the colder months I have also had good polaroiding along the shore between Hatchery Bay and Minnihaha Point. Big brown trout searching for small yabbies give a good sight at times. My best afternoon was four browns from 1.3 to two kilograms, all taken on a black Woolly Bugger fly.

It's my personal view that Jindabyne is one of the top trout waters in Australia. As well as brown and rainbow trout, it has Atlantic salmon and a few brook trout. Each year there is much excitement as the ex-brood stock of salmon are released into the lake. These fish can be up to six kilograms and are quite awesome.

For the non-specialist angler I can thoroughly recommend

Jindabyne as a bread-and-butter type trout water. And there are not too many of them around. There are good-quality hire boats, plenty of good shores to fish, as well as one of the top trout guides around in Steve Williamson from Lake Jindabyne Trout Fishing Adventures.

Lower Thredbo River

The lower Thredbo River, or Crackenback as it is also known, is a fine small to medium-size stream. Classified by New South Wales Fisheries as a 'Blue Ribbon' stream, the Thredbo is off limits to bait fisherman and is subject to strict size and bag limits and a closed season. Anglers can take two fish over 25 centimetres per day and cannot be in possession of more than four fish at any time.

I've had very good fishing for trout between 350 and 800 grams prior to Christmas, when the stream is high and clear with the snow-melt water coming down from the mountains. I prefer to lure fish at these times and I have found that revolving blade lures like Vibrax and Celta are very good. I prefer gold as the main colour. Late in the season towards the close, I have had better success with much bigger trout, up to three kilograms, by casting and retrieving Rapala bibbed lures in the rainbow and brown trout patterns. I have also found that the gold 'fluoro' colour is very well received.

Conclusion

The Snowies area is one of my all-time favourite places to fish. I've been going there for over 30 years and never tire of the trout fishing on offer. The session catching trout on scrubworms in the Frying Pan Arm of Lake Eucumbene rates highly as one of the most enjoyable segments I've filmed for the TV cameras.

Piscatorial Compass

Snowy Mountains, New South Wales

How to get there: From Sydney it is approximately 460 kilometres to Lakes Jindabyne and Eucumbene via the Hume and Federal highways. From Melbourne it's around 560 kilometres via the Hume and Murray Valley highways and the Alpine Way.

Where to stay: Accommodation is plentiful in the major towns in the district, with excellent caravan parks, motels, holiday units and lodges.

What to catch: Brown and rainbow trout, Atlantic salmon and brook trout.

Gear to take: Try a light threadline rod and reel with a good variety of lures. A fly-fishing outfit from four to seven weight is best.

When to go: Year round for both lakes. The closed season for the rivers and streams starts at midnight on the Monday of the Queen's Birthday long weekend in June and finishes on the Friday night of the October long weekend.

Guides and charters: I can highly recommend Steve Williamson at Lake Jindabyne – he is excellent. There are many other quality guides.

Rex reckons: For most for the year you will need warm, protective clothing. These lakes are at a high elevation and snow is always a possibility in winter.

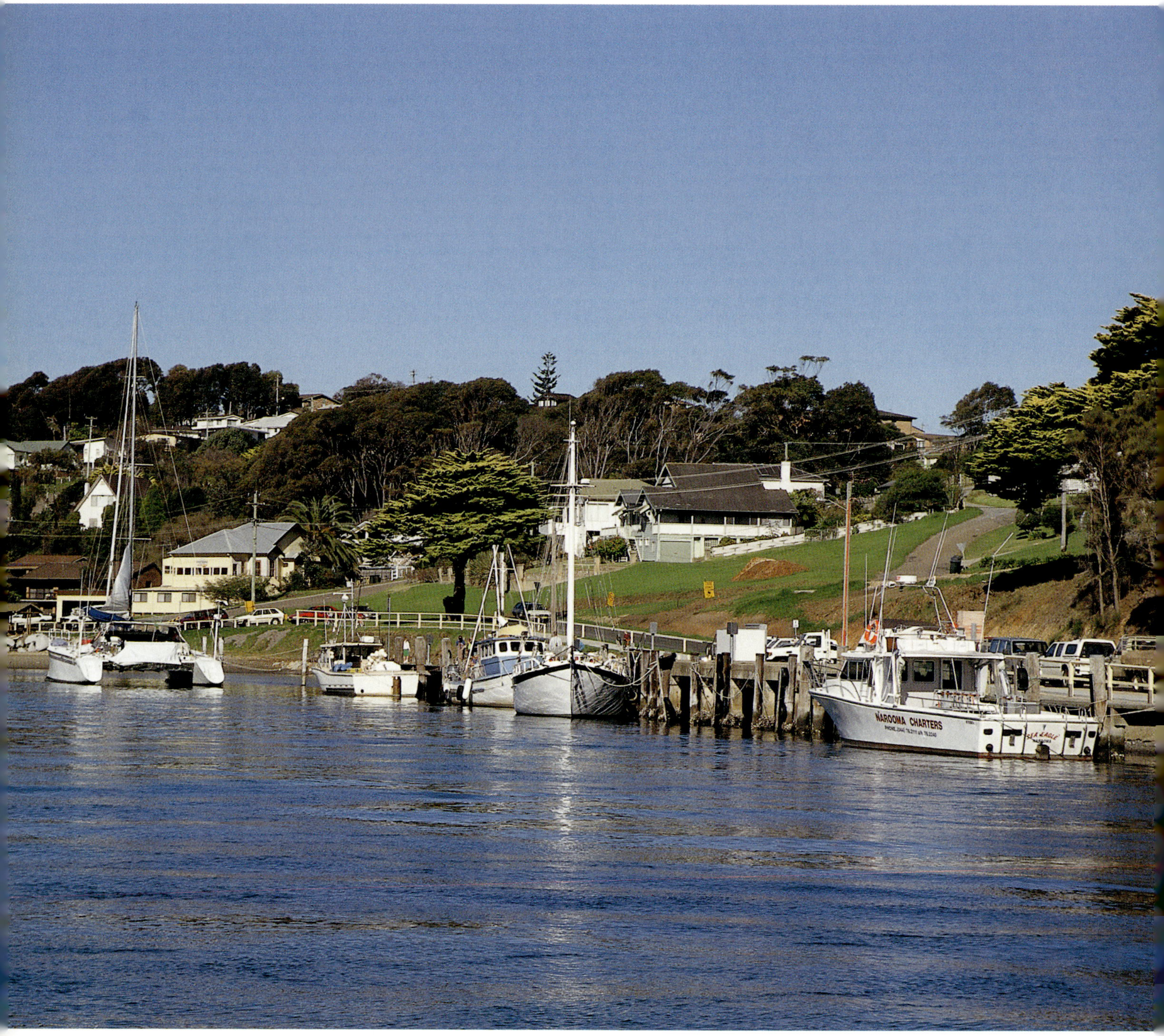
NAROOMA CHARTERS

Narooma

I have been a regular visitor to the south coast of New South Wales since the late seventies, and I really love the place.

Narooma has a permanent population of around 4000 people, many of them retirees. I guess I might be one of them one day! In summer, though, it is a holiday town and the population swells with tourists – mostly fishermen and their families. Apart from the fishing there are good beaches for swimming, nature walks and a spectacular coastal golf course.

'The Bar'

Narooma has an entrance from the sea to Wagonga Inlet that has a reputation for being a killer. There have been some tragic incidents there over the years but, and I say this with the greatest respect, I feel that all of these tragedies could and should have been avoided.

There are some simple rules for going through a bar, both moving into the ocean and

OPPOSITE: *The beautiful seaside town of Narooma.*

coming back from the ocean. One is that 'If in doubt, don't go out'. I'm sure that thousands of offshore anglers have avoided Narooma in favour of the Bermagui and Batemans Bay areas. In many cases the reason is their fear of the wretched bar. It has cost the Narooma area dearly in lost tourist dollars, and people who enjoy their fishing have missed out on some great fish.

Offshore Options

Offshore fishing from Narooma can be divided into four categories. The first is the famous blue water light sport fishing. This involves the catching of marlin, yellowfin tuna, albacore tuna, striped tuna and a variety of sharks on medium to light fishing gear (six to 24 kilograms). In some years there are even good numbers of dolphin fish (mahi mahi) as well as the odd wahoo. Most of this fishing is done between the 80- and 100-fathom line (150–180 metres) to the drop-off known as the Continental Shelf.

Then there is the fishing around Montague Island, located about nine kilometres south-east of Narooma. You can't miss it. With its trademark lighthouse built in 1881, it is one of the few major islands off the entire New South Wales coast. The main species of fish taken around the island are yellowtail kingfish, trevally, bonito, striped

ABOVE: *Lynne Hunt with a nice kingie caught offshore from Narooma.*

LEFT: *Montague Island – the game fishing capital of the south coast.*

OPPOSITE: *Ol' Rexy with a magnificent yellowfin tuna circa 1986. That's Montague Island in the background.*

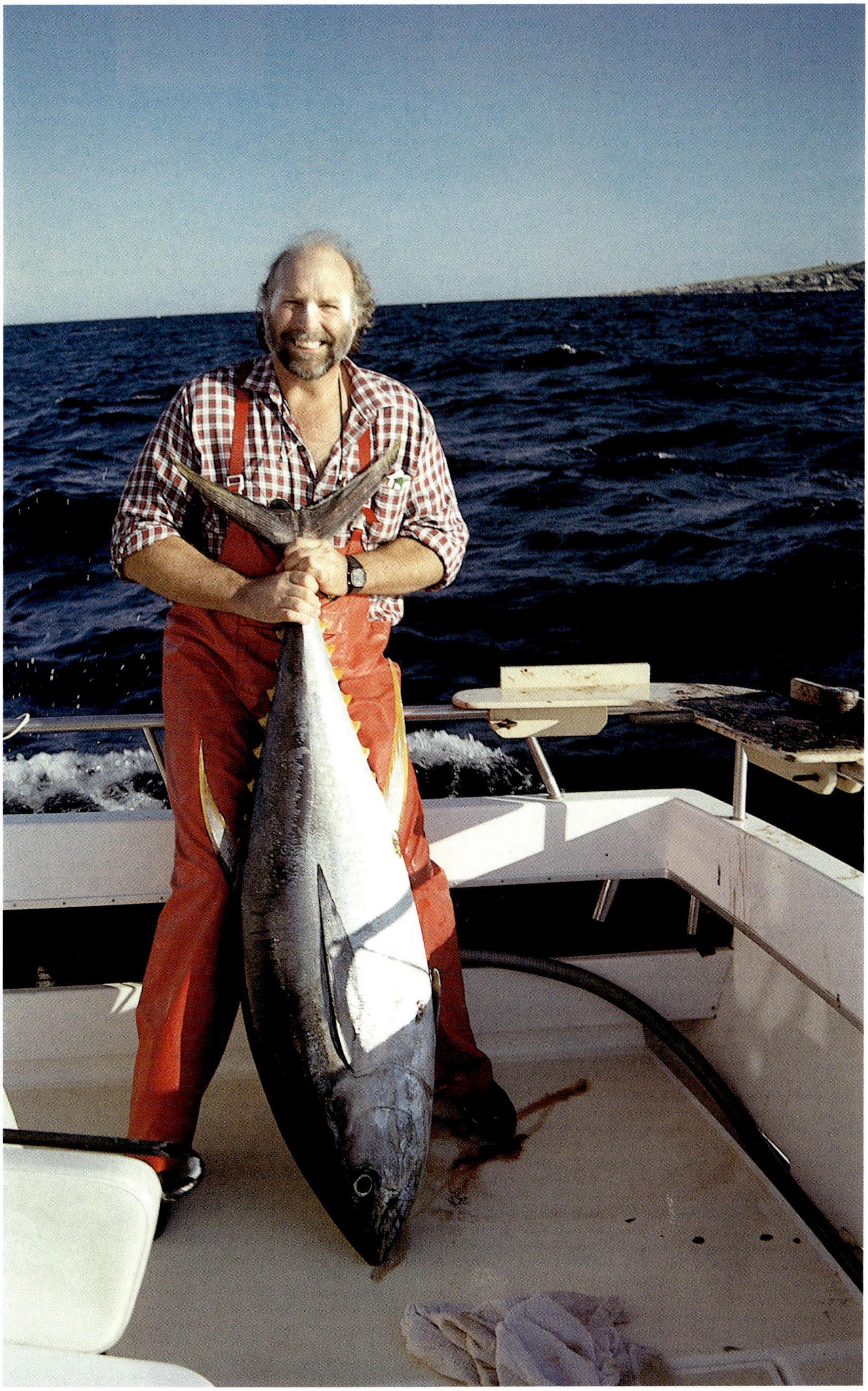

ABOVE: *A lovely striped marlin around the 100-kilogram mark, typical of the marlin caught in this area. This fish was caught around 'the Kink' on a skirted lure.*

LEFT: *A solid yellowtail kingfish caught circa 1980 off Narooma.*

OPPOSITE: *Yours truly and daughter Rachel with a pair of yellowfin whiting from Wagonga Inlet.*

and yellowfin tuna on or near the surface, and morwong and snapper on the bottom.

The prime target and most renowned fish at Montague Island is the mighty yellowtail kingfish. In the late 1980s and 1990s, however, their numbers were in decline due to commercial fishing pressure. Since the banning of kingfish traps off the New South Wales coast a few years ago, the numbers have rebounded strongly and we now enjoy some great sport fishing action from these lively fish. You can use a variety of methods to catch a kingfish, including trolling and casting lures, live baiting, dead baiting and jigging. Just anchor 50–100 metres off the island and give it a go.

Thirdly, there is the small boating craft enthusiast who just loves to drift on the waters off Narooma and dangle a baited line over the side. Bottom-bouncing is a very productive method involving one of the simplest forms of fishing. All you need is a sinker and a baited hook. The paternoster rig is the most effective in this form of fishing, with the hook rigged above the sinker.

Good captures of sand and tiger flathead up to two kilograms as well as flying gurnard, gummy shark, sergeant baker, morwong and snapper are regularly caught here. Sandy areas will produce various species of flathead, whilst 'reefy' ground will produce snapper and morwong. Without the aid of a depth sounder, you can literally tell the type of ground you're drifting over by the species being caught.

Finally, the main attraction offshore at Narooma is the marlin. All three marlin – black, striped and blue – have been taken here in good numbers. Water temperature plays a very important part in the marlin action.

The great Eastern Australian Current comes into play here, and can really mean the difference between a good day and a total blank. Seasoned anglers will readily recognise the water where the fish are likely to be. It should be cobalt blue, and there is usually some action around these patches of water that are regularly called eddies. More fastidious anglers will use a water temperature gauge; the ideal temperature is usually 21 degrees Celsius and above. One year I recorded 27 degrees Celsius at the area known as 'the Kink'. That season there was a sailfish caught on the northern tip of Montague Island, as well as a wahoo. These fish are usually caught a lot further north but had followed the water, proving that if the water's right, the fish will be there. Other years the 'warm' water does not arrive until after the Christmas break, but when it comes, the fishing hots up.

It is interesting to note that the methods of catching marlin at Narooma have changed a lot over the years. When the sport became very popular in the late '60s and early '70s the main method of catching marlin on the south coast of New South Wales was to catch a striped tuna, bridle-rig it and then slowly, and I mean slowly, troll the fish until it was eaten by a marlin or on many occasions a shark.

Then, as the 'stripies' became less frequent, anglers started to troll plastic skirt lures with various types of heads. Live bait is still used as well; slimy mackerel are used in trolling and switch-baiting methods are used too. But the main assault on the marlin these days is with a carefully laid pattern of lures of various sizes placed at varying intervals behind the moving boat. In addition to the skirted lures, a whole range of teasers or attractors are now employed to create a piscatorial blend of action designed to lure a hungry predator like a marlin to check out what's going on.

Beaches

There is also some good beach fishing along this part of the coast. Regular catches of Australian salmon, yellowfin bream and sand whiting are taken. I have had good success at Kianga, Dalmeny, north of the inlet and also at Handkerchief Beach. At times you can also take good numbers of tailor from these beaches. There are beach worms on most local beaches and these make terrific bait.

TOP: *Matthew Hunt hooked up to a large mako shark off the Continental Shelf.*

ABOVE: *Rachel Hunt with a solid yellowfin tuna caught off Narooma.*

Wagonga Inlet

The Wagonga Inlet at Narooma is the real gem of the area. It offers a diverse range of fish as well as very accessible and safe fishing water. The inlet is comprised of fast tidal shallow channels as well as a very deep lake. There are many good shore-based areas to fish as well as bait-pumping areas, launching ramps, hire boats and cafés.

A variety of species of fish have been caught in this inlet. However the main targeted fish are dusky flathead, snapper (small specimens are locally called squire), tailor, luderick, bream and yellowfin whiting. Jewfish or mulloway are also targeted on the full moon. The lake holds a good population of these fine fighting and eating fish.

For over 20 years I have fished for whiting almost exclusively and I can say quite confidently that marine worms are the best bait. These include blood worms, beach worms, long sandworms and soft sandworms. All these worms are available locally. If the small whiting are taking your bait or creating a nuisance, then two or three small blue soldier crabs are the go. I have also caught large whiting on nippers and live prawns.

Moving water is essential to consistent success with whiting. I prefer to fish shallow water only a metre or so in depth. I have taken fish on both tides, but if forced to state a preference I would say the last three hours of the ebb is absolutely prime time. Water temperature plays a huge part in whiting fishing in this area. If you have access to a temperature gauge or you have one on your depth sounder, then anything above 20 degrees Celsius is ideal. However if you don't have one, the estuary should appear cobalt blue on the run-in tide – just like the water offshore. If the colour is green it will be too cold for the whiting.

Conclusion

Narooma and its surrounds is one of my very favorite areas in the world, but then again I am biased. I guess I wouldn't have a holiday house there if I didn't think it was something special! The whole family enjoys the fishing offshore for marlin, tuna and yellowtail kingfish, although I'm just as content these days to jump in my tinnie and fish the beautiful clear waters of Wagonga Inlet for whiting.

Piscatorial Compass

Narooma, New South Wales

How to get there: Narooma is on the south coast of New South Wales, approximately 345 kilometres south of Sydney on the Princes Highway. It is around 690 kilometres from Melbourne, also via the Princes Highway.

Where to stay: Narooma is a holiday town and thus the full range of accommodation is available, with caravan parks, holiday units, motels and houses for rent.

What to catch: Striped and black marlin, yellowfin and striped tuna, yellowtail kingfish, mako shark, snapper, morwong, flathead, yellowfin whiting, dusky flathead, luderick, silver trevally, yellow-eye mullet, yellowfin bream and drummer.

Gear to take: Game-fishing tackle will typically consist of 15–30 kilogram rod and reels and skirted lures for trolling. A ten-kilogram rod and reel are the go for reef fishing. Use light threadline combos for estuary work.

When to go: Year round for the estuary and beaches. Game fishing is best from January to May.

Guides and charters: Several charter boats operate out of Narooma. An even bigger armada of game fishing charter boats base themselves at Bermagui.

Rex reckons: This is my home away from home. Top fishing for the whole family.

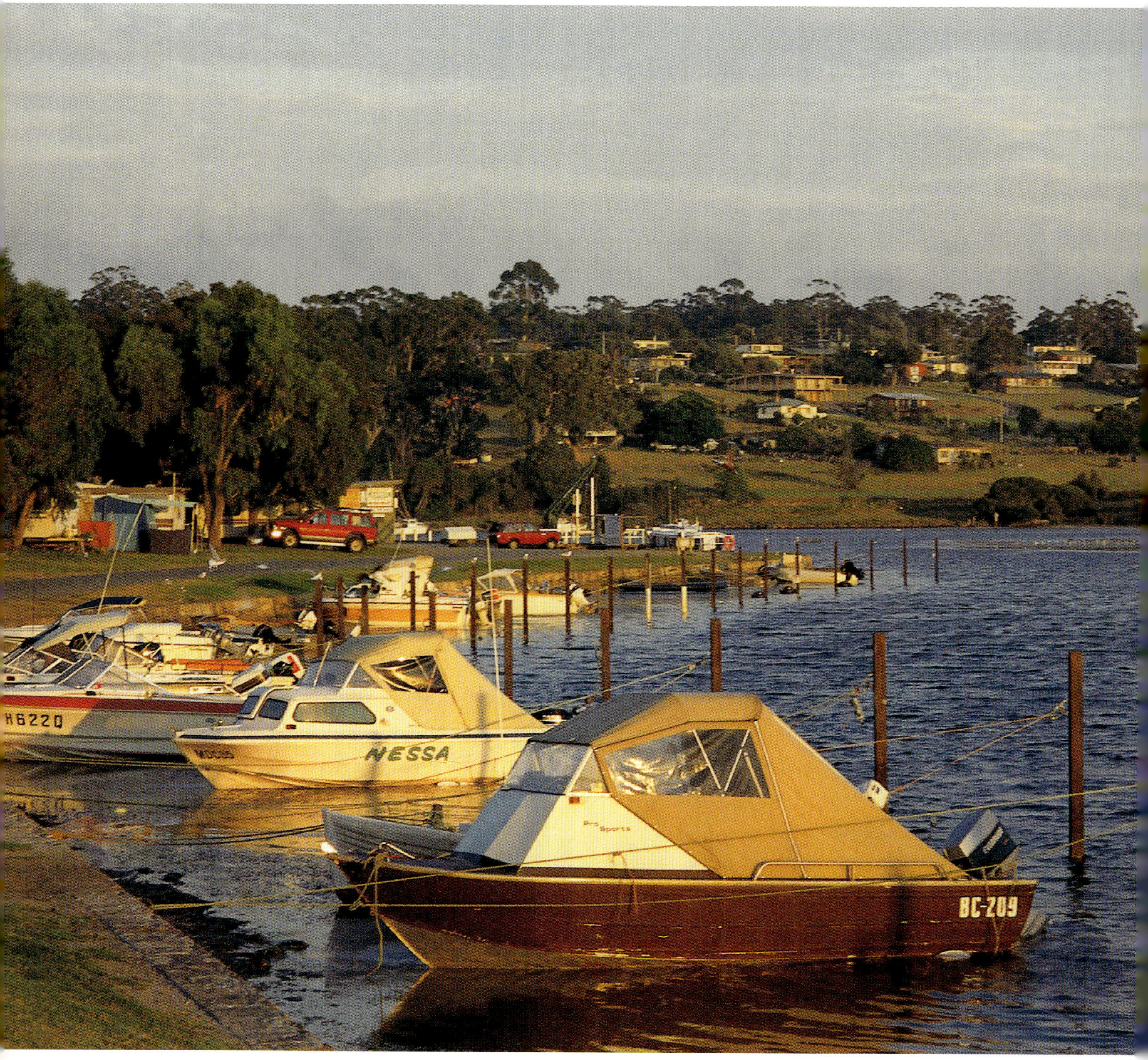
H6220
NESSA
BC-209

Mallacoota

Magnificent Mallacoota is a large estuarine system found near the Victoria–New South Wales border in the far south-eastern corner of Australia. The fishing is varied, with two major rivers, two estuarine lakes, bountiful surf beaches and offshore options aplenty to keep any angler happy.

My friend Bill Zuydwyk from the Metropolitan Angling Club introduced me to Mallacoota in the late 1970s. Around that time Bill was recognised as one of the best anglers in the area. His main go was big flathead on lures cast from the bank. Freddy Bayes, better known as 'Flathead Fred', has taken that mantle now, but back then Bill was the gun.

He took me to areas like Cemetery Bight, Swimming Point, Fairhaven and Goodwin Sands in

OPPOSITE: *The Foreshore Caravan Park allows anglers to moor their boats along the edge of the Bottom Lake at Mallacoota.*

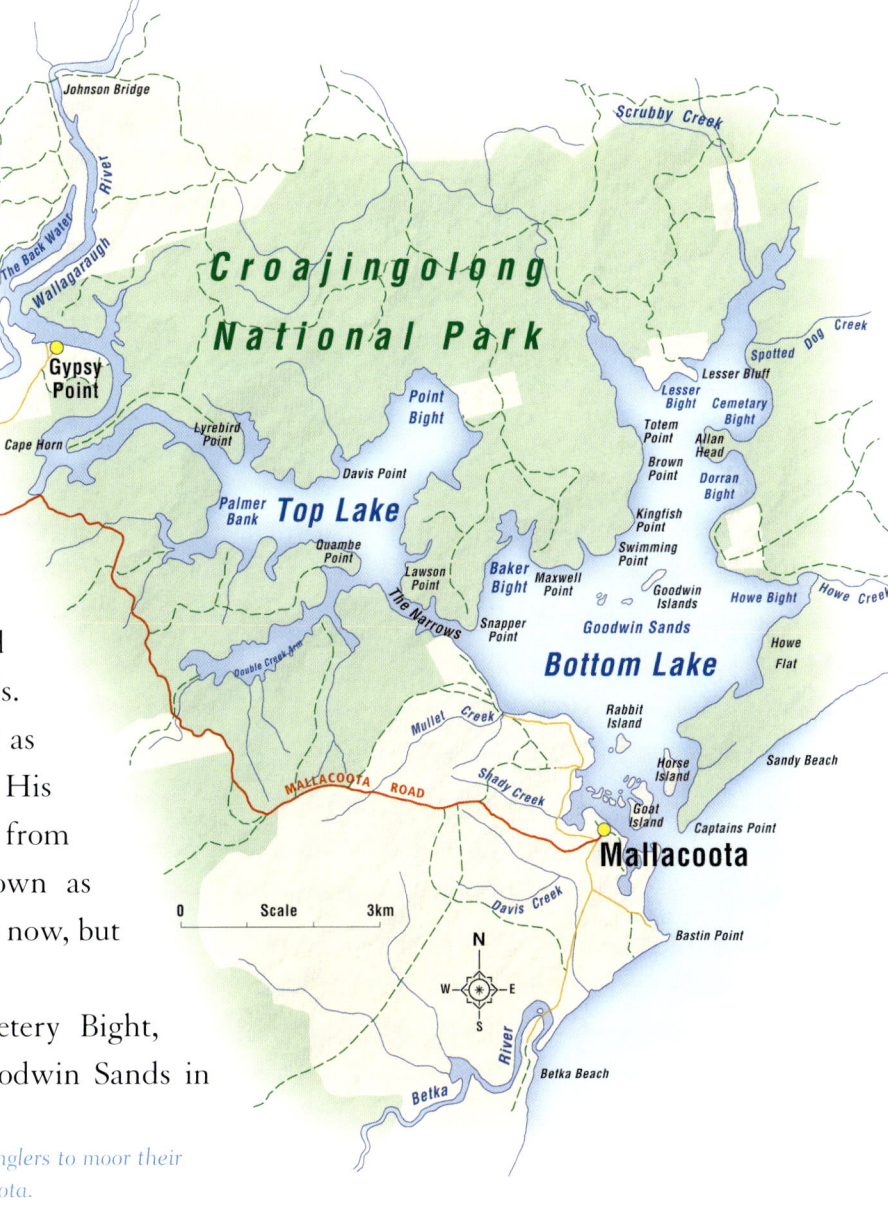

the Bottom Lake. He would cast relentlessly all day, and I mean all day. Cast after cast. He would understand where to fish. He'd look for any sign of a large flathead, which usually came in the form of a lie: a patch of sand where a big fish had lain in wait for a small prey, usually a mullet. Bill would then figure that the fish had to be somewhere close. It usually was, and Bill caught it. Many times they were over the magical ten-pound mark in the old scale.

I started to go to Mallacoota regularly and until I discovered Narooma in southern New South Wales a few years later, we always went there for our holidays. It was at Mallacoota that I cut my leg on a propeller, but that's another story. Suffice it to say that a propeller is not only dangerous when it is revolving, especially in sandy areas.

The flathead we were catching are 'dusky' flathead and are found throughout the Bottom Lake, Narrows, Top Lake and even upstream in the Genoa and Wallagaraugh rivers at Mallacoota. Duskies are one of the largest species of flathead in the world and are known to grow to in excess of ten kilograms.

They are ambush feeders, which means they are a little like my son Matthew in the kitchen when, as a teenager, he would 'lie in wait' for the fridge to be stocked. Dusky flathead are similar in that

LEFT: *View of Captains Point, a well-known luderick spot, looking back along the Bottom Lake.*

OPPOSITE: *An angler proudly displays his superb catch of luderick and yellowfin bream caught in the Bottom Lake.*

they are in no hurry to chase down their food; they prefer to make a snug hole for themselves and wait for a baitfish to swim by their noses before attacking.

Bottom Lake

It helps for an angler to study the habits of his target fish, and this is particularly so in Bottom Lake at Mallacoota. The lake is a vast shallow estuarine lake fed by water coming down from the Narrows and tidal forces when the entrance is open. In its lower reaches the lake is very shallow and is made up of channels and islands. Weed beds are scattered throughout the lake and these provide cover and food for the flathead and other species.

The best fishing spots within Bottom Lake include around the edge of the vast Goodwin Sands sandbank/island, where the bottom drops away, creating an ideal ambush point, and Harrison's Channel, Swimming Point and John Bull Light. If these areas are quiet, keep moving around and look for drops-offs and the edge of weed beds.

When it comes to bait, my advice is, when in Rome do as the Romans do. Mallacoota's dusky flathead population are very partial to the local 'poddy' mullet. They can be sourced from around the edge of the Bottom Lake or from the Betka River estuary just out of town. They should be rigged lightly to swim off the bottom. A live poddy mullet will rarely be knocked back by a ravenous dusky flathead.

The latest craze of soft plastic baits into Australia has seen this area become very popular with lure anglers chasing good-sized duskies. By drifting in a small boat or wading, the angler can cast these lures into a likely area with some expectation of getting onto a big dusky. As the bigger duskies are all females and therefore the breeders of the system, most sport-minded anglers release the fish to fight again another day.

Of all the environments within Mallacoota, the Bottom Lake offers the most variety in terms of species. Bream, King George whiting, Australian salmon, tailor, silver trevally, mullet, garfish and leatherjacket are the main species. There are in fact two species of bream at Mallacoota, black and yellowfin. The yellowfin is more common in New South Wales and Queensland estuaries, but can be caught in the entrance channel and off the beach at Mallacoota.

I took the TV crew to Bottom Lake a while ago and we caught some King George whiting for the cameras, although they didn't

LEFT: *The moon-like surface of the dusky flathead is a welcome sight for anglers fishing at Mallacoota.*

ABOVE: *Local Russell Paterson with a fine yellowfin bream he caught from the entrance of Mallacoota Inlet.*

really cooperate on the day. It illustrated how clean and healthy the system is, especially when the entrance is open.

Narrows

One of the most sought-after fish is the mulloway, also known further north as jewfish. The better places to look for these are the deeper parts of both the Bottom and Top lakes. However, by far the most popular and most productive place is the Narrows, which is a slender stretch of water that joins the two lakes.

Mulloway hunt at night, and so should the fisherman who wants to catch one. Free-swimming baits like juvenile salmon or tailor, 15–20 centimetre mullet and fresh squid are best. No one spot is better than another in the Narrows, so don't ignore the bank areas in preference to the deeper water.

Top Lake

Top Lake, as it is imaginatively called, is a year-round fishery for bream and good for dusky flathead at times. Bait and soft plastic lures work on both species here. The Top Lake is not as large as the Bottom Lake, nor is it as shallow throughout. It has a uniform depth except near Palmer Bank, where it is shallower. Some of the best fishing is in small bays and arms around the lake. Spots to try include Double Creek Arm, South West Arm and around Palmer Bank. Tailor, mullet and mulloway can also be caught in the Top Lake. Tailor are common in the warmer months and should be targeted with surface lures, usually metals.

Rivers

Bream abound in the entire Mallacoota system, but the feeder rivers, the Wallagaraugh and the Genoa, offer perfect spawning conditions. Prior to bag limits being introduced for bream, now ten a day per angler, there were some mass killings of breeding fish in

BELOW: *View of the lower section of the Bottom Lake. This area is made up of shallow flats and channels and it's always worth a look for schools of fish entering through the entrance.*

BOTTOM: *Mallacoota is one of the most reliable spots to catch luderick in Victoria.*

the area known as 'the Bull Ring' in the Wallagaraugh River. Fortunately this has now stopped. I am serious in saying that consideration must be given to protect spawning bream at the height of their run. I reckon allowing full attack on the species when they are at their most vulnerable is not good management – a little like allowing trout anglers to fish the spawners.

The main bream species found in the rivers is the black bream, although Wayne Grainger tells me there are a few hybrids about the system. These are a cross between the black and yellowfin bream. Live prawns, nippers (bass yabbies) and shrimp are the best baits, however soft plastics have taken their fair share of fish in recent years as anglers begin to warm to their effectiveness.

Beaches and Offshore

The main beach for surf fishing is found just off the road to Bastin Point. It straddles the entrance to the inlet and provides some great fishing for most surf species, but particularly Australian salmon, tailor, silver trevally and the tasty gummy shark. Yellowfin bream are taken off the beach in summer and autumn, which is something

LEFT: *The main surf beach fishes well for salmon, tailor, trevally and gummy shark.*

BELOW: *A darkly coloured southern black bream, sometimes encountered in the estuaries of far-eastern Victoria.*

BOTTOM: *Waiting for a bite on a dead calm day on Mallacoota Inlet.*

a bit different for Victorian surf anglers, unlike for our northern friends up the coast.

The offshore scene is relatively untouched. This is due to a poorly maintained ramp at Bastin Point, which is often covered in sand but still suitable for 4WD vehicles to use in good conditions. The options are wide and varied, including marlin and tuna out wide on the shelf and yellowtail kingfish around Gabo Island. There are also some major reef systems off Mallacoota. One known as the Starbank reef some distance offshore yields good snapper and morwong. Generally, if you arm yourself with some likely tackle you won't have to travel far to get amongst some striped tuna and other smaller pelagics on lures just offshore.

Conclusion

Mallacoota has long been recognised as a great area to fish. Tales of huge flathead and good runs of bream have been told about this area for many years.

One problem has been the perception that the netting of the lakes was having a detrimental effect on the system. In 2003, however, after heavy lobbying and outbursts by recreational anglers, the Victorian Government declared this water free of commercial netting for scale fish, particularly bream and flathead. That's got to be a good thing for the future of this marvellous estuary.

Piscatorial Compass
Mallacoota, Victoria

How to get there: Situated in the far south-east of Victoria on the Wilderness Coast, Mallacoota is approximately 515 kilometres from Melbourne on the Princes Highway.

Where to stay: Mallacoota is well served by angler-friendly caravan and camping parks, including one located right along the foreshore of the Bottom Lake. Holiday units and cabins are also available.

What to catch: Dusky flathead, black and yellowfin bream, King George whiting, yellow-eye mullet, estuary perch, mulloway, silver trevally, Australian salmon, tailor and gummy shark.

Gear to take: Use mostly light threadline rods and reels and a good lure selection, and light to medium beach-fishing gear.

When to go: A definite year-round fishing destination.

Guides and charters: There are one or two small guiding operations at Mallacoota, hire boats and offshore boat charters.

Rex reckons: Although the best way to fish Mallacoota is from a small dinghy, the area offers many opportunities for the shore-based angler, with many good spots from small jetties to relatively safe banks.

280 REX HUNT'S FISHING AUSTRALIA

Bemm River

I first heard of 'the Bemm' from my friend Wayne Christensen. Wayne and I were great mates in the late '50s and early '60s. We would fish most weekends, either from the local pier or for trout around Eildon. Most of the time we rode around on bikes, and on the long trips we hitchhiked – a 'no-no' in today's society. Wayne went to the Bemm as a kid with his father. He told me of very big bream, large brown trout in the fresh water and giant salmon from the beach.

It was only a matter of time before I went there for a fish; it happened late in my teens when I first got my driver's licence. I went down with some friends and while we did not set the world on fire, we caught enough fish to assure us the

OPPOSITE: *Early morning over Sydenham Inlet – there is something magical about this place.*

Bemm was a 'special place'. From that moment on I visited the river on a regular basis, at least two trips a year, one in November and the other with the Police Angling Club on the holiday weekend in March.

Bemm River is probably Victoria's premier bream fishing destination. The reason for this is that since the mid 1930s the Bemm has been free of professional netting, and a bag limit of ten bream per angler was in force at Bemm long before many other locations in Victoria. Thankfully this has ensured that this pristine bream water remains in excellent condition.

The Bemm River area comprises the river itself, which begins in the Victorian high country and the magnificent Errinunda National Park, as well as the estuarine lake known as Sydenham Inlet, the entrance channel and various surf beaches. The river crosses the Princes Highway and is largely inaccessible until about three

ABOVE: *Fishing a bait under a float through the snags in the river produces some excellent estuary perch.*

kilometres by road before the township of Bemm River. At this point a bridge crosses the river just downstream from some beautiful waterfalls. Snag-ridden in its upper reaches, the river meanders down through pastoral land for several kilometres before entering Sydenham Inlet. The inlet is an expansive estuarine lake about three kilometres long and five kilometres wide and is one of the main haunts of the southern black bream. The lake then flows into an entrance channel of about two kilometres length before reaching the ocean. The entrance opens and closes throughout the year depending on rainfall and at times, weather conditions.

ABOVE: *Float-fishing remains a passion for me.*

LEFT: *Local guru Don Cunningham is the man the TV crew and I go fishing with when we come to Bemm River.*

The River

November was always a top time in the river. The bream had usually schooled up and were moving upstream to spawn. We always pumped the soft sandworms on the sandbanks just into the lake outside the river mouth – worms to bream are like party pies and lollies to kids. With the entrance sometimes closed at the Bemm, the water level can reach a height where it is nearly impossible to pump worms. We used to bring our own from

Bairnsdale if that was the case. Later in the trip, when the worms were very tired, we used shrimps and live prawns with a lot of success, particularly on the bigger bream.

In the early years of my membership with the Police Anglers, the annual trip would consist of an estuary and a surf competition. Long before lures and soft plastics became popular in Australia, an exciting method of fishing for estuary perch was a live prawn under a small bubble float. The night before we'd have good fun collecting the live prawns for the fishing next morning. The prawn would be suspended about a metre under the float and dropped alongside snags in the river like fallen trees and other structures. But you had to be there before sun-up: the perch action was on when you got there and would cease immediately the sun was up and shining on the water.

In years to follow, some of the senior anglers like Keith Fleming found a method of angling the perch out of the snags in the river. The 'cat was let out of the bag' by local legend Gordon Fields, who ran a few huts and a milk bar at Bemm. The locals were really dirty on Gordon for telling our members. There was no bag limit on perch then, and some cricket-score bags brought bad publicity and

ABOVE: *A fine black bream caught from the bank under the cover of night. Bream and Bemm go hand in hand.*

OPPOSITE LEFT: *A brace of salmon caught by yours truly off the surf at Pearl Point, circa 1978.*

OPPOSITE: *Sensational scenery! This is Pearl Point, one of the main surf-fishing spots at Bemm River.*

the wrath of locals. This was around the time that Jarvis Walker conducted a fishing competition there and 3000 anglers turned up in the quest for one of the ten boats and motors on offer for the winners. It was angling, on for one and all. There were allegations of foul play. Locals said that with the slaughter of bream during the comp, the Bemm would never be the same. The next year without a comp, the fishing was again brilliant.

The only problem facing the Bemm is drought. Floods flush the system every now and again. The lack of rain, however, can cause major disruptions to the right spawning conditions for the bream. This, at times, has caused a lack of certain numbers in various year classes of fish. In years of low rainfall there is less spawning activity.

Sydenham Inlet

One thing I learnt early about fishing Sydenham Inlet is that if you did not have a bite in a few minutes, you had to move. Moving was quite easy as the lake is not a deep estuary for the most part. We used long poles at either end of the boat. They are simply forced into the soft mud and the boat is tied fore and aft to the poles. It is a terrific way to fish from a stationary and steady craft.

The lake is a series of weed banks and sand patches. If the water is clear, you can use polarising sunglasses to pick out the sand holes. If the water is murky, you have to use trial and error. If you cast out and don't get a bite in a few minutes, it means one of two things: first, you may have cast straight into the ribbon weed, and second, there are no fish. It is as simple as that.

Live prawns or sandworms are the prime baits, and I've learnt over the years that you need to allow the bream to take the bait down a bit and let it run before striking. The inlet also has possibly the largest population of estuary perch in Victoria. At times they are in huge schools working the prawns or small bait fish around weed beds. A live prawn under a bubble float is a sure-fire recipe for success, even at night.

Some of the more famous 'marks' within Sydenham Inlet

include the Mahoganies, Bob's Bay, Pelican Point (which is usually submerged) and the sensationally named Siberia. Siberia is an area in the far west of the inlet that can only be adequately boat-fished when the entrance is closed and the water levels in the lake are rising, as it is quite shallow and weedy. Then there are Mud Lake and Swan Lake, two small lakes that run off Sydenham Inlet but are also usually only accessible when the lake is closed and the water level up.

Summer through to autumn is a terrific time to fish the inlet – the joint is alive with fish. If the entrance has been opened by late winter and heavy spring rains, migrating seasonal fish like silver trevally, large yellow-eye mullet, yellowfin bream, tailor and Australian salmon will enter from Bass Strait. One year there was a terrific run of small to medium-sized King George whiting along the sandy patches near the Mahoganies. This area is one of my favourite spots within the Inlet.

While the Bemm has never been known for its flathead fishing, it does hold some monsters, particularly in the entrance channel towards the mouth before it spills into the Tasman Sea. Fish over the five-kilogram mark are taken here each year by specialist anglers using a variety of rubber-tail lures or live poddy mullet. You can catch the poddy mullet around the shallows near the entrance.

Beach Fishing

The beach can really turn on the surf-fishing action at times. Favourite spots like Pearl Point, First Beach and the Entrance Beach have all seen their fair share of hot bites. There is a road that leads west out of Bemm River and running off it are a succession of sand tracks that will lead you to the beach access points, the final turn-off being Pearl Point itself. The Entrance Beach can only be accessed by boat. All of these beaches have good deep gutters at times and this is what you are looking for, folks, as the fish will school up in these deeper areas.

Apart from Australian salmon from 500 grams through to three kilograms, there are good schools of yellow-eye mullet and, during the warmer months, some large 'yank' flathead and trevally. Balmy nights in the summer always see a sprinkling of lights where anglers are fishing the gutters for gummy sharks.

Conclusion

With modest, clean accommodation and good launching facilities that cater for varying lake levels, the Bemm offers the family angler a superb and pristine environment in which to fish. The sporting angler can tangle with a range of lure crunchers from big bream to estuary perch, and at times, Australian salmon.

Bemm River has been able to maintain its simple mystery from the early days. It has not been over-developed and I thoroughly enjoy every return trip I make to the area.

OPPOSITE: *Mates from my old Police Angling Club days clean their catch on a trip to Bemm River in 1980.*

Piscatorial Compass
Bemm River, Victoria

HOW TO GET THERE: Bemm River is in eastern Victoria just east of the timber town of Orbost. It is 440 kilometres from Melbourne via the Princes Highway and Sydenham Inlet Road.

WHERE TO STAY: There are a couple of caravan parks and many holiday units and houses to stay at when in town. There is a general store but no fuel at Bemm River.

WHAT TO CATCH: Black bream, estuary perch, yellow-eye mullet, Australian salmon, tailor, dusky flathead, garfish, silver trevally and luderick in the estuary. Salmon, gummy shark and flathead off the surf beach.

GEAR TO TAKE: Take light spinning rod and reels with nibble tips, and surf-fishing gear.

WHEN TO GO: Year round.

GUIDES AND CHARTERS: Have a chat to Don or Mark Cunningham at the general store for fishing advice.

REX RECKONS: This water contains some large bream that can be difficult to catch. Persevere with harder baits like spider crabs and whole prawns in the shell. Soft plastic and hard-bodied lures also account for some stud fish.

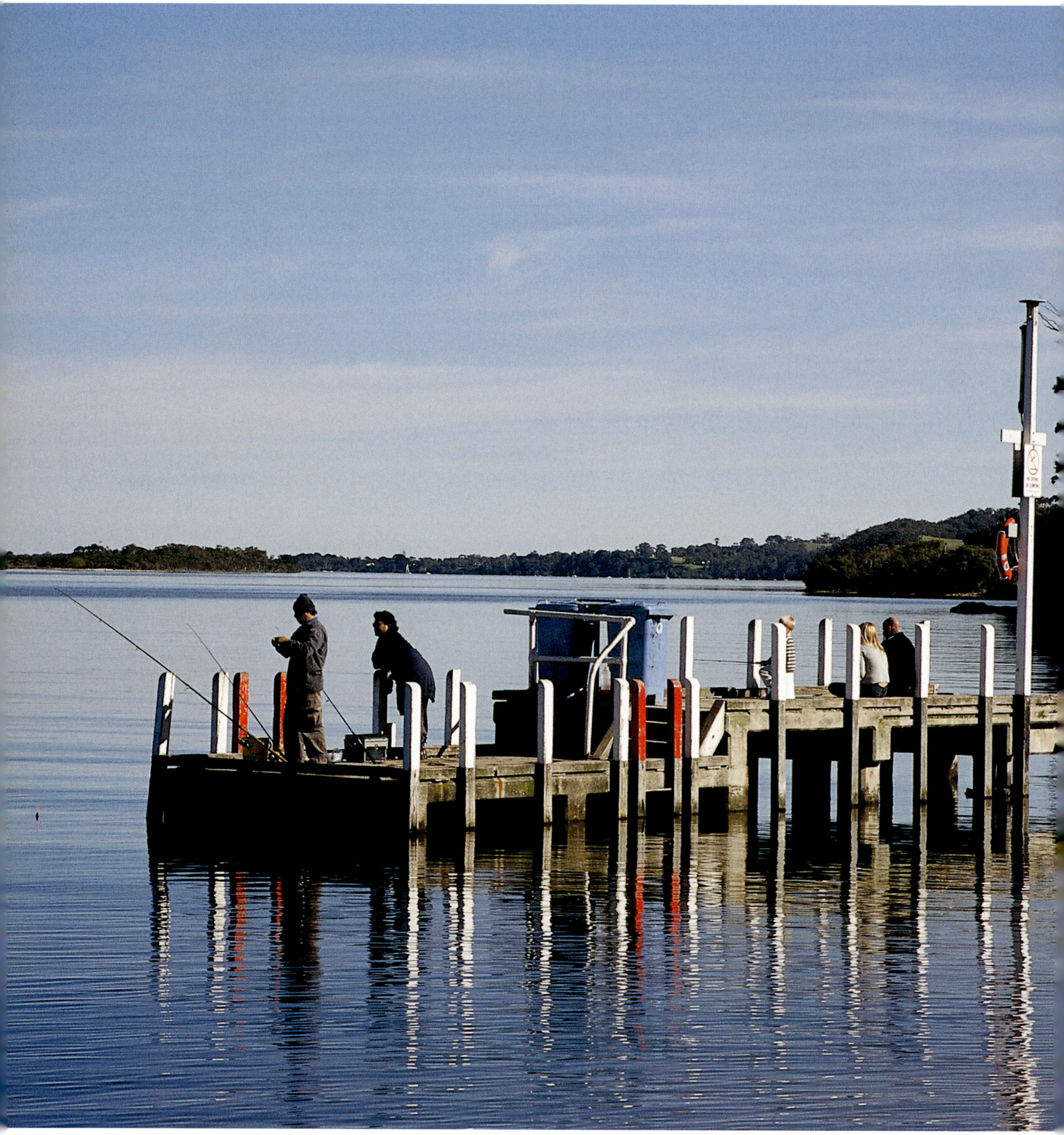

Gippsland Lakes and Rivers

A favourite haunt of mine for a number of years, the Gippsland Lakes and rivers offer some of the best light estuary fishing within a three-hour drive of Melbourne. The Lakes has been a popular fishing and holiday location for well over a century, particularly at places like Lakes Entrance, Metung and Paynesville. Today its popularity continues with improved boating facilities and great access to Ninety Mile Beach.

Western Lakes and Rivers

Lake Wellington, McLennan Strait, the Latrobe River and the Avon and Perry rivers form the western portion of the Gippsland Lakes. This

OPPOSITE: *A typical scene on the Gippsland Lakes.*

area has the lowest profile in the region. Some commercial fishing takes place here, mainly for huge carp and some bream and mullet.

Lake Wellington is a large, exposed body of water. As it is shallow, I would not advise anglers with small boats to go out in windy conditions. During winter and spring the lake is almost completely fed by fresh water from the rivers flowing down from the nearby mountain range. The best places to fish for bream and mullet are near the river mouths and near the entrance to McLennan Strait.

The lower stretches of the Latrobe River produce a few bream at times and can be very productive in dry periods. The lower regions of the Avon and Perry, however, are very good for bream, both from the bank and small dinghies. Lee Rayner from my TV show has had many good sessions in these two rivers. He has caught both bream and estuary perch on soft plastics worked along the reed beds and the many snags. He has seen a lot of shore-based anglers catch many quality bream during the springtime.

ABOVE: *Rachel at only six years of age with a fine bream she caught in the Mitchell River.*

OPPOSITE: *Calm evenings are a terrific time to fish for bream and mullet on Lake Victoria.*

McLennan Strait

One of my favourite areas in this region is McLennan Strait. This is a large, river-like tidal channel that joins Lake Wellington and Lake Victoria. The beauty of 'the Straits' is that they can be fished in most weather conditions, even in small boats. There are many shore-based areas that offer very good angling for bream and mullet. Estuary perch can be caught by casting soft plastic lures in amongst the snags that line the shore.

Seacombe Landing offers good access to shore-based fishing areas and also has a very good boat ramp where boats up to six metres can be launched quite easily. The area also has very large quantities of both sandflies (midges) and mosquitoes in summer. Some protection is advised (RID, Aeroguard, etc).

I have had very good fishing at times along the entire length of the strait. I like to fish this area with a tide running, and I've found that the direction of the flow means little, as long as it is running. In dry times the fish seem to be best from the local area known as 'the Woodpile', right up to the point where the strait becomes Lake Wellington. When fresh water comes down after rain, I have found the best fishing to be in the strait's lower areas.

At Holland's Landing there are excellent facilities. There is a comfortable caravan park that welcomes anglers and a store that sells tackle and quality bait, including live sandworms. The landing itself is a good spot for daytrippers to park their cars right at the water and fish from the landing. The boat ramp is also excellent, taking craft up to six metres in length.

I can recall one unusual trip that I had many years ago. It was the last leg of the Victorian Estuary Championships and I was head-to-head with two of the top estuary anglers in the state, Henry Humphries and Guenter Schnelle. The other fellows headed off upstream on a morning that saw huge amounts of dirty brown floodwater coming down the strait from the mountains.

I had spoken to a couple of locals during the week on one of my 'practice' sessions. They advised me that if the water was fresh after rain, the best spot would be in the deep water at the eastern end of

McLennan Strait. I remembered their message but after 15 minutes at the spot I decided to move. I pulled up my line, only to discover a mighty bream on the end. I continued in this vein for the rest of the comp and won by a bee's diaphragm.

What was happening was that the fresh water was running fast on the surface and the salt water was running upstream underneath. This was causing a bow in the line, which made it impossible for me to see the bite. It was just a matter of checking the line every few minutes and whenever I did, I had a bream on the end.

I have had many days like this. It is well worth a go. Each winter my friend Neil 'Thommo' Thompson and I do several trips to Holland's Landing just for the day. We buy our sandworms at the store and usually take home a nice catch of bream and mullet.

My main point here is that many people try to cast as far into the middle of the stream as they can. I have found no shortage of medium to small and sometimes undersized fish in this area. I have, however, been very successful when fishing one rod very close to the bank with a 'harder' bait like spider crab or small freshwater yabby.

Lake Victoria

Lake Victoria is the largest of the Gippsland Lakes in terms of physical size, stretching from McLennan Strait to below Raymond Island and almost to Metung, where it merges with Lake King. Bream and yellow-eye mullet form the bulk of the fish caught, but other fish like flathead, Australia salmon and in particular tailor, are taken regularly. There are many sandy shores where sandworms can be gathered with a bait pump.

Lake Victoria offers more sheltered bays than Lake Wellington and in parts is a lot deeper. Like Lake King, it does not suffer as much from freshwater inflows as the upper reaches of the system, so eels and carp are not the problem they are in 'the Straits' and Lake Wellington.

Toms Creek, in the north-western corner of Lake Victoria, is a very good sheltered fishery. Although it can be reached by foot, it is best accessed in a small boat launched at Holland's Landing. There

TOP: *The bream in the Gippsland Lakes will supposedly never take a lure. That myth has been well and truly debunked in recent years.*

ABOVE: *Bream will also take flies in the Gippsland Lakes.*

OPPOSITE: *Anglers fishing for salmon on Ninety Mile Beach.*

are some very good bream in this water. The usual bunch of sandworms will always get a response, but for the bigger bream I prefer harder baits like crabs or prawns. The new soft plastic baits have also taken some nice fish here. I think the best patterns are in the smaller sizes, with red and green the preferred colors. Hard-body minnow-style lures will also work when cast into submerged timber, particularly upstream in clear conditions near 'the Junction'.

Loch Sport

Loch Sport is a small holiday town located on the southern shore of Lake Victoria and offers both boat- and land-based anglers the chance to catch bream, mullet and tailor. Several boat ramps and a

ABOVE: *An angler casts from the Ninety Mile Beach at Loch Sport.*

marina service the area. As a bonus, Ninety Mile Beach, where salmon and gummy shark are the main targets, is only a five-minute drive from town.

Some good land-based fishing spots are the rock groynes built to prevent erosion along the shore. The best fishing is late afternoon on calm, warm days, with fresh sandworm cast into or near the weed beds. The ol' paternoster rig works best, particularly with the fast-biting mullet.

Boating anglers will find bream in any number of deeper holes. The best places to try include Storm Point on the opposite side of Lake Victoria, Pelican Bay and the 'Cliffs' area. Remember, folks, schools of bream move around a bit, so you should, too.

Access to the Ninety Mile Beach is from a road causeway that leads out of Loch Sport. The surf fisherman has two options here: stay on the road until the end, where there is a large car park and a short walk to the beach, or turn off just before this car park and travel on a dirt track for a few kilometres to another car parking area. Both spots offer good fishing for salmon – which one you choose just depends on how crowded the beaches are.

Paynesville

Paynesville is a typical fishing village and offers enormous opportunities for both the bank and boat angler. McMillan Strait separates the mainland from Raymond Island at Paynesville, and I have had some very good bream fishing there just near the Raymond Island ferry.

The new canals within Paynesville fish well for bream and mullet, and there are also areas that have good populations of luderick and garfish in the warmer months. Some big flathead weighing up to four kilograms have also been taken here on live mullet and soft plastic baits. Many retirees are living in the area and the bream and mullet are ideal 'tourist' type fish to catch. Good bait and tackle is available locally.

I can remember making many school-holiday trips to this area with my wife and kids. With a few local sandworms and a rod and reel for bream fishing, we rarely missed. One time, many years ago in one of the biggest floods the area had seen in years, my son Matthew and I caught bream in one metre of water in the launching ramp car park.

McMillan Strait is similar to McLennans Strait, except there is not as much tidal influence. In the warmer months tailor enter the area and I have taken good catches trolling bibbed lures or throwing silver metal lures to feeding schools.

Taking the car across to Raymond Island on the car ferry is worthwhile, as the many tracks on the island offer some excellent land-based fishing. Apart from the small jetties that line the Raymond Island side of McMillan Strait, the southern, more remote, shoreline offers fishing for bream, flathead, garfish and tailor.

ABOVE: *The Lakes region is a boating paradise, with many sheltered anchorages like this one at Picnic Arm inside Duck Arm.*

Mitchell River

The Mitchell is one of three main rivers that flow into Lake King, and all three offer great fishing. The Mitchell is the first river you encounter as you move north out of Paynesville and it winds its way up to and beyond Bairnsdale.

The lower reaches of the Mitchell have been a happy hunting ground for me, both competition-wise and for family outings. There is a very good springtime run of bream, which runs up this river as far as Bairnsdale. I have also caught garfish, flathead, estuary perch and tailor along the entire length of the Mitchell.

The river is a great supplier of fresh water to the Gippsland Lakes as it has no dams in its upper reaches and flows unbroken through rich pastoral land before entering Lake King. Around late winter and early spring there can be quite a flow coming down the river. This is a combination of run-off from rain and melting snow. I have caught good bream in the backwater just above the highway bridge in the spawning run of the bream around October. The best bait to use here is sandworms, which I prefer to pump myself in Jones Bay. It offers the perfect environment for bait gathering: silty sand and acres of it. I use shrimp and prawns in the Mitchell as well, when the small 'underweights' are a nuisance.

The Mitchell is a very good river for bank access on both sides; cars can literally be parked right where you fish. In the school holidays and again at peak holiday times like Christmas and Easter this is a perfect river for family fishing. A boat is an advantage though – by having all your gear on board it can be a mobile fishing platform.

The area from the Bluff to the river mouth at the Silt Jetties is my favourite area. In this lower region the bream can sometimes be rather small, so using 'harder' baits like shell, crabs and whole prawns can be beneficial for catching larger fish.

Yellow-eye mullet also frequent the lower reaches of the Mitchell River all year round. They are best caught by first using berley to attract them to your fishing area. If you are lucky enough to attract a large school of fish, the action can be quite frantic. The summer months and into autumn, when the water is clear, can be a very good time for garfish, flathead and tailor. All species enter the river at this time and can be taken regularly.

I have caught good-sized luderick around the trees and weed beds below the area known as 'the Cut'.

I would also recommend trying the boat ramp at Eagle Point if you want a chance at catching a big flathead. Bait your hook with live mullet or whole pilchards. There is a cleaning table here and the remains of the fish certainly attract big flatties.

ABOVE: *A box of sandworms is the most reliable of all bream baits in the Gippsland Lakes.*

OPPOSITE: *This McLennan Strait yellow-eye mullet responded well to some berley.*

Nicholson River

The Nicholson is a very productive river. It does not have the same reputation for bream as the Mitchell and Tambo rivers have, but I have had some great days out here. A boat is certainly an advantage. The best shore-based areas are located between the road and the railway bridges. While walking will create other opportunities for the shore-based angler, it is fair to say that the best way to fish the 'Nicho' is by small boat.

The boat ramp is very good. The drive to the river mouth will not excite with regard to structures that might hold bream, but don't let this bother you as this part of the river is typical of many bream rivers in Victoria. The bream schools can be anywhere. The only way to locate feeding fish is to try an area and, once located, the action can be hot. Above the bridges the river has well-known areas like 'the Tyres' 'the Poplars' and 'the Straight six'.

Tambo River

This is the best-known bream river in Victoria. I first fished here with my friend David Clark. It was a hot March in 1967 and we had both just obtained our driver's licence. We fished near the cliffs well above the road bridge and really got into the fish. The thing that amazed me was the variety – it was unbelievable. We caught bream, mullet, flathead, tailor, eels and estuary perch, and I have since caught luderick here too.

There are several areas where shore-based anglers can park and virtually fish beside their cars. It is just a matter of finding the schools of fish. This is usually easy – look for the anglers. I have found the area opposite the Johnsonville boat ramp and Rough Road very good. There are plenty of others. Again, sandworms are the best bait. For slower fishing but better quality fish I have found spider crabs, soft-shell clams and peeled prawns all good. This is one place where I have consistently caught bream on chicken fillet. I slice the chicken very long and thin and thread it on the hook like a worm.

The Tambo is definitely one river where it doesn't matter if

LEFT: *Thommo with a thumping European carp taken from McLennan Strait during winter, when loads of fresh water comes down the system.*

BELOW: *Gippsland anglers are catching on to how much estuary perch love lures.*

you're boat- or land-based, because there are plenty of opportunities for both types of fishing. The exception is the river entrance, where a boat is desirable as bank access is difficult. The entrance to Lake King is a prime spot when fresh water is moving down the river after rain, as many species prefer a little salt in their diet. Try for big flathead here as well as bream, luderick and estuary perch. A live prawn for bait is absolute dynamite in this situation.

Metung

Metung is an extremely popular holiday town with abundant accommodation options. Located on a thin strip of land ending at Shaving Point, the town has a marina, a rock breakwall and jetties servicing boat- and land-based anglers, though not all are open to the public.

I have had some good sessions on the tailor at Shaving Point near the boat ramp, where the water fairly charges past at times of big tides. I have cast silver wobblers here and caught tailor weighing over a kilogram. It is great sport! I also fish for bream from the edge of the point. It is essential to use very heavy barrel sinkers to get to the bottom. However, many of you will know my liking for fast-water fishing. As long as you use a running sinker and a leader of at least half a metre, you should be fine.

The boat ramp at Shaving Point is very good and offers access to some excellent fishing from small boats. Try some of the small inlets like Boxes and Chinaman's creeks; they carry some very good-sized bream and mullet.

There are also some fine fish to be taken from Bancroft Bay. If you have a boat there is a real chance of a mulloway in the deeper holes. You will always encounter large flathead on both dead and live baits, and there are small snapper, bream, salmon, tailor and mullet to be taken with fresh bait.

Around the corner from Shaving Point towards Melbourne are some good areas to pump your own sandworms. There are good patches of soft shell as well. Many locals net prawns here at night when conditions are right.

Lakes Entrance

Lakes Entrance is the most famous holiday town in the Gippsland Lakes. It is home to a large commercial fishing fleet and an infamous man-made entrance built back in the late 1800s. Being so close to the entrance to Bass Strait, the water here is very tidal, unlike much of the rest of the Gippsland Lakes.

ABOVE: *Anglers fish for luderick and trevally from one of the town jetties at Lakes Entrance.*

I have had great success on bream, trevally, mullet and flathead from the town jetties on the Cunninghame Arm. Live baits such as sandworms and prawns work best, and the best set-up for luderick is fresh green cabbage weed presented under a float and drifted amongst the moored commercial fishing vessels.

Sandworms can be pumped right at the end of the Cunninghame Arm, and when the prawns are running they can be netted here at night. A footbridge crosses Cunninghame Arm, connecting the township to the surf beach, where salmon, mullet and gummy shark can be caught.

When I was younger I trolled up some good tailor opposite Bullock Island and I've also caught quality silver trevally from the island itself. The nearby North Arm, which runs behind the township, is good for garfish.

I filmed at Fraser Island in the early days of the Rex Hunt TV show. We took some quality King George whiting from the Barrier Landing area. I can remember fishing very fast-running water for some big bream on striped tuna pieces and good-sized flathead on pilchards.

Other options at Lakes Entrance include Eastern Beach, which is a very good surf-fishing beach, and the offshore reefs, which hold good stocks of small to medium-sized snapper. Negotiating the entrance bar should only be undertaken by experienced boaters, though, and a charter boat is probably the best option here.

Conclusion

The Gippsland Lakes offers much to the angler, particularly the family fisherman. It's a great place to get kids hooked on fishing and folks, that's the kind of addiction that can be healthy and lifelong.

Piscatorial Compass

Gippsland Lakes and Rivers, Victoria

How to get there: The Gippsland Lakes are located midway along the eastern coast of Victoria. Sale is the first major town in the region, and is about 215 kilometres from Melbourne via the Princes Highway. Lakes Entrance is at the eastern end of the Lakes and is 320 kilometres from Melbourne via Sale and Bairnsdale on the Princes Highway.

Where to stay: Accommodation is available in all of the major towns around the Lakes.

What to catch: Black bream, yellow-eye mullet, estuary perch, tailor, Australian salmon, gummy shark, dusky and sand flathead, garfish, flounder, silver trevally, luderick, King George whiting and pinky snapper (mature snapper can be found offshore).

Gear to take: Light rods and threadline reels are great for the lakes and rivers generally. Use three-metre rods for beach fishing.

When to go: Year round. The rivers are best in winter and spring. The summer and autumn months offer variety and better weather.

Guides and charters: There are a few charter-boat operators based at Lakes Entrance.

Rex reckons: Many of the rivers that feed into the Gippsland Lakes offer superb land-based angling opportunities.

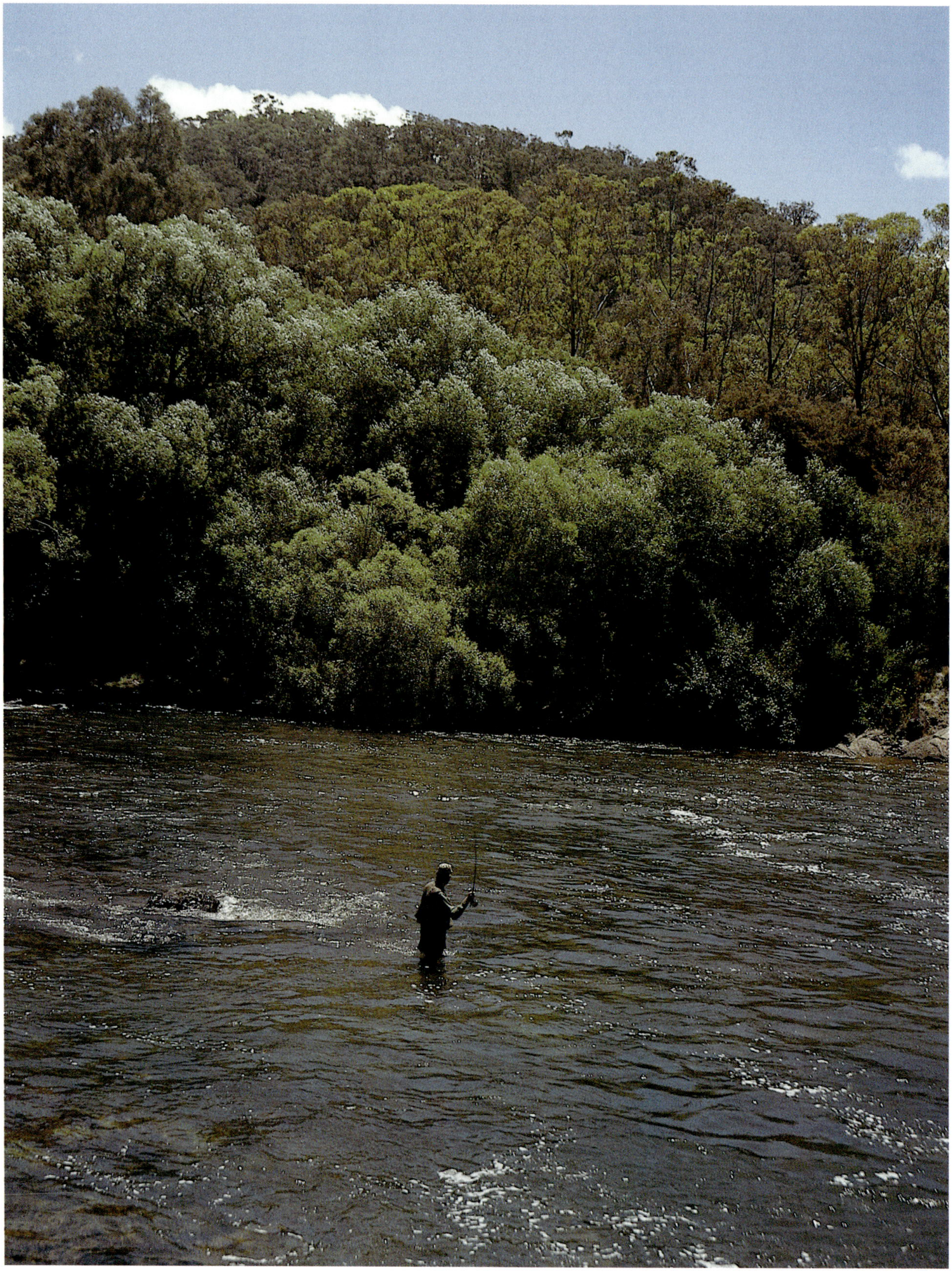

Eildon and Goulburn River

I suppose in the history of my fishing career, apart from the Mentone and Mordialloc piers on the eastern seaboard of Port Phillip Bay, this area holds the greatest affection for me. I love the landscape and also the waters of the Eildon region, which comprise the Goulburn River and its main tributaries, Lake Eildon and Eildon Pondage. To me the area used to be the pinnacle of trout fishing on the mainland of Australia. It is sad to have to say 'used to'.

Goulburn River

I first fished on the Goulburn River in 1963, travelling there in the back of a brand new EK Holden Special Sedan. I can remember the day clearly. My uncle Bill was driving, and with me were Bill Jenkins and Les

OPPOSITE: *The magnificent Goulburn River.*

ABOVE: *Yours truly 'drifts' spinning lures on the Goulburn.*

ABOVE OPPOSITE: *A ripper three-kilogram brown trout taken in the Big River Arm of Lake Eildon.*

BELOW OPPOSITE: *A feisty brown caught from the Goulburn River on worms.*

Thorogood. It was around the same time that I had caught my first trout in the Macallister River below Glenmaggie Weir. I used to work part-time on Saturdays in the back of Bill's grocery shop in Parkdale. Those days the business closed at midday and we were off over the mountains to the Goulburn River.

My most vivid memories of the river at Thornton are of its clarity. You could see well into the river and in fact, you could actually see the trout. That first day I caught a brown trout – it was quite small if I remember rightly, but still I was happy! I used a small bunch of worms downstream from the Thornton bridge. From that day on I regularly fished this area, and still do. Sadly after five years of drought the turbidity has turned the river into a 'sometime' fishery, especially because the trout rely on clear water to see the fly or the lure. The Goulburn is a tailrace fishery, which means that it relies on the amount of water being released from the Eildon Dam for its flow. I have regularly called the river an irrigation channel, because that's essentially what it is. At times the flows are also regulated by the call for electricity production.

The flow rate of the Goulburn is measure by megalitres (a megalitre is a million litres). The flow ranges from 120 megalitres a day in the winter through to over 10,000 megalitres in the height of the summer season. My ideal flow for fishing is between 2000 and 3000 megalitres a day.

As the water that feeds the Goulburn comes from very deep in Lake Eildon, the water can be too cold for many insects to hatch. However, most evenings in the summer there are sufficient hatches of midges, caddis and mayfly to give good sport. I have had success with all methods in this river. I certainly have my favourite areas, but it is fair to say that from the pondage gates at Eildon right down to the Hume Highway bridge at Seymour, there are some fine stretches of trout water.

The lower Goulburn is essentially a trout water, relying mainly on the recruitment of fish by natural spawning. The bee I had in my bonnet for many years is that Victorian Fisheries took away the closed season, size limit, and bag limit and many anglers found it hard to accept (especially when Tasmania has such harsh closed seasons and penalties for disturbing trout spawning).

The area between the pondage gates and Thornton is quite accessible through farm areas, but please ask for permission to enter. It has a series of good runs, deep holes and slow-moving areas. I have had good success in this stretch early in the season (September to December) using saltwater mussels and garden worms. I prefer to use the flat-tail worms that I gather under the cow pats.

Other types of bait and lures are always worth a try, though. I can also remember one show day in September many years ago. It was really blowing from the south-west and was very cold indeed. My friend David Clark and I had tried everything and had had no success at all. I tied on a yellow Dickson lure that looked more like Tina Turner's earring than a lure. This immediately triggered something in the trout's behaviour and I caught six brown trout in eight casts to rescue a disastrous day.

The area below the Thornton bridge down to the bridge at Alexandra is my favourite stretch. I have fond memories of fishing every inch of it with my mentor from Thornton, Bob Gibb. Bob was a spinner man and taught me that the Tiger Devon is the deadliest lure on the river. His famous teaspoon lure was not too bad either – it was simply an old handle from a teaspoon cut to size, and it was lethal.

When the river is moving between 3000 and 5000 megalitres a day the stretch below Gilmours Bridge is a delight to fish. This level creates good runs in the main stream and backwaters away from the flow. A good channel run dropping into a deeper hole is always worth some casts.

Many of you would be familiar with a place known as 'the Breakaway'. This is a stretch of the river that carved a new track after farmers altered the course across their land many years ago.

The river here is a delight to fish when conditions are right. Bait such as worms fished on the bottom, maggots fished in the runs with a berley cage, and grasshoppers or crickets drifted close to the bank are all fine fish takers. For the fly enthusiast, 'the Breakaway' is where you have a real chance. My preference is to fish blind with a bright fly like Royal Wulff or White Moth used as an indicator, dropping a metre down to a bead-head nymph.

Cast up and slightly across. This method is really good when no fish are seen to be moving. I have also had very good success when casting Celta-type lures slightly up and across stream, and another of my favourite lures here is the gold Wobbler.

Below Alexandra the river becomes more difficult to access. The best areas are where the road comes close to the river or where a bridge crosses it. Once again, there are several methods that will work, but I think the best is the bait option as the river becomes more sluggish as it winds its way towards Yea.

OPPOSITE: *Hooked up whilst spinning lures on the Goulburn River during a session for the TV cameras.*

RIGHT: *Some great 'cover' to be found on the lower Goulburn River – prime trout country.*

I have not encountered overly big trout on the Goulburn, although a fish of nearly three kilograms from a river is certainly not to be sneezed at. The average fish in the river is about 500 grams.

My most unusual day on the river was back in the early 1980s, when, as a member of the Metropolitan Anglers Club, I was fishing in the Victorian Trout Championships.

There were many good anglers participating and many were experts in their field. Most used worms or mussels exclusively. I preferred the lures, namely Tylos, Celtas or Wobblers.

This particular day was tough. Not many reports had arrived about any fish at all. I played a hunch and wandered onto a pebble bank just above the Stonecrusher Quarry at the top end of 'the Breakaway'. I decided to tie on a gold Celta. It was overcast and the water, while reasonably clear, was slightly coloured. I considered that my bag, which at that stage contained only three small brown trout, would be insufficient for me to finish in the top ten. I required a top-ten finish to retain my lead in the overall championship. I was really desperate to win the title that year, because I was going for a record three consecutive Champion of Champion titles. It was important for my CV, as I was trying to get into writing, radio and ultimately TV.

After making my way onto this bank I decided that with 45 minutes to go before lines up I had to work the area with a plan. The bank was flanked by two shallow fast channels. They both emptied into a rather large deep pool. That pool had trout written all over it.

Well, my punt paid off. In the 45 remaining minutes I hooked and landed six brown trout ranging from 550 to 850 grams. It was a hot session and one that was witnessed by several anglers who had decided that the day was so poor they would head back to the weigh-in early. The wash-up was that I won the day and those points enabled me to win my third championship. The lesson here is twofold. Firstly, the fish have to eat sometime somewhere, and secondly, never give up until the final bell.

Many people can relate to trout fishing being something special. I am one of them. Not for one moment do I consider trout to be difficult to catch. The rules of fishing I learnt early apply to them. Use a properly balanced outfit, fish to suit the fish's feeding times and use something for a bait or lure that they like to eat. So keep looking if you can't find them, there is definitely something there.

The Goulburn was where I cut my teeth on trout fishing. From

LEFT: *Eildon Pondage – some big trout lurk here.*

BELOW: *The result of a drift-spinning session on the Goulburn.*

ABOVE OPPOSITE: *A recent shot of Lake Eildon taken from the dam wall. Note the low water level.*

BELOW OPPOSITE: *A fine redfin (also called English perch) taken in Lake Eildon circa 1985.*

the mighty Tongariro River in New Zealand's North Island and the crystal-clear streams of the South Island, to Tasmania's best trout waters and the majestic River Itchen, a tributary of the famous chalk stream the River Test in the United Kingdom, I have taken the skills learnt on the banks of the Goulburn River to some of the best trout waters on earth.

Eildon Pondage

There are actually two bodies of water here, the upper and lower pondages. They are used as regulating ponds, so that the water can be sent down the Goulburn for irrigation in the agricultural areas of the Goulburn Valley. Water also comes through the power station to generate electricity. The water is very cold because it comes from the bottom of Lake Eildon. It can be quite turbid due to the eroding of the banks during low water levels.

The pondage is really a put-and-take fishery, with fishing possible all year round as the fish do not spawn; ex-brood stock from Snobs Creek Hatchery are liberated into this water. Some reach five kilograms, but most are between 1.5 and two kilograms. There are also frequent releases of two-year-old fish, as well as brown and rainbow trout that give very good sport.

In days gone by a mudeye presented under a bubble float was my preferred method of fishing. I also had very good success on lures such as the Supa Dupa and Tylos. Now the main method for bait anglers is the use of the dough mixture called Powerbait. Traditional trout anglers raise their eyebrows at this bait because of its technicolours. I remember the old bait called Catchit – it smelt like a 'soddy' mixture of salted potato crisps, but boy was it a good bait. Horses for courses, it's all fishing.

Mudeyes are still very good bait, especially when angling for trout that may have acclimatised to the water over a period of time. Some of these wily trout are selective feeders and can only be caught on mudeyes or a carefully presented fly in a nymph or longtail pattern.

ABOVE: *Preparing to fish the Goulburn River always fires ol' Rexy up.*

LEFT: *The Rex Hunt Futurefish Foundation stocks Murray cod into Lake Eildon so that these kids can catch 'em in a few years time.*

Lake Eildon

I can remember some great days on the main lake. Earlier on, late '50s I think, Lake Eildon was regarded as the premier trout water on the mainland of Australia. Then, of course, Lake Eucumbene in New South Wales took over, and later still Lake Pedder in Tasmania became the 'mecca' of Australian trout fishing.

I have had some good success in Lake Eildon. In my earlier years I used to spin lures from the shore at Fraser National Park, then called Devils River, with some success. Bob Gibb and I walked for miles and threw various lures (mainly Wobblers). The trout were not big but they were respectable at between 450 and 700 grams.

Trolling for trout was very good then, and in fact has become so again along the front of the main wall between the Eildon boat harbour and Jerusalem Creek. To access the really big trout (up to 4.5 kilograms) switched-on anglers use downriggers, paravanes or lead lines to get the lure down deep where the big fish lurk.

Trolling for natives like Murray cod and golden perch is on the increase, with some anglers getting excellent results using deep-diving large bibbed lures trolled over drop-offs, sunken timber and around points on the lake.

The Big River Arm is a traditional big fish hot spot, particularly late in the season as the trout move into the rivers to spawn. Each year a massive trout or two are reported from Eildon; usually they come from the Big River Arm and are taken on a deep-diving large Rapala bibbed lure. I also like to fish the Big River in the late summer to early autumn. I have found the stretch above the bridge on the Eildon–Jamieson Road to be particularly productive for small to medium-sized trout on small lures like Celta or Vibrax, or the ever-popular nymph with an indicator fly rig.

My other favourite area of Eildon is the Howqua Arm. For a ten-year period in the late '70s to '80s I haunted the area, both in a small dinghy and from the bank. Redfin were a main target here in summer. Tying up to any old stump was the go. Not all snags had someone home, but once you found the reddy schools it was on. My favourite lure with these was a long barrel sinker in natural lead colour squashed onto a long shank number 6 hook. Believe me, it is lethal. Another very good lure is the yellow Dickson revolving blade model. It is inexpensive and a great redfin lure.

Where it runs into the main lake, the Howqua River is a proven trout producer. The deep channel holds some very big fish and the smaller trout will always give a sight. Mudeyes under a float, worms on the bottom and lures cast into the lines of trees are all worth a try. The Howqua is a delightful little stream chock full of hungry little trout.

Conclusion

The Rex Hunt Futurefish Foundation was more or less conceived in the Eildon region. One of the foundation's core aims was born from a desire to return Victoria's greatest freshwater fishing arena to its former glory. The foundation regularly stocks Lake Eildon with trout and native fish like Murray cod, over and above the number of fish stocked there by Victorian Fisheries. We want to see a vibrant mixed fishery for Lake Eildon that generations to come will enjoy.

Piscatorial Compass

Eildon and Goulburn River, Victoria

How to get there: Eildon is 150 kilometres north of Melbourne via the Maroondah Highway, Taggerty Thornton Road and the Goulburn Valley Highway.

Where to stay: There are several excellent caravan and camping parks around Lake Eildon itself and along the Goulburn River. Houseboats can be rented for Lake Eildon.

What to catch: Brown and rainbow trout, Murray cod, golden perch and redfin.

Gear to take: Use light threadline rods and reels with small spinning lures. Fly-fishing outfits should be from four to five weight.

When to go: September to May. The river is closed to fishing during the winter months; for exact dates.

Guides and charters: There are many fly-fishing guides for the Goulburn River. Mick Hall of Blackridge Fly Fishing is an excellent guide, and Goulburn Valley Fly Fishers is a good place to start.

Rex reckons: Bait fish with flat-tail earthworms or use revolving blade lures cast slightly upstream across shallow gravel areas on the Goulburn River from September to November. For fly anglers, cast a nymph with an indicator upstream and allow it to flow back to you.

Photograph Credits

Phil Bennett	**South West Rocks**: pp 233, 234 (bottom), 235.
Kaj Busch	**Dirk Hartog Island**: pp 150, 151 (left), 152, 154 (top left) **Cape York**: pp 203 (bottom) **South West Rocks**: pp 232 (left).
Rocky Carosi	**St Helens**: pp 42, 44–48.
Gary Crombie	**Lord Howe Island**: pp 236, 238, 239, 240.
Rex Hunt	**Port Phillip Bay**: pp 3, 5, 7 **Western Port**: pp 20, 22 **Central Highlands**: pp 52 (below left), 54 **Lake Burbury**: pp 56, 58 **Strahan**: pp 65 (middle) **Apollo Bay**: pp 68 **Lakes Purrumbete and Bullen Merri**: pp 83 **Warrnambool**: pp 92 **Port Lincoln to Ceduna**: pp 139 (bottom) **Dirk Hartog Island**: pp 148, 151 (right), 153, 154 (top right and bottom) **Kimberley**: pp 158 (right), 160 (top), 161 **Tiwi Islands**: pp 166 (right), 167 (right), 169 (right), 172 **Mary River**: pp 182 **South Alligator River**: pp 188, 190, 191, 192 **Liverpool River**: pp 194, 196–198 **Cape York**: pp 202 **Narooma**: pp 266 (top), 267, 268 (left) **Bemm River**: pp 284 (left), 286 **Gippsland Lakes and Rivers**: pp 291, 297, 298 (left) **Eildon and Goulburn River**: pp 302, 304, 305, 307, 308, 309 (bottom).
Craig McGill	**Hawkesbury River**: pp 242, 244 (right), 245, 246 (bottom) **Sydney**: pp 248, 250, 251 (top), 252, 253, 254.
Shane Mensforth	**Kangaroo Island**: pp 104, 106–109 **Adelaide**: pp 110, 112–115 **Marion Bay**: pp 116 **Whyalla**: pp 122, 124–126 **Tumby Bay**: pp 128, 130–132 **Port Lincoln to Ceduna**: pp 134, 136, 137, 138, 139 (top), 140, 141.
John Mondora	**Lake Tinaroo**: pp 208, 210–213.
Leeann Payne	**Cape York**: pp 205 (top left and right), 206 (top) **Noosa**: pp 214, 217, 218, 220 (left) **Gold Coast**: pp 225, 227, 228 (left and top right).

Lee Rayner **Port Phillip Bay**: pp iii, xii, 2, 8, 15, 16, 18 **Western Port**: pp 24 **Central Highlands**: pp 50, 52, 53 (top and below right) **Marion Bay**: pp 120 **Cape York**: pp 200, 203 (top), 204 **Noosa**: pp 216, 220 (right) **Lord Howe Island**: pp 241 **Snowy Mountains**: pp 256, 259, 260 (right), 261, 262 (top) **Narooma**: pp 269, 270 (bottom) **Gippsland Lakes and Rivers**: pp 292 (bottom).

Darren Reid **Port Phillip Bay**: pp 4, 6, 9, 10 (right), 11, 12, 13, 14 **Western Port**: pp 25 (below), 26 (left) **Port Albert**: pp vi–vii, 28, 30, 31, 32, 34, 35 **Flinders Island**: pp 36, 40 (bottom left) **Lake Burbury**: pp 59, 60, 61 **Strahan**: pp 62, 64, 65 (top and bottom left), 66 **Apollo Bay**: pp 70–77 **Lakes Purrumbete and Bullen Merri**: pp 78, 80, 81, 85 **Warrnambool**: pp 86, 88–91, 93, 94 **Portland**: pp 96, 98, 99, 100, 101 (top), 102 **Esperance**: pp 142, 144–147 **Tiwi Islands**: pp 164, 166 (left), 167 (left), 168, 169 (left), 170, 171 **Cape Don**: pp 174, 176 (right), 177, 178, 179 **Mary River**: pp 183–187 **Noosa**: pp 219 **Gold Coast**: pp 222, 224, 226, 228 (bottom right) **South West Rocks**: pp 230, 232 (right), 234 (top) **Hawkesbury River**: pp 246 (top) **Sydney**: pp 255 **Snowy Mountains**: pp 258 (left), 262 (bottom) **Narooma**: pp 264, 266 (bottom), 268 (right), 270 (top) **Mallacoota**: pp 272, 274–278 **Bemm River**: pp x–xi, 280, 282, 283, 284 (right), 285 **Gippsland Lakes and Rivers**: pp 288, 290, 292 (top), 293–296, 298 (right), 300 **Eildon and Goulburn River**: pp 309 (top), 310 (left).

Bruce Smith **Lakes Purrumbete and Bullen Merri**: pp 82, 84 **Eildon and Goulburn River**: pp 306, 310 (right).

Steve Starling **Kimberley**: pp 156, 158 (left), 159, 160 (bottom), 162 (left) **Cape Don**: pp 176 (left) **Mary River**: pp 180 **Hawkesbury River**: pp 244 (left) **Sydney**: pp ix, 251 (bottom).

Paul Worsteling **Port Phillip Bay**: pp 10 (left) **Western Port**: pp 23, 25 (top), 26 (right), 27 **Port Albert**: pp 33 **Flinders Island**: pp 38, 39, 40 (top and bottom right), 41 **Portland**: pp 101 (bottom) **Marion Bay**: pp 118, 119 **Kimberley**: pp 162 (right) **Cape York**: pp 205 (bottom), 206 (bottom) **Snowy Mountains**: pp 258 (right), 260 (left) **Narooma**: pp 269.

Index

A
abalone
　bait, as, 145
　St Helens, 43
Adelaide, 106, 109, 111–115, 121, 127, 133, 140, 141, 143
　artificial reefs, 111
　boating facilities, 112
　fishing restrictions, 111
　land-based opportunities, 114
　launching ramps, 112
　offshore, 113–114
Adelaide River, 187
Admiralty Gulf, 161
Aire River, 76
Akuna Bay, 246
albacore tuna
　Flinders Island, 41
　Narooma, offshore, 266
　St Helens, 47, 49
Alexandra, 305, 306
American River, 106, 107
Anglers Reach, 259
Anonyma Shoal reef, 9
Ansons Bay, 48–49
Apollo Bay, 68, 69–77, 92
　boat harbour, 71
Apsley Strait, 172
Arafura Sea, 173, 177, 179
Archipelago of the Recherche, 143, 145, 146–147
Arnhem Land, 175, 191, 195, 199
arrow squid
　Lawrence Rocks, 100
　Portland, 103
Arthurs Lake, 51, 52–54, 55
　closed season, 52
Atherton Tablelands, 209
Atlantic salmon
　Creel Bay, 261
　Gordon River, 66
　Lake Bullen Merri, 83
　Lake Jindabyne, 262
　Snowy Mountains, 263
　Strahan, 67
Australian bass
　fry, 221
　Hawkesbury River, 247
　Lake Bullen Merri, 83–84
　Lake Macdonald, 221
　Noosa, 217, 221
　Noosa River, 216
Australian salmon
　Adelaide, 115
　Aire River, 76
　Apollo Bay, 72, 73, 77
　Bastin Point, 278
　Beaumaris Bay, 7

Bemm River, 286, 287
Bottom Lake, 276
Broken Bay, 246
Ceduna, 140
Convention Beach, 138
Emu Bay, 107
Esperance, 144, 147
Flinders Island, 38, 41
Georges Bay, 47
Gippsland Lakes and rivers, 301
Hawkesbury River, 247
Johanna Beach, 77
Kangaroo Island, 109
Lady Bay, 92
Lake Victoria, 292
Lord Howe Island, 239, 241
Macquarie Harbour, 65
Mallacoota, 279
Marengo, 74
Narooma beaches, 270
Ninety Mile Beach, 31
Ocean Beach, 67
Port Albert, 35
Port Phillip Bay, 3
Portland, 103
Pot Boil Point, 39
Snelling Beach, 107
St Helens, 49
Stokes Bay, 107
Strahan, 67
Sydney, 250, 251, 255
Warrnambool, 93
Whyalla, 127
Avalon ramps, 16
Avon River, 289, 290

B
Bairnsdale, 284, 295, 296, 301
bald-chin groper, 151, 153, 155
Balls Pyramid, 240, 241
Bamanga, 207
Bancroft Bay, 299
bar-tailed flathead, 154
Barham River, 73–74
barracouta, 45
　Apollo Bay, 72, 73, 77
　Flinders Island, 41
　Lady Bay, 92
　Lee breakwater, 99
　McLoughlins Beach, 31
　Marion Bay, 121
　Mary River, 187
　Mornington Pier, 7
　Parakary River, 171
　Port Hurd, 192
　Portland, 103
　St Helens, 45, 49
　Tumby Bay, 133

barracuda
　Burford Island, 177
　Cape Don, 179
　Kimberley, 163
　Liverpool River, offshore, 198
　Rex's Cay, 177
　Vansittart Bay, 163
barramundi
　Adelaide River, 187
　Apsley Strait, 172
　Cape Don, 176, 179
　Cape York, 205, 207
　Chamberlain River, 163
　Corroboree Billabong, 182
　Crocodile Islands, 199
　Doughboy River, 203
　Dudwell Inlet, 169, 172
　electro-fished, 210, 212–213
　fingerlings, 211
　Goose Creek, 167, 173
　Gulf of Carpentaria, 204
　Jessie River rock bar, 173
　Junction Bay, 199
　Kimberley, 163
　Lake Tinaroo, 209–213
　Liverpool River, 195–196, 198, 199
　Mary River, 183
　Melville Island, 172
　Nourlangie Creek, 193
　Port Hurd, 166, 169
　Red Lily Billabong, 191
　Shady Camp, 184, 186
　South Alligator River, 192, 193
　Tiwi Islands, 166, 173
　Tomkinson River, 196
　Trepang Creek, 178
　Vansittart Bay, 162, 163
　world-record, 211
　Yellow Waters, 191
Barrenjoey Head, 246, 247
Barron River, 209
Barwon Banks, 219
bass, 244
Bass Strait, 30, 33, 34, 37, 38, 41, 153, 286, 299
bass yabbies
　bream, for, 48, 103, 234, 278
　mullet, for, 234
　Port Albert, 30
　whiting, for, 217, 271
Bastin Point, 278, 279
Batemans Bay, 266
Bathurst Island, 165, 166, 167–172, 192
Beagle Gulf, 173
Beaumaris, 4, 7
Bellarine Peninsula
　Werribee River to, 16–19
Bemm River, 281–287

beach fishing, 287
　drought, 285
　fishing restrictions, 282
berley, 6, 45, 160, 253
　bluefish, for, 239
　cage, 305
　garfish, for, 8, 114
　Lake Purrumbete, 81
　mullet, for, 114, 296
　sharks, for, 101
　snapper, for, 127, 155, 229
　tommy ruff, for, 114
　trout, for, 65
　whiting, for, 24, 217
Bermagui, 266
Betka River, 276
big eye trevally, 221
Big River Arm, Lake Eildon, 311
Bird Rock, 17
Birregurra, 71
black backed salmon, 140
black bream
　Adelaide, 115
　Bemm River, 285, 287
　Esperance, 147
　Gippsland Lakes and rivers, 301
　Hopkins River, 88
　Mallacoota, 276, 279
　Port River, 115
　southern **see** southern black bream
　St Helens, 49
　Wallagaraugh River, 278
　Warrnambool, 95
　yellowfin bream cross, 278
black jewfish
　Apsley Strait, 172
　Cape Don, 179
　Jessie River rock bar, 173
　Mary River, 187
　Port Hurd, 169–170
　Shady Camp, 186
　Snake Bay, 171
　South Alligator River, 193
　Tiwi Islands, 173
black kingfish **see** cobia
black marlin
　Gold Coast, 227, 229
　Lord Howe Island, 240, 241
　Narooma, 269, 271
　South West Rocks, 233, 235
　Sydney, 250, 255
Black Rock, 4
　Clocktower reef, 8
black-tip reef shark, 240
blackfish **see** luderick
Blacknose Point, 99
Blanket Bay, 74
blue-eye trevalla, 41

blue groper
    Cape du Couedic, 107
    Investigator Islands, 138
    Kangaroo Island, 108, 109
Blue Johanna Beach, 76, 77
Blue Lake, 52
blue marlin
    Flinders Island, 41
    Lord Howe Island, 240, 241
    Narooma, offshore, 269
blue morwong
    Archipelago of the Recherche, 146, 147
    Esperance, 145, 147
    Investigator Strait, 108
    Kangaroo Island, 108, 109
    Marion Bay, 119, 121
    Thistle Island, 136, 137
    Warrnambool, 92, 95
blue salmon
    Junction Bay, 199
    Mary River, 187
    Shady Camp, 186
    South Alligator River, 193
    Tiwi Islands, 173
blue shark, 100
blue-spotted flathead, 137, 138
blue swimmer crab
    Adelaide, 114, 115
    Whyalla, 124, 127
blue-throated wrasse, 35
bluebone see bald-chin groper
bluefin tuna see northern bluefin tuna; southern bluefin tuna
bluefish, 239, 241
Blyth River, 199
Bob Bay, 286
bonito
    bait, as, 233
    Broken Bay, 246
    cobia, for, 233
    Montague Island, 266
    Sydney, 250, 251, 255
Bonnet Rock, 9
bony bream, 210
Boston Bay, 136
Boston Island, 136
Botany Bay, 249, 253–254
    fishing restrictions, 253
Bottom Lake, 273, 274, 275–277, 279
Bouchier and Boulton channels, 25
Boxes Creek, 299
Brazendale Island, 52, 53
break-sea cod
    Archipelago of the Recherche, 146
    Esperance, 147
bream
    Aire River, 76
    Ansons Bay, 48
    Apollo Bay, 77
    Avon River, 290
    Bancroft Bay, 299
    Barham River, 74, 75
    Bemm River, 281, 283, 287
    black see black bream
    bony see bony bream
    Botany Bay, 253

Bottom Lake, 276
Broken Bay, 247
fingermark, see fingermark bream
Fraser Island, 301
Geelong jetties, 17
Gippsland Lakes, 290
Glenelg River, 103
Gold Coast Seaway, 227
Hawkesbury River, 246
Holland's Landing, 292
Hopkins River, 88, 90
Jumpinpin, 227
Kangaroo Island, 109
Lake King, 298
Lake Victoria, 290, 292
Lakes Entrance, 300
Latrobe River, 290
Loch Sport, 293, 294
Macleay River, 233, 234
McLennan Straits, 291
Mallacoota, 277, 279
Merri River, 91
Metung, 299
Middle Harbour, 253
Mitchell River, 295
Mordialloc Pier, 8
Moyne River, 94
Nerang River, 225
Newport Power Station outflow channel, 14
Nicholson River, 297
Noosa, 218, 219
Noosa River, 217
North Harbour, 253
Patterson River, 6
Paynesville, 294, 295
Pelican Bay, 294
Perry River, 290
Port Hacking, 254
Port River, 115
sea see warehou
Shaving Point, 299
South West Rocks beaches, 234
Station Pier, 11
Storm Point, 294
Sydney, 249, 250, 251
Tambo River, 297
Toms Creek, 292–293
Top Lake, 277
Vaucluse, 251
Wagonga Inlet, 270
Werribee River mouth, 15
Williamstown Pier, 14
yellowfin see yellowfin bream
Brennans Wharf, 136
Bridgewater Bay, 102
Bridgewater Beach, 98
Brighton, 9
Brisbane, 215, 221, 229, 235, 255
Brisbane Waters, 246, 247
Broadbeach, 224
Broadwater, 224, 225, 226
Broken Bay, 244, 246–247
bronze whaler shark
    Dirk Hartog Island, 153
    Port Hurd, 166
    South Alligator River, 193

brook trout
    Central Highlands, 55
    Lake Jindabyne, 262
    Snowy Mountains, 263
Broome, 157, 158–161
brown trout
    Apollo Bay, 77
    Arthurs Lake, 52, 54
    Barham River, 74
    Bemm River, 281
    Buckenderra Arm, 261
    Central Highlands, 55
    Creel Bay, 261
    Eildon Pondage, 309
    Gordon River, 66
    Goulburn River, 304, 305, 308
    Great Lake, 54
    Lake Bullen Merri, 83
    Lake Burbury, 57, 61
    Lake Eildon, 304
    Lake Eucumbene, 258, 259, 260
    Lake Jindabyne, 262
    Lake Purrumbete, 80, 81, 83
    Lake Sorell, 55
    Lower Thredbo River, 263
    Merri River, 91
    Snowy Mountains, 263
    Strahan, 67
    Tasmanian Highlands, 54
    Wild Dog Creek, 72
Buckenderra Arm, 260–261
Bullock Island, 300
Burford Island, 176, 177
Burley Heads, 224
butterfish see dusky morwong

C
Cactus Beach, 140
Cairns, 207, 209, 212, 213
calamari squid
    Adelaide, 115
    Apollo Bay Harbour, 72
    bait, as, 103
    Flinders Island, 41
    Lady Barron, 40
    Point Gellibrand reef areas, 13
    Portland, 103
    Sydney, 250, 255
Cambridge Gulf, 163
Cameron Inlet, 41
Campbell's Cove, 13, 16
Camperdown, 79, 85
Canal Bay, 54
Cape Arid, 144, 147
Cape Barren Island, 40
Cape Cassini, 109
Cape Don, 175–179
Cape Du Couedic, 107
Cape Dutton, 107
Cape Helvetius, 171
Cape Jervis, 109
Cape Le Grand, 144
Cape Nelson, 102
Cape Otway, 74
Cape Patton, 70, 71
Cape York, 201–207
    beaches, 200, 206–207

Cape York Peninsula, 201
carp
    European see European carp
    Gippsland Lakes, 290
Carrum, 5–8
catfish
    Corroboree Billabong, 182
    Mary River, 187
    Shady Camp Lagoon, 186
Ceduna, 140–141
Cemetery Beach, 25
Cemetery Bight, 273
Central Highlands, 51–55
    lakes, 54–55
Chamberlain River, 163
Chambers Bay, 184, 186
Chardons reef, 219
Chinamans Creek, 299
chinook salmon
    Central Highlands, 55
    Lake Bullen Merri, 83
    Lake Purrumbete, 80, 81
chopper tailor, 229
Clarke Island, 40
Clift Island, 171
Clocktower reef, 8
Clonmell Island, 30
Cobden, 85
cobia
    Broome, 160
    Cape York beaches, 206
    Dirk Hartog Island, 155
    Gold Coast, 229
    Kimberley, 163
    Noosa, 218, 219, 221
    South West Rocks, 233, 235
Cobourg Peninsula, 175–176
cockles see pipis
cod
    break-sea see break-sea cod
    estuary see estuary cod
    Kangaroo Island, 108, 109
    maori see maori cod
    Murray see Murray cod
    Noosa, offshore, 219
    reef see reef cod
Coffin Bay, 138, 141
Coffs Harbour, 231, 241
Convention Beach, 138, 139
Cooinda, 191
Coolangatta, 224, 229
Coomera River, 226
Cooroy, 221
Coral Creek, 246
Coral Sea, 218, 229
coral trout
    Cape Don, 179
    Dundas Strait, 177
    Gulf of Carpentaria, 205
    Kimberley, 163
    Liverpool River, 198, 199
    Noosa, 218, 219, 221
    Tiwi Islands, 173
Corio Bay, 4, 16, 17
    ramps, 16
Corner Inlet, 34
Corroboree Billabong, 181, 182–183

Covisart Bay, 139
Cow Paddock Bay, 53
Cowan Waters, 244
Cowes, 23
crab
  bait, as, 115, 216, 296
  blue swimmer see blue swimmer crab
  bream, for, 293
  mud see mudcrabs
Crackenback see Lower Thredbo River
Crawfish Rock, 23
crayfish, 69
Creel Bay, 261
Crocodile Islands, 199
Cunninghame Arm, Lakes Entrance, 300

D
Dalmeny Beach, 270
Darling Point, 251
dart
  Dirk Hartog Island, 155
  Gold Coast, 229
  Noosa, 219, 221
  snub-nosed see permit
  South West Rocks, 233, 234, 235
Darwin, 105, 165, 166, 173, 179, 181, 187, 189, 193, 199, 203
D'Estress Bay, 107
Deep Mornington, 5–7
deep-sea trevalla, 43
Dendy Street reef, 9
Denham, 155
Denham Sound, 150
Dennington, 91
depth sounder, 5, 84, 85, 99, 229, 234, 262, 269, 271
Derby, 163
Devils River, 310
Dirk Hartog Island, 149–155
  rock fishing, 150–154
Discovery Bay, 98, 102
Dog Island, 30, 33
dolphin fish
  Dirk Hartog Island, 155
  Macleay River, 234
  Narooma, offshore, 266
  South West Rocks, 233, 235
  Sydney Harbour, 249
Double Bay, 251
Double Creek Arm, Top Lake, 277
Doughboy River, 202
downrigger, 82, 85, 310
drift-spinning, 58, 61
Dromana, 5
drummer
  Narooma, 271
  Sydney, 250, 255
Duck Arm, Gippsland Lakes, 295
Dudley Peninsula, 107
Dudwell Inlet, 169, 172, 173
Dundas Strait, 177, 178
dusky flathead
  Bemm River, 287
  Botany Bay, 253

Bottom Lake, 274–276
Broadwater, 226, 228
Genoa River, 274
Gippsland Lakes and rivers, 301
Gold Coast, 229
Hawkesbury River, 244, 246, 247
Macleay River, 233, 235
Mallacoota, 274, 279
Narooma, 271
Narrows, the, 274
Noosa, 221
Noosa River, 220
Port Hacking, 254
South West Rocks, 235
Sydney, 255
Top Lake, 274, 277
Wagonga Inlet, 270
Wallagaraugh River, 274
dusky morwong
  Port Phillip Bay, 9
Dutton, 99

E
Eagle Point, 296
Eagle Rock, 23
East Alligator River, 189
East Beach, 85, 88, 95
Eastern Beach, 300
Eastern Cove, 107
eel
  Lake Victoria, 292
  Tambo River, 297
Eildon, 281, 311
Eildon and Goulbourn River, 303–311
Eildon Pondage, 303, 309
Eldon River, 58
electro-fishing, 210, 212–213
elephant fish, 24
Elephant Rock, 39, 40
Eleven Mile Beach, 144
Elizabeth Island, 23
Elliston, 135, 138, 141
Emu Bay, 107
English perch see redfin
Entrance Beach, 287
Entrance Island, 198
Esperance, 143–147
  beaches, 144–146
estuary cod
  Burford Island, 177
  Cape Don, 178, 179
  Dundas Strait, 177
estuary perch, 33
  Aire River, 76
  Apollo Bay, 77
  Avon River, 290
  Barham River, 74
  Bemm River, 282, 287
  Gippsland Lakes and rivers, 301
  Hawkesbury River, 244, 247
  Hopkins River, 88, 89, 90
  Lake King, 298
  McLennan Straits, 291
  Mallacoota, 279
  Merri River, 91
  Mitchell River, 296

Perry River, 290
Sydenham Inlet, 285
Tambo River, 297
Eucumbene River, 258
European carp
  Lake Sorell, 55
  McLennan Strait, 298
Everglades, 217
Eyre Peninsula, 121, 130, 135, 136

F
Fairhaven, 273
False Bay, 123
Farmers Channel, 32
fingermark bream
  Cape Don, 179
  Dundas Strait, 177
  Goose Creek, 173
  Junction Bay, 199
  Kimberley, 163
  Port Hurd, 166
  Tiwi Islands, 173
  Vansittart Bay, 162
First Beach, 287
fish attracting devices (FADS), 233
Fish Rock, 232, 234, 235
fishing lines
  braided line, 120, 146, 147
  gelspun, 173
  lead, 310
  light, 228, 240, 247, 260
  monofilament, 85
  threadline, 121, 127, 147, 192, 221, 229, 235, 247, 271
Fitzroy River, 101
flathead
  Altona Pier, 15
  Apollo Bay, 70
  Bancroft Bay, 299
  bar-tailed see bar-tailed flathead
  Bemm River, 286, 287
  Bird Rock area, 18
  blue-spotted see blue-spotted flathead
  Boston Bay, 136
  Botany Bay, 253
  Broken Bay, 247
  D'Estress Bay, 107
  Deep Mornington to Carrum, 6
  Dirk Hartog Island, 155
  dusky see dusky flathead
  Eagle Point, 296
  Elliston, 138
  Esperance, 147
  Flinders Island, 38, 40
  Frankston Pier, 6
  Fraser Island, 301
  Georges Bay, 47
  Gold Coast Seaway, 229
  Half Moon Bay Pier, 10
  Kangaroo Island, 109
  Kerford Road Pier, 11
  Kilcunda, 27
  Lagoon Pier, 11
  Lake King, 298
  Lake Victoria, 292
  Lakes Entrance, 300

McLoughlins Beach, 30, 31
Mallacoota, 273–275, 279
Manns Beach, 32
Middle Harbour, 253
Mitchell River, 296
Mordialloc Pier, 7, 8
Mornington Pier, 7
Narooma, 269, 271
Nerang River, 225
New Street groynes and reef, 10
Ninety Mile Beach, 31
Noosa River, 217
North East River, 39
North Harbour, 253
Paynesville, 294, 295
Point Gellibrand reef areas, 13
Point Henry area, 19
Port Albert, 30, 34
Port Fairy, 95
Port Hacking, 254
Port Phillip Bay, 3
Port Welshpool, 34
Portland, 103
Pot Boil Point, 39
Prince George bank, 19
Rabbit Island, 35
sand see sand flathead
Smoky Bay (SA), 141
St Helens, 49
St Kilda Pier, 11
Station Pier, 11
Sydney, 249, 251
Tambo River, 297
tiger see tiger flathead
Venus Bay, 139
Werribee River mouth, 15
Western Port, 24
Whyalla, 127
'yank' see 'yank' flathead
Fleurieu Peninsula, 106
Flinders, 24–25
Flinders Island, 35, 37–41
flounder
  Gippsland Lakes and rivers, 301
  McLoughlins Beach, 30
  North East River, 39
  Port Albert, 30
  Port Phillip Bay, 3
  Strahan, 67
  Venus Bay, 139
fly-fishing, 184, 186, 226, 233, 309
  anchovy imitation flies, 207
  beaches, for, 155
  bread flies, 239
  Broome, 161
  Cape Don, for, 179
  Cape York, for, 207
  Clouser fly, chartreuse-coloured, 217
  Clouser fly, pink, 207
  crab fly, 203
  dolphin fish, for, 233
  Lake Burbury, 60–61
  Lake Purrumbete, 83
  Longtail fly, 260, 261
  Lord Howe Island, 239
  Mary River, for, 187

Matuka fly, green, 55
Matuka Longtail fly, 259
Montgomery reef, 161
nymph pattern fly, 309
Red Tag fly, 53
Royal Wulff fly, 60, 306
Tom Jones fly, 55
White Moth fly, 306
'wind-lane' style, 58, 60–61
Woolly Bugger fly, black, 262
Yellow Peril fly, 55
flying gurnard, 268
Forrest, 71, 77
Frankston, 5
Fraser Island, 300
Furneax Group, 37, 40

G
Gabo Island, 279
ganged hook, 151
Garden Point, 166, 172
garfish
    Adelaide, 114, 115
    Altona Pier, 15
    bait, as, 10, 127, 138
    Beaumaris Bay, 7, 8
    Bemm River, 287
    Bottom Lake, 276
    Cape Otway, 74
    Coffin Bay, 138
    Deep Mornington to Carrum, 6
    Elliston, 138
    Flinders Island, 41
    Frankston Pier, 6
    Georges Bay, 47
    Gippsland Lakes and rivers, 301
    Half Moon Bay Pier, 9
    Kangaroo Island, 109
    Kerford Road Pier, 11
    Kingscote, 107
    Lady Bay, 92
    Lagoon Pier, 11
    Lord Howe Island, 240, 241
    Manns Beach, 32
    Marion Bay, 121
    Mitchell River, 296
    Mordialloc Pier, 8
    Mornington Pier, 7
    New Street reef, 10
    North Arm, Lakes Entrance, 300
    Paynesville, 294, 295
    Point Cook reef areas, 14
    Point Gellibrand reef areas, 13
    Point Henry area, 19
    Port Albert, 30
    Port Phillip Bay, 1, 3
    Prince George bank, 19
    Reevesby Island, 131
    Ricketts Point, 8
    Robertsons Beach, 33
    Sandringham breakwater, 9
    Seaford Pier, 6
    St Helens, 49
    Station Pier, 11
    Tumby Bay, 129, 133
    Werribee River mouth, 16
    Western Port, 24
    Whyalla, 127
    yellowtail kingfish, for, 138
Geelong, 77, 95, 103
Geelong Grammar School Lagoon, 17
Genoa River, 274, 277
Georges Bay, 45, 47
giant clams, 162
giant groper, 166
giant herring
    Bathurst Island, 171
    Cape York, 206, 207
    Liverpool River, offshore, 198
giant trevally
    Bathurst Island, 171
    Broome, 160
    Burford Island, 177
    Cape Don, 176, 179
    Cape York, 202, 207
    Dundas Strait, 177
    Gold Coast, 229
    Kimberley, 163
    Liverpool River, 198, 199
    Melville Island, 172
    Montgomery reef, 160, 161
    Nerang River, 225
    Noosa, 221
    Noosa River, 217
    Port Hurd, 167
    Tiwi Islands, 173
    Trepang Creek, 178
    Vansittart Bay, 158
Gippsland, 87
Gippsland Lakes and rivers, 49, 288–301
    commercial fishing, 290
    Western Lakes and rivers, 289–290
Glenelg River, 98, 102, 103
Glenelg tyre reefs, 113
Glenmaggie Weir, 304
Gold Coast, 214, 223–229
    beaches, 224
    offshore, 229
Gold Coast Seaway, 226, 228, 229
gold spot trevally, 153
golden perch, 310
golden snapper
    Cape Don, 179
    Gulf of Carpentaria, 205
    Liverpool River, 198, 199
    South Alligator River, 192, 193
golden trevally
    Bathurst Island, 171
    Broome, 160, 161
    Cape York, 207
    Gulf of Carpentaria, 205
    Kimberley, 163
    Liverpool River, 198, 199
    Montgomery reef, 161
    Noosa, 221
    Tiwi Islands, 173
Goodwin Sands, 273, 275
Goose Creek, 167, 173
Gordon Bay, 170
Gordon River, 64, 66–67
Goulburn River, 303–309
    flow rate, 304
    tailrace fishery, 304
Goulburn Valley, 309
Grange tyre reef, 110, 114
Great Australian Bight, 139, 140, 145
Great Lake, 51, 54, 55
great white shark, 101
grey-black gudgeon, 88
Griffith Island, 95
groper
    bald-chin see bald-chin groper
    blue see blue groper
gudgeon
    grey-black see grey-black gudgeon
    Lake Bullen Merri, 83, 84
    twin, 85
Gulf of Carpentaria, 202, 204
Gulf of St Vincent, 111, 114, 115, 117
Gullala Creek, 172
gummy shark
    Bass Strait, 153
    Bastin Point, 278
    Bemm River, 287
    Bridgewater Bay, 102
    Cape Otway, 74
    Esperance beaches, 144, 145, 147
    Flinders, at, 25
    Flinders Island, 38, 40, 41
    Gippsland Lakes and rivers, 301
    Johanna Beach, 77
    Lady Barron, 40
    Lady Bay, 92
    Lakes Entrance, 300
    McLoughlins Beach, 31
    Mallacoota, 279
    Manns Beach, 33
    Narooma, offshore, 268
    Narrawong Beach, 98
    Ninety Mile Beach, 31, 294
    Port Albert Channel, 34
    Port Welshpool, 34
    Portland, 101, 102, 103
    Pot Boil Point, 39
    Warrnambool, 93
    Western Port, 24
Gunnamatta, 26
gurnard
    flying see flying gurnard
    Glenelg tyre reefs, 113
    McLoughlins Beach, 31
    Marion Bay, 121

H
hairtail, 244, 246
Halls reef, 219
hammerhead shark
    Cape Don, 179
    Lord Howe Island, 240
    Rex's Cay, 177
Handkerchief Beach, 270
Hanson Bay, 107
harlequin fish
    Archipelago of the Recherche, 146, 147
    Esperance, 147
harpuka, 41
Harrison's Channel, 275
Hastings, 23
Hat Head, 232
Hatchery Bay, 262
Hawk Island, 52
Hawkesbury River, 243–247
Hayley Point, 74
Hayley reef, 74
Hell Rock, 177
Henty reef, 73, 74
Henty River, 64, 65, 66
herring
    bait, as, 235
    giant see giant herring
    ox-eye see ox-eye herring
    wolf see wolf herring
Highland Lakes, 61
Hobart, 48, 55, 60, 61, 66, 202
Holland's Landing, 291, 292
Hopkins River, 87, 88–90, 93, 94
Horans Point, 82
Horden Vale, 76
Horseshoe Bay, 235
Hoses Rocks, 82
Howqua Arm, Lake Eildon, 311
hump-headed wrasse, 241
Huon Bay, 262

I
Indian Ocean, 150, 151, 160
Investigator Islands, 138
Investigator Strait, 108, 120

J
Jabiru, 183
Jackson River, 204
Jerusalem Bay, 246
Jerusalem Creek, 310
Jessie River, 172, 173
Jessie River Camp, 172
Jessie River rock bar, 172–173
Jew Shoal, 219
jewfish see also mulloway
    black see black jewfish
    Broken Bay, 247
    Hawkesbury River, 244, 246, 247
    Macleay River, 234–235
    Melville Island, 172
    Noosa Heads breakwall, 218
    Sydney, 250, 251, 255
    Wagonga Inlet, 271
Jindabyne, 262
Johanna surf beach, 70
John Dory, 250, 253, 254, 255
Johnsonville boat ramp, 297
Johnston River, 172, 173
Jonah Bay, 53
Jones Bay, 296
Jubilee Park, 90
Jumpinpin, 226, 227–229
Junction Bay, 199

K
Kakadu, 181, 189, 191, 193
Kalgoorlie, 144
Kalkite Point, 262
Kangaroo Island, 105–109, 120
    beaches and rocks, 107
    jetties, 106–107
    offshore, 108–109

Kate Kearney, 30, 33
Kellidie Bay, 138
Kempsey, 235
Kianga Beach, 270
Kilcunda, 25–27
Killarney Beach, 95
Killiecrankie Bay, 41
Kimberley, 157–163
King Edward River, 158, 162
King George whiting
    Adelaide, 113, 115
    American River, 107
    Apollo Bay, 72, 77
    Bottom Lake, 276
    Bouchier and Boulton channels, 25
    Coffin Bay, 138
    Esperance, 147
    Flinders, at, 25
    Gippsland Lakes and rivers, 301
    Gulf of St Vincent, 112
    Kangaroo Island, 108, 109
    Lady Bay, 92
    Lawrence Rocks, 100
    McLoughlins Beach, 31
    Mallacoota, 279
    Marengo, 74
    Marion Bay, 119, 121
    Point Gellibrand reef areas, 13
    Point Henry area, 19
    Port Albert, 30
    Port Phillip Bay, 2, 3, 7
    Portland, 99, 103
    Rabbit Island, 35
    Sandy Point, 25
    Skenes Creek, 71
    Streaky Bay, 139
    Thevenard, 141
    Thistle Island, 137
    Tumby Bay, 133
    Western Port, 22
    Whyalla, 127
King River, 57
king salmon **see** chinook salmon
King Sound, 161
kingfish
    Balls Pyramid, 240
    Boston Bay, 136
    Fish Rock, 234
    Lady Barron, 40
    Lord Howe Island, 241
    Narooma, offshore, 266
    North Harbour, 253
    Sydney, offshore, 250
    Tumby Bay, 129
    Wave Break Island, 229
    yellowtail **see** yellowtail kingfish
kingfish traps
    banning of, 268
Kings Head, 89, 90
Kirk Point
    Long Reef, 17
    ramps, 16
Kununurra, 157

L
Lady Barron, 39–40, 41
Lady Bay, 88, 92
Lady Julia Percy Island, 95, 101
Lake Bullen Merri, 79, 80, 83–85
Lake Burbury, 57–61
    fly-fishing, 60–61
    land-based opportunities, 58–59
    trolling lures, 59–60
Lake Craven, 76
Lake Eildon, 303, 304, 309, 310–311
Lake Eucumbene, 258–261, 263, 310
    Frying Pan Arm, 260, 263
    Providence Portal Arm, 258, 259
Lake Gnotuk, 80
Lake Jindabyne, 261–262
Lake King, 292, 295, 296, 298
Lake Macdonald, 220
Lake Pedder, 310
Lake Purrumbete, 79, 80–83
Lake Sorell, 55
Lake Tinaroo, 209–213
    environmental make-up, 210
Lake Victoria, 290, 291, 292–293, 294
Lake Wellington, 289, 290, 291, 292
Lakes Entrance, 289, 299–301
Lakes Purrumbete and Bullen Merri, 77–85
    stocking program, 80
Lane Cove River, 251
Latrobe River, 289, 290
Launceston, 55
Lawrence Rocks, 100
leatherjacket
    Adelaide, 115
    Altona Pier, 15
    Apollo Bay Harbour, 72, 73
    Bottom Lake, 276
    Bouchier and Boulton channels, 25
    Coffin Bay, 138
    Flinders, at, 24
    Frankston Pier, 6
    Half Moon Bay Pier, 10
    horseshoe, 121
    Kangaroo Island, 107, 109
    Lady Bay, 92
    Long Reef, 17
    Marion Bay, 121
    Middle Harbour, 253
    Point Henry area, 19
    Port Phillip Bay, 3
    Portland, 99, 103
    six-spined **see** six-spined leatherjacket
    Sydney, 250, 251, 255
    Warrnambool, 88
Lee breakwater, 98, 99, 103
Levys Beach, 88, 91, 94–95
Liawenee Canal, 54
Lingi Point, 177
Little Pine Lagoon, 55
Liverpool River, 195–199
Loch Sport, 293–294
Locks Well, 138
Logans Beach, 88, 93
Long Reef, 17
long-tail tuna, 198
long tom
    Dirk Hartog Island, 151
    Kimberley rivers, 162

Lord Howe Island, 237–241
    inshore and offshore, 239–240
    land-based opportunities, 240–241
    tourism restrictions, 238
    World Heritage listing, 238
Lower Thredbo River, 263
    fishing restrictions, 263
luderick
    Bemm River, 287
    Gippsland Lakes and rivers, 301
    Hawkesbury River, 247
    Lake King, 298
    Lakes Entrance, 300
    Macleay River, 233, 234
    Macquarie Harbour, 65
    Narooma, 271
    Noosa, 217, 218, 221
    Paynesville, 294
    South West Rocks, 233, 235
    Strahan, 67
    Sydney, 250, 255
    Tambo River, 297
    Wagonga Inlet, 270
lures
    bait-fish profile, 251
    bibbed, 60, 103, 263, 295, 310, 311
    CD 11 Rapala, 19, 198
    CD 13 Rapala, 198
    Celta, 263, 306, 307, 311
    Cobra-style, 60
    Dahlberg Diver, 182, 191
    deep-diving, 82, 85, 103, 160, 163, 167, 173, 179, 183, 186, 192, 193, 196, 198, 213, 226, 259, 261, 310, 311
    Dickson, yellow, 305, 311
    diving, 191, 193, 203
    ford-fender attractors, 262
    frog imitation, rubber, 182
    Gold Bomber Fly, 184
    Halco Trembler, 177
    hard-bodied, 251, 287, 293
    long barrel sinker, natural lead, 311
    Magnum Barra, 196
    Manns 10+, 196
    medium-diving, 191
    metal, 39, 277, 295
    mice imitation, rubber, 182
    minnow, 60, 85, 89, 179, 293
    Nilmaster, 203
    Nilmaster Spearhead, 192, 198
    Pink Things, 161, 191
    plastic skirt, 270
    poppers, 198, 217, 234
    Rapala bibbed, 263, 310
    Rapala Rainbow Trout, 261
    rattling, 162, 172, 179
    rattling silver spot, 196
    revolving blade, 60, 263, 311
    rubber-tail, 286
    scum frog, 182
    shallow-diving, 191
    silver, 39, 239
    skirted, 40, 47, 160, 229, 268, 271
    sliced metal, 233
    Sliders, 221
    Sluggos, 251

    soft plastic, 10, 184, 193, 216, 221, 226, 235, 244, 251, 276, 277, 278, 287, 290, 291, 293, 295
    soft plastic jig-type, 6
    spinning, 59, 61, 72, 304, 307, 311
    Stumpjumper, 206
    Super Duper, 259, 309
    surface, 277
    surface popper, 217
    Tasmanian Devil, 53, 60, 82, 85, 259
    teaspoon, 305
    Tiger Devon, 305
    Tylos, 307, 309
    Vibrax, 263, 311
    Wobbler, 306, 307, 310

M
Macallister River, 304
Macdonald River, 204
mackerel tuna, 218, 219, 221
Macleay River, 232–233, 234–235
McLennan Strait, 289, 290, 291–292, 295
McLoughlin's Beach, 30–31, 34
McMillan Strait, 294, 295
Macquarie Harbour, 63, 64–66
maggots
    garfish, for, 10
mahi mahi **see** dolphin fish
mako shark
    Narooma, 271
    Portland, 100
    St Helens, 45, 47, 49
Mallacoota, 273–279
    beaches and offshore, 278–279
    fishing restrictions, 279
mangrove jack
    Cape Don, 177, 179
    Cape York, 207
    Doughboy River, 203
    Dundas Strait, 177
    Gold Coast, 228, 229
    Goose Creek, 173
    Gullala Creek, 172
    Junction Bay, 199
    Kimberley, 161, 163
    King Edward River, 159
    Liverpool River, 199
    Melville Island, 172
    Nerang River, 225
    Port Hurd, 166
    Tiwi Islands, 173
    Trepang Creek, 178
    Vansittart Bay, 162
Manifold Clock Tower, 79
Maningrida, 195, 199
Manly, 253
Manns Beach, 30, 32–33
Manns Point, 251
manta rays, 205
maori cod, 221
Marengo, 73, 74
Marion Bay, 117–121
    inshore opportunities, 121
marlin
    black **see** black marlin
    blue **see** blue marlin

Mallacoota, offshore, 279
methods of catching in Narooma, 270
Narooma, offshore, 266, 269
South West Rocks, 232
striped see striped marlin
Sydney Harbour, 249
Marlo, 26
Mary River, 181–187, 191
Melbourne, 4, 6, 35, 77, 95, 103, 124, 166, 255, 261, 263, 271, 279, 287, 289, 299, 301, 311
Melville Island, 105, 165, 172–173
Merri River, 88, 91
Metung, 289, 292, 299
Middle Harbour, 253
Middle Island, 145, 146
Middle River, 108
Miena, 55
Milikapiti, 173
Minnihaha Point, 262
Mitchell River (Vic), 291, 295–296, 297
Mitchell River (WA), 162
Monkey Mia, 155
Montague Island, 266
Montgomery reef, 161
Mornington, 5
Mornington Peninsula, 26
morwong
blue see blue morwong
dusky see dusky morwong
Lady Julia Percy Island, 95
Montague Island, 268
Narooma, 268, 269, 271
Starbank reef, 279
Sydney, 250, 255
Mosman Bay, 251
Mount Dutton Bay, 138
Mount Gower, 237
Mount Lidgbird, 237
Mount Martha, 5
Mounts Bay, 73
Mouth Flat beaches, 107
Moyne River, 94, 95
Mud Lake, 286
mudcrab
Crocodile Islands, 199
Trepang Creek, 178
mudeyes, 54, 58, 61, 81, 311
bait, as, 85, 259, 262, 309
Lake Burbury, 59
trout, for, 309
mullet
Adelaide, 114, 115
Aire River, 76
Apollo Bay, 72, 73, 77
bait, as, 102, 103, 162, 226, 235, 251, 277
Bancroft Bay, 299
Barham River, 75
barramundi, for, 162, 171
Bathurst Island, 167
Bottom Lake, 276
dusky flathead, for, 226
Elliston, 138
Emu Bay, 107
flathead, for, 251, 295, 296

Geelong jetties, 17
Gippsland Lakes, 290
Glenelg River, 103
Hawkesbury River, 246, 247
Holland's Landing, 292
Investigator Strait, 108
Kangaroo Island, 108, 109
Kerford Road Pier, 11
Kilcunda, 27
Lady Bay, 92
Lake Victoria, 290
Lakes Entrance, 300
Levys Beach, 90, 95
Loch Sport, 293
Logans Beach, 94
Macleay River, 234
McLennan Straits, 291
Metung, 299
Mordialloc Pier, 8
Moyne River, 94
mulloway, for, 277
New Street groynes, 10
Newport Power Station outflow channel, 14
Noosa, 219, 221
Patterson River, 6
Paynesville, 294
Port Hacking, 254
Portland Harbour, 99
Pot Boil Point, 39
Sandringham breakwater, 9
Shady Camp Lagoon, 183
Skenes Creek, 71
Snelling Beach, 107
St Kilda Pier, 11
Station Pier, 11
Stokes Bay, 107
Strahan, 67
Sydney, 249, 255
Tambo River, 297
Top Lake, 277
Tumby Bay, 133
Venus Bay, 139
Warrnambool, 93
Western River, 108
Whyalla, 127
Williamstown Pier, 14
yellow-eye see yellow-eye mullet
mulloway
Bancroft Bay, 299
Bottom Lake, 277
Bridgewater Bay, 102
Ceduna beaches, 140
Esperance beaches, 144, 145, 147
Glenelg River, 103
Gold Coast, 227, 229
Hawkesbury River, 246, 247
Hopkins River, 89
Kangaroo Island, 109
Lagoon Pier, 11
Logans Beach, 94
Macleay River, 233, 234
Mallacoota, 279
Middle Harbour, 253
Narrows, the, 277
Newport Power Station outflow channel, 14

Port River, 115
Portland, 99, 101, 102, 103
Smoky Bay, 141
South West Rocks, 233, 235
Station Pier, 11
Sydney, 251, 255
Thevenard, 141
Top Lake, 277
Wagonga Inlet, 271
Warrnambool, 93
Wave Break Island, 229
Murray cod, 310, 311
mussels
bait, as, 8
farms, 19
saltwater, 305
whiting, for, 24
Williamstown Pier, 14

N
nannygai
Adelaide, 112, 113
Archipelago of the Recherche, 146
Esperance, 147
Investigator Islands, 138
Investigator Strait, 120
Kangaroo Island, 108, 109
Lady Bay, 92
Marion Bay, 118, 119, 121
Thistle Island, 136
Narooma, 265–271
beaches, 270
marlin, methods of catching, 270
offshore options, 266–270
water temperature, 269
Narrawong Beach, 98, 99, 101
Narrows, the, 274, 275, 277
Neds Beach, 241
Neil Island, 52
Nelson, 103
Nepean Bay, 106
Nerang River, 225, 226
New Street groynes and reef, 10
Newcastle, 247
Nicholson River, 297
Ninety Mile Beach, 26, 31, 289, 294
nipper see bass yabbies
Noorat, 87
Noosa, 215–221
beaches, 219
offshore, 219
Noosa Heads, 217, 218
Noosa River, 216–217, 219
Noosaville, 216
Norfolk Island, 237
North Arm, Lakes Entrance, 300
North Cape, 109
North East River, 38–39
North Harbour, 253
North Head, 251
North reef, 219
North Shore Beach, 219
North Stradbroke Island, 227
northern bluefin tuna
Cape York, 204
Dirk Hartog Island, 155
Liverpool River, 199

Noosa, 221
Tiwi Islands, 173
Nourlangie Creek, 193
Nullarbor Plain, 140, 143
nymph, 309, 311
bead-head, 306

O
Ocean Beach, 67
ocean perch, 250
Olivers Hill, 6
Omeo, 29
orange roughy, 43
Orbost, 287
Otway Ranges, 69, 70, 73, 76, 77
Outer Harbour Channel, 113
ox-eye herring
Corroboree Billabong, 182, 183
Mary River, 187
Nourlangie Creek, 193
Shady Camp Lagoon, 186
South Alligator River, 193
Tiwi Islands, 173
oysters
Ceduna, 140
Coffin Bay, 138

P
Pacific Ocean, 237
Palm Beach, 247
Parakary River, 170–171
paravane, 310
Parkdale, 304
Parramatta River, 251
parrotfish
Kangaroo Island, 107
Macquarie Harbour, 65
Marion Bay, 121
Middle Island, 145
Patagonian toothfish, 153
paternoster rig, 120, 145, 268, 294
Patterson River, 5, 49
boat ramps, 5
Paynesville, 289, 294–295
pearl perch
Gold Coast reefs, 229
Noosa, 221
South West Rocks, offshore, 233
Pearl Point, 284, 287
Pearson Island, 134
Pelican Bay, 294
Pelican Point, 286
Penneshaw, 109
Penneshaw River, 106
Pennington Bay, 107
Penstock Lagoon, 55
perch
English see redfin
golden see golden perch
ocean see ocean perch
pearl see pearl perch
Sydney, 254
Perisher Valley, 257
permit
Cape York beaches, 206
Doughboy River, 203, 206
Peron Peninsula, 154, 155

Perry River, 289, 290
Perth, 143, 147, 155, 163
Peterborough, 93
Picnic Arm, Gippsland Lakes, 295
pike *see* snook
pilchard
    bait, as, 81, 99, 100, 102, 103, 120, 127, 145, 151, 153, 229, 234, 236, 251
    cobia, for, 206
    flathead, for, 296, 301
    gummy shark, for, 145
    King George whiting, for, 31
    mullet, for, 39
    salmon, for, 39, 145
    snapper, for, 155
    snook, for, 39
    tailor, for, 234
    Western Australian, 127
pinky snapper, 8
    Beaumaris Pier, 8
    Bouchier and Boulton channels, 25
    Clocktower reef, 10
    Gippsland Lakes and rivers, 301
    Kerford Road Pier, 11
    Kilcunda, 27
    Lagoon Pier, 11
    Long Reef, 17
    Manns Beach, 33
    New Street groynes, 10
    Point Gellibrand reef areas, 13
    Point Henry area, 19
    Port Albert, 30, 34
    Port Phillip Bay, 4
    Portland Harbour, 99
    Ricketts Point, 8
    Station Pier, 11
pipis
    bait, as, 8, 74, 100, 114, 115, 246
    dart, for, 224
    flathead, for, 224
    King George whiting, for, 133
    luderick, for, 65
    sand whiting, for, 224
    snapper, for, 6
    Surfers Paradise, 224
    whiting, for, 24
    yellowfin bream, for, 224
Pittwater, 244, 247
Point Cook
    marine park, 13
    reef areas, 13
Point Danger, 99, 100
Point Gellibrand
    reef areas, 13
Point Henry, 18
Point Wilson, 17
Port Adelaide, 115
Port Albert, 29–35
Port Augusta, 117
Port Douglas, 138
Port Essington, 178
Port Fairy, 88, 93, 94, 95, 101
Port Hacking, 249, 254
Port Henry, 18
Port Hurd, 166, 167, 169–171, 192
Port Jackson, 253

Port Lincoln, 117, 129, 133, 135–136, 138, 141
    aquaculture farms, 136
Port Lincoln to Ceduna, 135–141
Port Macquarie, 231
Port Melbourne, 5
Port Phillip Bay, 1–19, 81, 113, 126, 303
Port River, 114, 115
Port Welshpool, 30, 34–35
Portarlington, 5, 18
Portland, 92, 96–103
Possession Island, 201
Pot Boil Point, 39
Potters Point, 85
Powlett River, 26
prawns
    bait, as, 115, 216, 246, 251, 285, 287, 296, 297, 298, 300
    Bancroft Bay, 299
    bream, for, 103, 278, 284, 293
    estuary perch, for, 284
    garfish, for, 10
    King George whiting, for, 133
    snapper, for, 6
    whiting, for, 271
Prince Regent River, 162
Pump House Bay, 53

Q
queen snapper *see* blue morwong
queenfish
    Bathurst Island, 171
    Burford Island, 177
    Cape Don, 176, 179
    Cape York, 206, 207
    Cobourg Peninsula, 177
    Gulf of Carpentaria, 205
    Kimberley rivers, 163
    Liverpool River, 198 199
    Melville Island, 172
    Port Hurd, 166
    Rex's Cay, 177
    Skardon River, 202
    Tiwi Islands, 173
    Trepang Creek, 178
    Vashon Head, 179
Queenscliff, 19
Queenstown, 57, 61
quinnat salmon *see* chinook salmon

R
Rabbit Island, 35
Rainbow Beach, 219
Rainbow Point, 82
rainbow trout
    Central Highlands, 55
    Eildon Pondage, 309
    Gordon River, 66
    Great Lake, 54
    Lake Bullen Merri, 83
    Lake Burbury, 57, 61
    Lake Eucumbene, 258, 259
    Lake Jindabyne, 262
    Lake Purrumbete, 80, 83
    Lower Thredbo River, 263
    Macquarie Harbour, 64–65

Snowy Mountains, 263
    Strahan, 67
Raymond Island, 292, 294, 295
razor fish
    bait, as, 139
    Streaky Bay, 139
    whiting, for, 139
Red Bluff, 41
Red Bluff reef, 8
red claw crayfish, 210, 213
red emperor
    Cape Don, 179
    Dirk Hartog Island, 154, 155
    Gulf of Carpentaria, 205
    Kimberley, 163
    Noosa, offshore, 219
red gurnard, 38
Red Johanna beach, 76, 77
Red Lily Billabong, 191
redfin
    Howqua Arm, Lake Eildon, 311
    Lake Eildon, 308
reef cod, 221
reef shark
    black-tip *see* black-tip reef shark
    Dirk Hartog Island, 153
reels *see* rods and reels
Reevesby Island, 130, 131
Rex's Cay, 177
Ricketts Point
    marine sanctuary, 8
    Yarra River, to, 8–11
River Itchen, 309
River Test, 309
Robertsons Beach, 33
rock cod
    Mordialloc Pier, 8
    Port Phillip Bay, 3
Rocky Point, 171
rods and reels
    baitcaster, 55, 173, 179, 182, 187, 193, 207, 213
    beach, 77, 95, 147, 221, 229
    light rod, 19, 41, 109, 133, 287, 301
    light to medium rod, 27, 35, 77, 95, 103, 121, 141, 229, 235, 279
    long rod, 48, 154
    medium rod, 19, 115, 121, 127, 133, 147, 241, 247, 255
    medium to heavy, 103, 235
    overhead reel, 120, 121, 141, 147, 155, 221, 229, 235, 241, 247, 255
    overhead rod, 41, 115, 127, 147, 155, 221, 229, 235, 241, 247, 255
    soft-action long rod, 228
    spinning, 247, 255, 287
    surf, 41, 109, 141, 287
    taper, 260
    threadline, 19, 35, 41, 49, 61, 67, 77, 85, 95, 127, 140, 221, 235, 247, 255, 263, 271, 279, 301, 311
    three-metre, 301
    whiting-type, 81
Roebuck Bay, 158, 160
Rose Bay, 251
Roxby Island, 130
running sinker rig, 81, 260, 262, 299

S
sailfish
    Broome, 158, 162
    Kimberley, 163
    Montague Island, 269
    South West Rocks, 234
Sale, 301
salmon
    Apollo Bay Harbour, 73
    bait, as, 127, 277
    Bancroft Bay, 299
    Bemm River, 281, 287
    black-backed *see* black-backed salmon
    blue *see* blue salmon
    Boston Bay, 136
    Botany Bay, 253
    Brennans Wharf, 136
    Bridgewater Bay, 102
    Cape Otway, 74
    Eleven Mile Beach, 144
    Elliston, 138
    Esperance beaches, 145
    Frankston Pier, 6
    Georges Bay, 47
    Hanson Bay, 107
    Kangaroo Island, 107, 109
    Kerford Road Pier, 11
    Kilcunda, 27
    Lady Barron, 40
    Lagoon Pier, 11
    Lakes Entrance, 300
    Lawrence Rocks, 100
    Lee breakwater, 99
    Levys Beach, 90, 94, 95
    Locks Well Beach, 138
    Logans Beach, 94
    Macquarie Harbour, 65
    Marengo, 74
    Mordialloc Pier, 8
    Moyne River, 94
    Ninety Mile Beach, 292, 294
    North East River, 38, 39
    Port Albert, 30
    Port Fairy, 88, 95
    Portland, 99, 101, 102
    Skenes Creek, 71
    Smoky Bay, 141
    St Kilda Pier, 11
    threadfin *see* threadfin salmon
    Trousers Point, 39
    Tuckamore Beach, 140
    Tumby Bay, 129
    Venus Bay, 139
    Warrnambool, 88, 93
    Western Port, 24
    Wild Dog Creek, 71
Sampan Creek, 184
samson fish
    Archipelago of the Recherche, 146, 147
    Dirk Hartog Island, 155
    Esperance, 147
    Kangaroo Island, 108
    Marion Bay, 119
sand flathead
    Apollo Bay, 77

Flinders Island, 38, 41
Gippsland Lakes and rivers, 301
Gold Coast, 228, 229
Narooma, offshore, 268
Sand Lake, 52
sand whiting
   Dirk Hartog Island, 154
   Gold Coast, 229
   Hawkesbury River, 246, 247
   Narooma beaches, 270
   Nerang River, 225, 226
   Noosa, 219, 221
   Noosa River, 216, 217
   Pittwater, 247
   Port Hacking, 254
   South West Rocks, 233, 234, 235
   Sydney, offshore, 250
Sandringham breakwall, 8
Sandy Point, 23
Sarah Island, 63
saratoga
   Corroboree Billabong, 182
   Liverpool River, 199
   Mary River, 187
   Shady Camp Lagoon, 186
   South Alligator River, 192, 193
   Tiwi Islands, 173
scallops, 43
scarlet sea perch, 160
Schnapper Point, 6
school shark
   Flinders Island, 38, 40
   McLoughlins Beach, 31
   Western Port, 24
'schoolies' see jewfish
Scotts Beach, 140
sea bream, 95
sea-run trout
   Aire River, 76
   Barham River, 74
   Henty River, 64, 67
   Merri River, 91
seaspray, 34
Second Creek, 167
Seisia, 203, 204, 205, 207
sergeant baker, 268
seven gill shark, 40, 41
Seven Spirit Bay, 178
Seymour, 304
Shady Camp, 182, 184–186
   boat ramps, 184
   fishing restrictions, 184
Shady Camp Barrage, 184, 186
Shady Camp Lagoon, 181
Shags Rocks, 82
shark
   Adelaide, 115
   Apollo Bay, 70, 77
   bait, as, 172
   blue see blue shark
   Cape Don, 179
   Gold Coast Seaway, 227
   great white see great white shark
   hammerhead see hammerhead shark
   Kangaroo Island, 109
   Kimberley, 163

Lady Bay, 92
Lady Julia Percy Island, 95
Logans Beach, 94
Lord Howe Island, 240, 241
Narooma, offshore, 266
Noosa Heads breakwall, 218
Port Fairy, 95
Portland, 103
reef see reef shark
Rex's Cay, 177
school see school shark
Sydney, 255
Tumby Bay, 133
Wave Break Island, 229
whaler see whaler shark
Shark Bay, 149, 150, 154–155
   snapper fishing restrictions, 155
Shaving Point, 299
Shelly Beach, 102
short-finned eel, 85
Siberia, 286
silver trevally
   Apollo Bay, 70, 72, 77
   Bastin Point, 278
   Bemm River, 286, 287
   Bottom Lake, 276
   Bullock Island, 300
   Esperance beaches, 144, 145, 147
   Flinders Island, 38, 41
   Georges Bay, 47
   Gippsland Lakes and rivers, 301
   Investigator Strait, 120
   Kangaroo Island, 107
   Kingscote, 107
   Lady Barron, 40
   Lady Bay, 92
   Lee breakwater, 99
   McLoughlins Beach, 30, 31
   Mallacoota, 279
   Marion Bay, 121
   Middle Island, 146
   Narooma, 271
   North East River, 39
   Port Albert, 35
   Port Hacking, 254
   Port Phillip Bay, 3
   Portland, 99, 103
   Pot Boil Point, 39
   Skenes Creek, 71
   Spilsby Island, 132
   Sydney, 250, 255
   Thevenard, 141
   Tumby Bay, 133
   Warrnambool, 88, 93
   Western River Cove, 107
   Wild Dog Creek, 71
Singapore Deep, 30, 34, 35
Sir Joseph Banks Group, 129, 130–131, 133
six-spined leatherjacket
   Marion Bay, inshore, 121
   Port Hacking, 254
Skardon River, 202, 204
Skenes Creek, 71, 73
skipjack see also silver trevally, 145
slides, 196
Smoky Bay, 141

Smoky Cape, 234
Snake Bay, 171, 173
Snake Channel, 34
Snake Island, 34
snapper
   Adelaide, 111, 113, 115
   Altona Pier, 15
   Apollo Bay, 70, 72, 73, 77
   Archipelago of the Recherche, 146
   Bancroft Bay, 299
   Beaumaris Bay, 7
   Bird Rock area, 18
   Boston Bay, 136
   Botany Bay, 253
   Brennans Wharf, 136
   Brighton breakwater, 11
   Cape Otway, 74
   Cape Patton, 71
   Carrum to Ricketts Point, 7
   Corio Bay, 17
   Deep Mornington to Carrum, 5–6
   Dirk Hartog Island, 155
   Eastern Beach, 301
   Esperance, 147
   Flinders, at, 25
   Glenelg tyre reefs, 113
   Gold Coast, 229
   golden see golden snapper
   Hayley Point, 76
   Investigator Islands, 138
   Johanna Beach, 77
   Kangaroo Island, 108, 109
   Kerford Road Pier, 11
   Lady Bay, 92
   Lady Julia Percy Island, 95
   Logans Beach, 94
   McLoughlins Beach, 31
   Manns Beach, 33
   Marengo, 74
   Marion Bay, 119, 121
   Montague Island, 268
   Mordialloc Pier, 7
   Mornington Pier, 7
   Narooma, 268, 271
   Narrawong Beach, 98
   New Street groynes, 10
   Ninety Mile Beach, 31
   Noosa, 218, 219, 221
   North Harbour, 253
   Outer Harbour Channel, 113
   Point Cook reef areas, 13
   Port Albert Channel, 34
   Port Fairy, 95
   Port Phillip Bay, 2–4
   Port Welshpool, 35
   Portland, 99, 101, 103
   queen see blue morwong
   red see nannygai
   Sandringham breakwater, 9, 10
   Shark Bay, 153, 154
   Shelly Beach, 102
   South West Rocks, 233, 235
   Spencer Gulf, 125–127, 132
   St Kilda Pier, 11
   Starbank reef, 279
   Steep Point, 154
   Sydney, 250, 255

Thevenard, 141
Thistle Island, 136
Tumby Bay, 129, 133
Wagonga Inlet, 270
water temperature, 3
Werribee River mouth, 16
Western Port, 23
Whyalla, 123, 127
Snelling Beach, 107
snook
   Apollo Bay, 77
   bait, as, 247
   Elliston, 138
   Flinders, at, 24
   Flinders Island, 41
   jewfish, for, 247
   Kangaroo Island, 109
   Marion Bay, 121
   Mordialloc Pier, 8
   Point Gellibrand reef areas, 13
   Point Henry area, 19
   Port Welshpool, 35
   Portland, 103
   Reevesby Island, 131
   Trousers Point, 39
   Tumby Bay, 133
   Western Port, 24
   Whyalla, 127
snotty-nose trevally
   Kerford Road Pier, 11
   Portland Harbour, 99
Snowdens Beach, 115
Snowy Mountains, 257–263
   closed season, 263
   hydroelectric scheme, 257, 258, 261
snub-nosed dart see permit
Snug Cove, 108
'soapies' see jewfish
South Alligator River, 189–193
   billabongs, 191–192
   lower reaches, 193
South Eldon River, 58
South Passage, 154
South Stradbroke Island, 222, 224, 226, 227
South West Arm, Top Lake, 277
South West Rocks, 231–235
   beaches and rocks, 234
   offshore, 233
southern black bream, 283
southern bluefin tuna
   Kangaroo Island, 109
   Lawrence Rocks, 100
   Port Lincoln, 134
   Portland, 101, 103
southern calamari, 8
Southern Ocean, 71, 72, 92, 100, 121, 135, 154
Southport, 225, 226
Southport Spit, 226
spangled emperor, 155
Spanish mackerel
   Bathurst Island, 171
   Broome, 160
   Cape Don, 176, 179
   Cape Helvetius, 171
   Cape York, 207

Dirk Hartog Island, 154, 155
Dundas Strait, 177
Gold Coast, 229
Kimberley, 163
Melville Island, 172
South West Rocks, 233, 235
Tiwi Islands, 173
Vashon Head, 179
Spencer Gulf, 117, 123, 125–127, 130, 131
Spilsby Island, 132
spotted mackerel
　Gold Coast, 229
　Sydney Harbour, 249
Squeaky Beach, 144
squid
　Adelaide, 114
　Apollo Bay Harbour, 73
　arrow see arrow squid
　bait, as, 74, 99, 100, 114, 127, 229, 251, 253, 277
　Bird Rock area, 18
　Brennans Wharf, 136
　calamari see calamari squid
　Elliston, 138
　Flinders, at, 24
　Kangaroo Island, 109
　mullet, for, 39
　mulloway, for, 277
　Port Welshpool, 35
　silver trevally, for, 40
　Sydney, offshore, 250
　Warrnambool, 88
squire see also snapper
　Gold Coast reefs, 229
　Wagonga Inlet, 270
St Helens, 42–49
　offshore, 45–47
St Kilda, 9
St Margaret Island, 33
Starbank reef, 279
Steep Point, 154
stingrays
　Manns Beach, 33
　Port Phillip Bay, 3
　Werribee River mouth, 15
Stokes Bay, 107, 108
Stony Point, 25
Storm Point, 294
Strahan, 61–67
Streaky Bay, 139, 141
striped marlin
　Flinders Island, 41
　Lord Howe Island, 240, 241
　Narooma, 269, 271
　St Helens, 47, 49
　Sydney, 250, 255
striped trumpter
　Flinders Island, 40, 41
　St Helens, 45, 47, 49
striped tuna
　bait, as, 254
　bream, for, 301
　Broken Bay, 246
　Flinders Island, 41
　Montague Island, 266
　Narooma, 266, 271

St Helens, 45
Starbank reef, 279
Sydney, offshore, 250
Strzelecki Peaks, 39
Sunday Island, 30
Sunday Island Channel, 34
Sunshine Coast, 214, 221
Sunshine reef, 219
Surf Point, 155
surf reel
　beach fishing, for, 141
surf rod
　beach fishing, for, 141
Surfers Paradise, 223
Surrey River, 101
Swan Lake, Bemm River, 286
sweep
　Cape Du Couedic, 107
　Cape Jervis, 106
　Cape Otway, 74
　Cape Patton, 71
　Coffin Bay, 138
　Flinders Island, 41
　Investigator Islands, 138
　Kangaroo Island, 107, 109
　Lady Bay, 92
　Lady Julia Percy Island, 95
　Tumby Bay, 129, 133
sweetlip
　Cape Don, 179
　emperor see sweetlip emperor
　South West Rocks, offshore, 233
sweetlip emperor, 221
Swimming Point, 272, 275
switch-baiting, 270
Sydenham Inlet, 281, 282, 283, 285–286
Sydney, 136, 235, 241, 242, 247, 249–255, 257, 263, 271

T
tackle see fly-fishing; rods and reels
tailing trout, 53
tailor
　bait, as, 277
　Bancroft Bay, 299
　Bastin Point, 278
　Bemm River, 286, 287
　Botany Bay, 253
　Bottom Lake, 276
　Broken Bay, 246
　chopper see chopper tailor
　Dirk Hartog Island, 151, 153, 155
　Georges Bay, 47
　Gippsland Lakes and rivers, 301
　Gold Coast, 227, 229
　Hawkesbury River, 247
　Lake Victoria, 292
　Lakes Entrance, 300
　Loch Sport, 293
　Mallacoota, 279
　McMillan Strait, 295
　Mitchell River, 296
　mulloway, for, 277
　Narooma beaches, 270
　Newport Power Station outflow channel, 14
　Noosa, 215, 218, 219, 221

Noosa River, 217
Paynesville, 295
Port Albert, 30
Shaving Point, 299
Smoky Bay, 141
South West Rocks, 233, 234, 235
St Helens, 49
Sydney, 250, 251, 255
Tambo River, 297
Top Lake, 277
Wagonga Inlet, 270
Talbot Bay, 161
Tambo River, 297–298
tarpon see ox-eye herring
Tarraville, 33
tarwhine, 218, 219, 221
Tasman Sea, 232, 286
Tasmania, 105
Teewah Beach, 219
teraglin, 229
Terang, 87
Thevenard, 141
Thistle Island, 136–137
Thornton, 304, 305
threadfin salmon
　Bathurst Island, 167–168
　Cape Don, 179
　Cape York, 205, 207
　Crocodile Islands, 199
　Goose Creek, 173
　Junction Bay, 199
　Kimberley, 163
　Liverpool River, 196, 198, 199
　Mary River, 182, 187
　Port Hurd, 166, 169
　Second Creek, 166, 169
　Shady Camp, 186
　South Alligator River, 193
　Tiwi Islands, 173
Thredbo, 257
Thredbo River, 261
thresher shark, 100, 103
tiger flathead
　Flinders Island, 38, 41
　Narooma, offshore, 268
tiger sharks, 166
Timor Sea, 165, 173
Tiwi Islands, 165–173
Tomkinson River, 196
tommy ruff
　Adelaide, 114, 115
　Aire River, 76
　bait, as, 127
　Brennans Wharf, 136
　Elliston, 138
　Esperance beaches, 144, 147
　Kangaroo Island, 109
　Reevesby Island, 131
　Tumby Bay, 129, 133
　Venus Bay, 139
Toms Creek, 292
Tongariro River, 309
Tooram Stones, 88, 90
Top End, 55, 105, 179, 182, 210
Top Lake, 274, 277
Torrens River, 111
Torres Strait, 201

Traralgon, 35
Trepang Bay, 176, 177, 178–179
Trepang Creek, 178
trevally
　Apollo Bay Harbour, 73
　Bemm River, 287
　big eye see big eye trevally
　Bird Rock area, 18
　Boston Bay, 136
　Cape Du Couedic, 107
　Cape York beaches, 206
　Dirk Hartog Island, 155
　Elliston, 138
　giant see giant trevally
　gold spot see gold spot trevally
　golden see golden trevally
　Kangaroo Island, 109
　Kerford Road Pier, 11
　Kilcunda, 27
　Kimberley rivers, 162
　Lagoon Pier, 11
　Lakes Entrance, 300
　Liverpool River, offshore, 198
　Logans Beach, 94
　Lord Howe Island, 239, 241
　Manns Beach, 32
　Marengo, 74
　Montague Island, 266
　Moyne River, 94
　Newport Power Station outflow channel, 14
　Noosa River, 216
　North Harbour, 253
　Port Albert, 30
　Rex's Cay, 177
　silver see silver trevally
　slimy or snotty-nose see snotty-nose trevally
　Station Pier, 11
　Tumby Bay, 129
　Vashon Head, 179
　Western Port, 24
　Wild Dog Creek, 71
　Williamstown Pier, 14
Trial Bay, 231, 232
trolling, 161
　Apsley Strait, 172
　Arthurs Lake, 53
　Bathurst Island, 171
　black marlin, for, 229
　Broadwater, 226
　Broken Bay, 246
　Creel Bay, 262
　dusky flathead, for, 226, 228
　Flinders Island, 41
　Gold Coast, offshore, 229
　golden perch, 310
　Huon Bay, 262
　jewfish, for, 247
　Kimberley, 163
　kingfish, for, 268
　Lake Burbury, 58, 59–60
　Lake Eildon, 310
　Lake Jindabyne, 261
　Lakes Entrance, 300
　Liverpool River, 196, 198
　Lord Howe Island, 240

marlin, 232, 240
McMillan Strait, 295
Melville Island, 173
Montague Island, 268
Murray cod, 310
Narooma, 270
Port Hurd, 166
Portland Bay, 100
Providence Portal Arm, Lake Eucumbene, 258
Shady Camp, 186
South Alligator River, 191, 193
sooty grunter, for, 213
sportsfish, for, 163
Sydney, 250
trout, 66, 310
Troubridge Shoal, 117
Trousers Point, 39
trout
　Arthurs Lake, 55
　Big River Arm, Lake Eildon, 311
　brook see brook trout
　brown see brown trout
　Central highlands, 51
　coral see coral trout
　Creel Bay, 261
　Eildon, 281
　Eildon Pondage, 308
　Goulburn River, 304–309
　Hopkins River, 88
　Howqua River, 311
　Lake Eildon, 310
　Lake Purrumbete, 81
　Lower Thredbo River, 263
　Merri River, 91
　rainbow see rainbow trout
　sea-run see sea-run trout
　tailing see tailing trout
Tuckamore Beach, 140
Tumby Bay, 127–133
Tummock Hill see Whyalla
tuna
　albacore see albacore tuna
　bait, as, 160
　Boston Bay, 136
　long-tail, see long-tail tuna
　mackerel see mackerel tuna
　Mallacoota, offshore, 279
　southern bluefin see bluefin tuna
　striped see striped tuna
　yellowfin see yellowfin tuna
Tunarama Festival, 135
turrum see gold spot trevally
turtles, 179
tusk fish, 240, 241

V

Van Diemen Gulf, 184, 191, 193
Vansittart Bay, 158, 161–163
Vashon Head, 179
Vaucluse, 251
Venus Bay, 139, 141
Vivonne Bay, 106

W

Wagonga Inlet, 265, 268, 270–271
wahoo
　Dirk Hartog Island, 155
　Lord Howe Island, 240, 241
　Montague Island, 269
　Narooma, offshore, 266
　South West Rocks, 234, 235
Walhalla, 29
Wallagaraugh River, 274, 277, 278
warehou
　Bird Rock area, 18
　Kerford Road Pier, 11
　Lady Julia Percy Island, 95, 101
　Lawrence Rocks, 100
　Portland, 99, 103
　Western Port, 24
Warrnambool, 87–95, 101, 103
Waterloo Bay, 138
Watsons Bay, 251
Wave Break Island, 229
Wedge Spit, 17
Weipa, 204, 205, 206, 207
Werribee River, 11
　Bellarine Peninsula to, 16–19
　mouth, 15
　ramps, 16
　Yarra River to, 12–15
West End, 41
West Lakes, 115
Western Port, 21–27
　species, 22–24
　tides, 22, 24
Western River, 108
Whalebone Creek, 71
whaler shark
　bait, as, 169
　bronze see bronze whaler shark
　Cape Don, 179
　Gulf of Carpentaria, 205
　jewfish, for, 169
　Lord Howe Island, 240
　Rex's Cay, 177
whitebait
　bait, as, 81
　salmon, for, 39, 66
Whitemark, 41
whiting
　Adelaide, 111, 114
　Altona Pier, 15
　Apollo Bay, 70, 73
　Beaumaris Bay, 7, 8
　Bird Rock area, 18
　Boston Bay, 136
　Cape Otway, 74
　Ceduna, 140
　Corio Bay, 17
　Deep Mornington to Carrum, 6
　Dirk Hartog Island, 155
　Elliston, 138
　Esperance beaches, 144
　Flinders, at, 24
　Investigator Strait, 108
　Kangaroo Island, 106, 109
　Kerford Road Pier, 11
　King George see King George whiting
　Lady Bay, 92
　Long Reef, 17
　Macleay River, 233
　McLoughlins Beach, 30
　Manns Beach, 32
　Marengo, 74
　Marion Bay, 121
　Middle Island, 145
　Mordialloc Pier, 7, 8
　New Street groynes and reef, 10
　Point Cook, 13–14
　Port Phillip Bay, 2
　Prince George bank, 19
　Reevesby Island, 131
　Ricketts Point, 8
　sand see sand whiting
　Sandringham breakwater, 9
　Smoky Bay, 141
　Streaky Bay, 139
　Tumby Bay, 129
　Venus Bay, 139
　Wagonga Inlet, 271
　water temperature, 3, 271
　Werribee River mouth, 15, 16
　Western Port, 24
　Whyalla, 127
　yellowfin see yellowfin whiting
Whyalla, 123–127, 133
　artificial reefs, 127
　boating facilities, 124
Wild Dog Creek, 71–72, 73
Williamstown, 4, 13
Wilsons Promontory, 34, 35, 144
wire trace, 100, 151, 179, 246
Wisemans Ferry, 244
wolf herring, 171
Woodside, 26
Woy Woy, 246
wrasse
　Apollo Bay Harbour, 72, 73
　blue-throated see blue-throated wrasse
　double-header see hump-headed wrasse
　Flinders Island, 41
　Glenelg tyre reefs, 113
　hump-headed see hump-headed wrasse
　Kangaroo Island, 107
　Marion Bay, 121
　Middle Island, 145
Wurrong Point, 85
Wyndham, 157, 163

Y

yabbies
　bait, as, 292
　freshwater, 292
　whiting, for, 24
Yalata Beach, 140
'yank' flathead
　Bemm River, 286
　scarcity of, 16
Yarra River
　Ricketts Point to, 8–11
　Werribee River, to, 12–15
Yea, 306
Yellow Waters, 191
yellow-eye mullet, 10, 26
　Barham River, 74
　Bemm River, 286, 287
　Gippsland Lakes and rivers, 301
　Hopkins River, 89
　Lake Victoria, 292
　Mallacoota, 279
　Mitchell River, 296
　Narooma, 271
yellowfin bream
　Bemm River, 286
　black bream cross, 278
　Gold Coast, 229
　Hawkesbury River, 247
　Macleay River, 234
　Mallacoota, 276, 278, 279
　Narooma, 270, 271
　Noosa, 221
　Noosa River, 216
　Pittwater, 247
　Port Hacking, 254
　South West Rocks, 233, 235
　Sydney, 255
yellowfin tuna
　Dirk Hartog Island, 155
　Flinders Island, 41
　Lord Howe Island, 240, 241
　Montague Island, 268
　Narooma, 266, 271
　South West Rocks, 233, 235
　St Helens, 45, 47, 49
　Steep Point, 155
　Sydney, 249, 250, 255
yellowfin whiting
　Manly, 253
　Narooma, 271
　Wagonga Inlet, 268, 270
yellowtail kingfish
　Boston Bay, 136
　Broken Bay, 246
　Coffin Bay, 138
　Fish Rock, 234
　Flinders, at, 25
　Gabo Island, 279
　Gold Coast, 229
　Kangaroo Island, 108, 109
　Lady Bay, 92
　Lord Howe Island, 239, 241
　Montague Island, 266, 268
　Narooma, 268, 271
　Port Welshpool, 35
　Portland, 99, 103
　South West Rocks, 233, 235
　Sydney, 250, 251, 255
　Tumby Bay, 133
　Whyalla, 124, 127
yellowtail scad
　bait, as, 251
　Botany Bay, 253
　flathead, for, 251
Yorke Peninsula, 117, 120, 121
Yorkies reef, 9